CompTIA®
Network+®
Review Guide
Second Edition

CompTIA®
Network+®
Review Guide
Second Edition

Bill Ferguson

WILEY

John Wiley & Sons, Inc.

Senior Acquisitions Editor: Jeff Kellum
Development Editor: Alexa Murphy
Technical Editor: Quentin Docter
Production Editor: Eric Charbonneau
Copy Editor: Kim Wimpsett
Editorial Manager: Pete Gaughan
Production Manager: Tim Tate
Vice President and Executive Group Publisher: Richard Swadley
Vice President and Publisher: Neil Edde
Media Project Manager 1: Laura Moss-Hollister
Media Associate Producer: Doug Kuhn
Media Quality Assurance: Shawn Patrick
Book Designers: Judy Fung and Bill Gibson
Compositor: Craig Woods, Happenstance Type-O-Rama
Proofreaders: Troy McMillan and Nancy Bell
Indexer: Ted Laux
Project Coordinator, Cover: Katherine Crocker
Cover Designer: Ryan Sneed

Dear Reader,

Thank you for choosing *CompTIA Network+ Review Guide, Second Edition*. This book is part of a family of premium-quality Sybex books, all of which are written by outstanding authors who combine practical experience with a gift for teaching.

Sybex was founded in 1976. More than 30 years later, we're still committed to producing consistently exceptional books. With each of our titles, we're working hard to set a new standard for the industry. From the paper we print on, to the authors we work with, our goal is to bring you the best books available.

I hope you see all that reflected in these pages. I'd be very interested to hear your comments and get your feedback on how we're doing. Feel free to let me know what you think about this or any other Sybex book by sending me an email at nedde@wiley.com. If you think you've found a technical error in this book, please visit http://sybex.custhelp.com. Customer feedback is critical to our efforts at Sybex.

Best regards,

Neil Edde
Vice President and Publisher
Sybex, an Imprint of Wiley

To my father, who in the 1980s told me to learn as much about computers as I could and to buy and hold Microsoft stock. Unfortunately, I took only part of his good advice. Seriously, his purchase of an IBM PC XT computer in 1983 has made all the difference in my life and in my IT career. Unfortunately, Dad passed away on March 6, 2011, at the tender age of 73. I still think about him every time I use a computer. Thanks, Dad, and may you rest in peace!

Acknowledgments

First I'd like to thank Jeff Kellum for giving me the opportunity to write this important book. Several people have assisted me in many ways, so I'd like to acknowledge their contributions and offer my sincere appreciation. Specifically, I'd like to thank Quentin Docter, Eric Charbonneau, and Pete Gaughan for technical and developmental editing and support and for keeping me on track throughout the process. My thanks also goes to Alexa Murphy for keeping me on track and helping me put all the final, professional touches on the book. To the many people involved in this effort with whom I never worked with one-on-one—thanks! It takes a great team to put together a great book.

Finally, I'd like to acknowledge the encouragement and prayers of my family and friends and the students in my technical classes and Sunday school classes. In Him, all things are possible!

About the Author

Bill Ferguson—MCT, MCSE, MCP+I, CCSI, CCNA, A+, Network+, Server+, Security+, VCP4, VCI4—has been in the computer industry for more than 20 years. Originally in technical sales and sales management with Sprint, Bill made his transition to Certified Technical Trainer in 1997 with ExecuTrain. Bill now runs his own company (Parallel Connections) as an independent contractor/author in Birmingham, Alabama, teaching classes for most of the national training companies and some regional training companies as well as international classes and virtual (online) classes. In addition, Bill writes and produces technical training videos for Quickcert, VTC, and Palaestra Training Company. He has written video titles including *A+, Network+, Windows 2000 Management, Windows XP Management, Windows MCDST,* and *Interconnecting Cisco Network Devices.* In addition, he wrote the *Microsoft Certified Desktop Support Technician (MCDST) Study Guide,* the previous *Network+ Review Guide,* and the *Network+ Fastpass* books for Sybex/Wiley Press. Bill says, "My job is to understand the material so well that I can make it easier for my students to learn than it was for me to learn."

Contents at a Glance

Contents

Introduction

The Computer Technology Industry Association (CompTIA) developed the Network+ certification to provide an industry-wide means of certifying the competency of computer service technicians in the basics of computer networking. The Network+ certification is granted to those individuals who have attained a level of knowledge and networking skills that show a basic competency with the networking needs of both personal and corporate computing environments.

CompTIA's exam objectives are periodically updated to keep its exams applicable to the most recent technological developments. The foundational elements, however, remain constant even as higher-end technology advances. The Network+ objectives have recently been changed to a small degree to reflect the very latest changes in technology. At the time of this writing, this book is current for the 2011 (N10-005) objectives as stated by CompTIA (www.comptia.org).

What Is Network+ Certification?

The Network+ certification offers an introductory step into the complex world of IT networking. You need to pass only a single exam to become Network+ certified. This is often the first step toward true networking knowledge and experience. By obtaining Network+ certification, you will be able to obtain more networking experience and gain an interest in networks in order to pursue more complex and in-depth network knowledge and certifications.

For the latest pricing on the exam and updates to the registration procedures, go to either www.vue.com or www.2test.com. You can register online for the exam. If you have further questions about the scope of the exam or related CompTIA programs, refer to the CompTIA website at www.comptia.org.

Is This Book for You?

CompTIA Network+ Review Guide is designed to be a succinct, portable exam review guide that can be used either in conjunction with a more complete study program (such as Sybex's *CompTIA Network+ Study Guide*, computer-based training courseware, or a classroom/lab environment) or as an exam review for those who don't need more extensive test preparation. It isn't my goal to give the answers away but rather to identify those topics on which you can expect to be tested and to provide sufficient coverage of these topics.

Perhaps you've been working with information technologies for many years. The thought of paying lots of money for a specialized IT exam preparation course probably doesn't sound too appealing. What can they teach you that you don't already know, right? Be careful, though. Many experienced network administrators have walked confidently into the test center only to walk sheepishly out of it after failing an IT exam. After you've finished reading this book, you should have a clear idea of how your understanding of networking technologies matches up with the expectations of the Network+ test makers.

Perhaps you're relatively new to the world of IT—drawn to it by the promise of challenging work at a higher salary? You've just waded through an 800-page study guide, or you've taken a class at a local training center. Lots of information to keep in your head, isn't it? Well, by organizing this book according to CompTIA's exam objectives and by breaking up the information into concise, manageable pieces, I've created what I think is the handiest exam review guide available. Throw it in your laptop bag and carry it to work with you or get a copy of it on Kindle. As you read the book, you'll be able to identify quickly those areas you know best and those that require a more in-depth review.

> The goal of the Review Guide series is to help Network+ candidates brush up on the subjects on which they can expect to be tested on the Network+ exam. For complete in-depth coverage of the technologies and topics involved, we recommend *CompTIA Network+ Study Guide*, from Sybex.

How Is This Book Organized?

This book is organized according to the official objectives list prepared by CompTIA for the Network+ exam. The chapters correspond to the six major domains of objective and topic groupings. In fact, the exam is weighted across these six domains as follows:

- Domain 1.0 Network Technologies (21 percent)
- Domain 2.0 Network Installation and Configuration (23 percent)
- Domain 3.0 Network Media and Topologies (17 percent)
- Domain 4.0 Network Management (20 percent)
- Domain 5.0 Network Security (19 percent)

Within each chapter, the top-level exam objective from each domain is addressed in turn. This discussion of each objective also contains an "Exam Essentials" section. Here you are given a short list of topics that you should explore fully before taking the test. Included in the "Exam Essentials" areas are notations on key pieces of information you should have taken out of *CompTIA Network+ Study Guide*.

At the end of each chapter you'll find the "Review Questions" section. These questions are designed to help you gauge your mastery of the content in the chapter.

Additional Study Tools

We've included several additional study tools available from the book's companion site. These tools will help you retain vital exam content as well as prepare you to sit for the actual exams:

Readers can get the additional study tools by visiting www.sybex.com/go/ netplusrg 2e. Here, you will get instructions on how to download the files to your hard drive.

Test engine   Using this custom test engine, you can identify weak areas up front and then develop a solid studying strategy using each of these robust testing features. Our thorough readme file will walk you through the quick, easy installation process.

Electronic flashcards   You'll find flashcards for on-the-go review. These are short questions and answers, just like the flashcards you probably used to study in school. You can answer them on your PC or download them onto a portable device for quick and convenient reviewing.

Glossary of Terms in PDF   The Glossary of Terms in PDF (Adobe Acrobat) format can easily be read on any computer. If you have to travel and brush up on any key terms, you can do so with this useful resource.

Tips for Taking the Network+ Exam

Here are some general tips for taking your exams successfully:

- Bring two forms of ID with you. One must be a photo ID, such as a driver's license. The other can be a major credit card or a passport. Both forms must include a signature.

- Arrive early at the exam center so you can relax and review your study materials, particularly tables and lists of exam-related information.

- Read the questions carefully. Don't be tempted to jump to an early conclusion. Make sure you know exactly what the question is asking.

- Don't leave any unanswered questions. Unanswered questions give you no opportunity for guessing correctly and scoring more points.

- There will be questions with multiple correct responses. When there is more than one correct answer, a message on the screen will prompt you to either "Choose two" or "Choose all that apply." Be sure to read the messages displayed so you know how many correct answers you must choose.

- Questions needing only a single correct answer will use radio buttons to select an answer, while those needing two or more answers will use checkboxes.

- When answering multiple-choice questions you're not sure about, use a process of elimination to get rid of the obviously incorrect answers first. Doing so will improve your odds if you need to make an educated guess.

- On form-based tests (non-adaptive), because the hard questions will eat up the most time, save them for last. You can move forward and backward through the exam.

- For the latest pricing on the exams and updates to the registration procedures, visit CompTIA's website at www.comptia.org.

How to Contact the Publisher

Sybex welcomes feedback on all of its titles. Visit the Sybex website at www.sybex.com for book updates and additional certification information. You'll also find forms you can use to submit comments or suggestions regarding this or any other Sybex title.

The Exam Objectives

The following are the areas (referred to as *domains*, according to CompTIA) in which you must be proficient in order to pass the Network+ exam:

Domain 1.0 Network Technologies   This domain illustrates the OSI model of communication and how all the network devices and network protocols are organized based on this model. I will discuss the functions of common network protocols, ports, addressing technologies, and addressing schemes. In addition, I will discuss routing and routing protocols used primarily with TCP/IP. Finally, I will discuss an emerging technology in regard to computers and switches: virtualization.

Domain 2.0 Network Installation and Configuration   This domain includes the installation and configuration of routers and switches in a wired network. I will discuss the installation and configuration of wireless networks. I will also discuss troubleshooting wired and wireless networks. Finally, I will identify and discuss an emerging type of network, the SOHO network.

Domain 3.0 Network Media and Topologies   This domain concerns the categorization of media types such as fiber and copper. It also touches on wireless standard and WAN technologies. In addition I will cover the basics of the logical and physical shapes of various networks and how the topology of the network affects the technologies used in the network. Finally, I will discuss common physical connectivity problems and their solutions.

Domain 4.0 Network Management   In this domain, I will start by discussing the purpose and features of various network appliances. I will continue by discussing ways to troubleshoot connectivity issues in a network and the common hardware and software tools you can use. In addition, I will discuss methods used to monitor resources and analyze traffic. Finally, I will explain methods and rationales for network performance optimization.

Domain 5.0 Network Security   This area includes recognizing and defending against common network threats. I will discuss the proper use of firewalls, IDS, VPN concentrators, and other network hardware and software that can help you combat network attacks. I will also discuss common authentication and encryption techniques used by network administrators for wired and wireless networks.

The Network+ Exam Objectives

At the beginning of each chapter, I have included a complete listing of the topics that will be covered in that chapter. These topic selections are developed straight from the test objectives listed on CompTIA's website. These are provided for easy reference and to assure you that you are on track with learning the objectives. Note that exam objectives are subject to change at any time without prior notice and at CompTIA's sole discretion. Please visit the Network+ Certification page of CompTIA's website (http://certification.comptia.org/network/default.aspx) for the most current listing of exam objectives.

Domain 1.0 Network Technologies

1.1 Compare the layers of the OSI Model and the TCP/IP models.

- OSI model:
    - Layer 1 – Physical
    - Layer 2 – Data Link
    - Layer 3 – Network
    - Layer 4 – Transport
    - Layer 5 – Session
    - Layer 6 – Presentation
    - Layer 7 – Application
- TCP/IP model:
    - Network Interface layer
    - Internet layer
    - Transport layer
    - Application layer

1.2 Classify how applications, devices, and protocols relate to the OSI model layers.

- MAC address
- IP address
- EUI-64
- Frames

- Packets
- Switch
- Router
- Multilayer switch
- Hub
- Encryption devices
- Cable
- NIC
- Bridge

1.3 Explain the purpose and properties of IP addressing.

- Classes of addresses:
  - A, B, C, and D
  - Public vs. private
- Classless (CIDR)
- IPv4 vs. IPv6 (formatting)
- MAC address format
- Subnetting
- Multicast vs. unicast vs. broadcast
- APIPA

1.4 Explain the purpose and properties of routing and switching.

- EIGRP
- OSPF
- RIP
- Link state vs. distance vector vs. hybrid
- Static vs. dynamic
- Routing metrics:
  - Hop counts
  - MTU, bandwidth
  - Costs
  - Latency
- Next hop
- Spanning-Tree Protocol
- VLAN (802.1q)

- Port mirroring
- Broadcast domain vs. collision domain
- IGP vs. EGP
- Routing tables
- Convergence (steady state)

1.5 Identify common TCP and UDP default ports.

- SMTP – 25
- HTTP – 80
- HTTPS – 443
- FTP – 20, 21
- TELNET – 23
- IMAP – 143
- RDP – 3389
- SSH – 22
- DNS – 53
- DHCP – 67, 68

1.6 Explain the function of common networking protocols.

- TCP
- FTP
- UDP
- TCP/IP suite
- DHCP
- TFTP
- DNS
- HTTPS
- HTTP
- ARP
- SIP (VoIP)
- RTP (VoIP)
- SSH
- POP3
- NTP
- IMAP4

- Telnet
- SMTP
- SNMP2/3
- ICMP
- IGMP
- TLS

1.7 Summarize the DNS concepts and its components.

- DNS servers
- DNS records (A, MX, AAAA, CNAME, PTR)
- Dynamic DNS

1.8 Given a scenario, implement the following network troubleshooting methodology:

- Identify the problem.
  - Information gathering.
  - Identify symptoms.
  - Question users.
  - Determine if anything has changed.
- Establish a theory of probable cause.
  - Question the obvious.
- Test the theory to determine cause:
  - Once theory is confirmed, determine next steps to resolve the problem.
  - If theory is not confirmed, re-establish new theory or escalate.
- Establish a plan of action to resolve the problem and identify potential effects.
- Implement the solution or escalate as necessary.
- Verify full system functionality and if applicable implement preventative measures.
- Document findings, actions and outcomes.

1.9 Identify virtual network components.

- Virtual switches
- Virtual desktops
- Virtual servers
- Virtual PBX
- Onsite vs. offsite
- Network as a Service (NaaS)

Domain 2.0 Network Installation and Configuration

2.1 Given a scenario, install and configure routers and switches.

- Routing tables
- NAT
- PAT
- VLAN (trunking)
- Managed vs. unmanaged
- Interface configuration:
    - Full duplex
    - Half duplex
    - Port speeds
    - IP addressing
    - MAC filtering
- PoE
- Traffic filtering
- Diagnostics
- VTP configuration
- QoS
- Port mirroring

2.2 Given a scenario, install and configure a wireless network.

- WAP replacement
- Antenna types
- Interference
- Frequencies
- Channels
- Wireless standards
- SSID (enable/disable)
- Compatibility (802.11 a/b/g/n)

2.3 Explain the purpose and properties of DHCP.

- Static vs. dynamic IP addressing
- Reservations
- Scopes

- Leases
- Options (DNS servers, suffixes)

2.4 Given a scenario, troubleshoot common wireless problems.

- Interference
- Signal strength
- Configurations
- Incompatibilities
- Incorrect channel
- Latency
- Encryption type
- Bounce
- SSID mismatch
- Incorrect switch placement

2.5 Given a scenario, troubleshoot common router and switch problems.

- Switching loop
- Bad cables/improper cable types
- Port configuration
- VLAN assignment
- Mismatched MTU/MUT black hole
- Power failure
- Bad/missing routes
- Bad modules (SFPs GBICs)
- Wrong subnet mask
- Wrong gateway
- Duplicate IP address
- Wrong DNS

2.6 Given a set of requirements, plan and implement a basic SOHO network.

- List of requirements
- Cable length
- Device types/requirements
- Environment limitations
- Equipment limitations
- Compatibility requirements

Domain 3.0 Network Media and Topologies

3.1 Categorize standard media types and associated properties.

- Fiber:
  - Multimode
  - Singlemode
- Copper:
  - UTP
  - STP
  - CAT3
  - CAT5
  - CAT5e
  - CAT6
  - CAT6a
  - Coaxial
  - Crossover
  - T1 Crossover
  - Straight-through
- Plenum vs. non-plenum
- Media converters:
  - Singlemode fiber to Ethernet
  - Multimode fiber to Ethernet
  - Fiber to coaxial
  - Singlemode to multimode fiber
- Distance limitations and speed limitations
- Broadband over powerline

3.2 Categorize standard connector types on network media.

- Fiber:
  - ST
  - SC
  - LC
  - MTRJ

- Copper:
  - RJ-45
  - RJ-11
  - BNC
  - F-connector
  - DB-9 (RS-232)
  - Patch panel
  - 110 block (T568A, T568B)

3.3 Compare and contrast different wireless standards.

- 802.11 a/b/g/n standards
  - Distance
  - Speed
  - Latency
  - Frequency
  - Channels
  - MIMO
  - Channel bonding

3.4 Categorize WAN technology types and properties.

- Types:
  - T1/E1
  - T3/E3
  - DS3
  - OCx
  - SONET
  - SDH
  - DWDM
  - Satellite
  - ISDN
  - Cable
  - DSL
  - Cellular
  - WiMAX
  - LTE

- HSPA+
- Fiber
- Dialup
- PON
- Frame relay
- ATMs
- Properties:
    - Circuit switch
    - Packet switch
    - Speed
    - Transmission media
    - Distance

3.5 Describe different network topologies.

- MPLS
- Point to point
- Point to multipoint
- Ring
- Star
- Mesh
- Bus
- Peer-to-peer
- Client-server
- Hybrid

3.6 Given a scenario, troubleshoot common physical connectivity problems.

- Cable problems:
    - Bad connectors
    - Bad wiring
    - Open, short
    - Split cables
    - DB loss
    - TXRX reversed
    - Cable placement
    - EMI/interference

- Distance
- Cross-talk

3.7 Compare and contrast different LAN technologies.

- Types:
  - Ethernet
  - 10BaseT
  - 100BaseT
  - 1000BaseT
  - 100BaseTX
  - 100BaseFX
  - 1000BaseX
  - 10GBaseSR
  - 10GBaseLR
  - 10GBaseER
  - 10GBaseSW
  - 10GBaseLW
  - 10GBaseEW
  - 10GBaseT
- Properties:
  - CSMA/CD
  - CSMA/CA
  - Broadcast
  - Collision
  - Bonding
  - Speed
  - Distance

3.8 Identify components of wiring distribution.

- IDF
- MDF
- Demarc
- Demarc extension
- Smart jack
- CSU/DSU

Domain 4.0 Network Management

4.1 Explain the purpose and features of various network appliances.

- Load balancer
- Proxy server
- Content filter
- VPN concentrator

4.2 Given a scenario, use appropriate hardware tools to troubleshoot connectivity issues.

- Cable tester
- Cable certifier
- Crimper
- Butt set
- Toner probe
- Punch down tool
- Protocol analyzer
- Loop back plug
- TDR
- OTDR
- Multimeter
- Environmental monitor

4.3 Given a scenario, use appropriate software tools to troubleshoot connectivity issues.

- Protocol analyzer
  - Throughput testers
  - Connectivity software
  - Ping
  - Tracert/traceroute
  - Dig
  - Ipconfig/ifconfig
  - Nslookup
  - Arp
  - Nbtstat

- Netstat
- Route

4.4 Given a scenario, use the appropriate network monitoring resource to analyze traffic.

- SNMP
- SNMPv2
- SNMPv3
- Syslog
- System logs
- History logs
- General logs
- Traffic analysis
- Network sniffer

4.5 Describe the purpose of configuration management documentation.

- Wire schemes
- Network maps
- Documentation
- Cable management
- Asset management
- Baselines
- Change management

4.6 Explain different methods and rationales for network performance optimization.

- Methods:
  - QoS
  - Traffic shaping
  - Load balancing
  - High availability
  - Caching engines
  - Fault tolerance
  - CARP

- Reasons:
  - Latency sensitivity
  - High bandwidth applications (VoIP, video applications, unified communications)
  - Uptime

Domain 5.0 Network Security

5.1 Given a scenario, implement appropriate wireless security measures.

- Encryption protocols:
  - WEP
  - WPA
  - WPA2
  - WPA Enterprise
- MAC address filtering
- Device placement
- Signal strength

5.2 Explain the methods of network access security.

- ACL:
  - MAC filtering
  - IP filtering
  - Port filtering
- Tunneling and encryption:
  - SSL VPN
  - VPN
  - L2TP
  - PPTP
  - IPSec
  - ISAKMP
  - TLS
  - TLS 1.2
  - Site-to-site and client-to-site

- Remote access:
    - RAS
    - RDP
    - PPPoE
    - PPP
    - ICA
    - SSH

5.3 Explain methods of user authentication.

- PKI
- Kerberos
- AAA (RADIUS, TACACS+)
- Network access control (802.1x, posture assessment)
- CHAP
- MS-CHAP
- EAP
- Two-factor authentication
- Multifactor authentication
- Single sign-on

5.4 Explain common threats, vulnerabilities, and mitigation techniques.

- Wireless:
    - War driving
    - War chalking
    - WEP cracking
    - WPA cracking
    - Evil twin
    - Rogue access point
- Attacks:
    - DoS
    - DDoS
    - Man in the middle
    - Social engineering
    - Virus

- Worms
- Buffer overflow
- Packet sniffing
- FTP bounce
- Smurf
- Mitigation techniques:
  - Training and awareness
  - Patch management
  - Policies and procedures
  - Incident response

5.5 Given a scenario, install and configure a basic firewall.

- Types:
  - Software and hardware firewalls
- Port security
- Stateful inspection vs. packet filtering
- Firewall rules:
  - Block/allow
  - Implicit deny
  - ACL
- NAT/PAT
- DMZ

5.6 Categorize different types of network security appliances and methods.

- IDS and IPS:
  - Behavior based
  - Signature based
  - Network based
  - Host based
- Vulnerability scanners:
  - NESSUS
  - NMAP
- Methods:
  - Honeypots
  - Honeynets

Domain 1 Network Technologies

COMPTIA NETWORK+ EXAM OBJECTIVES COVERED IN THIS CHAPTER:

✓ **1.1 Compare the layers of the OSI and TCP/IP models OSI model:**

- Layer 1 – Physical

- Layer 2 – Data Link

- Layer 3 – Network

- Layer 4 – Transport

- Layer 5 – Session

- Layer 6 – Presentation

- Layer 7 – Application

- TCP/IP model:

- Network Interface Layer

- Internet Layer

- Transport Layer

- Application Layer

✓ **1.2 Classify how applications, devices, and protocols relate to the OSI model layers.**

- MAC address

- IP Address

- EUI-64

- Frames

- Packets

- Switch

- Router

- Multilayer switch
- Hub
- Encryption devices
- Cable
- NIC
- Bridge

✓ **1.3 Explain the purpose and properties of IP addressing.**

- Classes of addresses
  - A, B, C, and D
  - Public vs. private
- Classless (CIDR)
- IPv4 vs. IPv6 (formatting)
- MAC address format
- Subnetting
- Multicast vs. unicast vs. broadcast
- APIPA

✓ **1.4 Explain the purpose and properties of routing and switching.**

- EIGRP
- OSPF
- RIP
- Link state vs. distance vector vs. hybrid
- Static vs. dynamic
- Routing metrics
  - Hop Counts
  - MTU, bandwidth
  - Costs
  - Latency
- Next hop
- Spanning-Tree Protocol

- VLAN (802.1q)
- Port mirroring
- Broadcast domain vs. collision domain
- IGP vs. EGP
- Routing tables
- Convergence (steady state)

✓ **1.5 Identify common TCP and UDP default ports.**

- SMTP – 25
- HTTP – 80
- HTTPS – 443
- FTP – 20, 21
- TELNET – 23
- IMAP – 143
- RDP – 3389
- SSH – 22
- DNS – 53
- DHCP – 67, 68

✓ **1.6 Explain the function of common networking protocols.**

- TCP
- FTP
- UDP
- TCP/IP suite
- DHCP
- TFTP
- DNS
- HTTPS
- HTTP
- ARP
- SIP (VoIP)
- RTP (VoIP)

- SSH

- POP3

- NTP

- IMAP4

- Telnet

- SMTP

- SNMP2/3

- ICMP

- IGMP

- TLS

✓ **1.7 Summarize the DNS concepts and its components.**

- DNS servers

- DNS records (A, MX, AAAA, CNAME, PTR)

- Dynamic DNS

✓ **1.8 Given a scenario, implement the following network troubleshooting methodology:**

- Identify the problem

  - Information gathering

  - Identify symptoms

  - Question users

  - Determine if anything has changed

- Establish a theory of probable cause

  - Question the obvious

- Test the theory to determine cause:

  - Once theory is confirmed, determine next steps to resolve the problem.

  - If theory is not confirmed, re-establish new theory or escalate.

- Establish a plan of action to resolve the problem and identify potential effects.

- Implement the solution or escalate as necessary.

- Verify full system functionality and if applicable implement preventative measures.

- Document findings, actions and outcomes.

✓ **1.9 Identify virtual network components.**

- Virtual switches

- Virtual desktops

- Virtual servers

- Virtual PBX

- Onsite vs. offsite

- Network as a Service (NaaS)

Computer communication in today's world is amazing, isn't it? We seem to be able to connect to each other from wherever we happen to be at that time. Networks seem to "stitch" themselves together almost magically with no effort on anybody's part! At least, that's what "seems" to happen.

In fact, there is a lot of technology behind that magic. In this book, I will discuss the components that make our communication possible. You will learn that, no matter what type of network you are using, three components are essential in order for you to be able to communicate: a common protocol, a common network media, and a common network client or service. In this chapter, I'll primarily discuss the first component—the protocol. Although many types of protocols are in use today, all protocols have one element in common: they are a set of rules by which a network or a group of components behaves in order to communicate. In fact, you can think of protocols like a language. If both of us can speak the same language, then we can talk to each other. Otherwise, we might have a real problem communicating. The same is true when protocols don't match on two sides of a network connection between computers or network devices.

I'll start by discussing the primary protocol in use today, TCP/IP. You will learn that TCP/IP is not just one protocol but instead an entire suite of protocols that each has a particular function in your network. I will define each of the protocols as it relates to the entire model of communication, namely, the Open Systems Interconnect (OSI) model. You should understand protocols in general terms as well as the many specific protocols in the TCP/IP protocol suite. I will also discuss how each of the devices in your network is dependent upon the second essential service, the network media. I will cover the purpose and use of devices such as routers, switches, and network interface cards and how each of the devices uses addresses that "stitch together" the communication magic. I will show you ways to understand your network connections and addressing so that you can efficiently troubleshoot your own networks and understand the troubleshooting questions on the test. Finally, I will discuss the very latest and most intriguing devices in use in today's networks, virtual devices.

For more detailed information on Domain 1's topics, please see *CompTIA Network+ Study Guide, 2nd Ed* (9781118137550) or *CompTIA Network+ Deluxe Study Guide, 2nd Ed* (9781118137543), both published by Sybex.

1.1 Compare the layers of the OSI and TCP/IP models

It's important to understand that TCP/IP is not just one protocol, or even two protocols; instead, it's an entire group of protocols that work together to support network communication. Although the OSI model is just a theoretical model, the TCP/IP suite represents the continual development of protocols, each of which loosely aligns itself to a portion of the OSI model. The Department of Defense (DOD) defines the TCP/IP suite of protocols as having four layers. In this section, I will discuss the relationship between the OSI model and the TCP/IP model (suite).

OSI model

The *Open Standards Interconnection (OSI) model* was developed by the International Organization for Standardization (ISO) in the 1980s. It defines seven layers of communication between two devices. The purpose of the model was to allow developers to focus on only the layers that applied to them and only on the protocols (rules) at those layers. The seven layers and their function in the OSI model are as follows:

Layer 1 – Physical   This layer defines the electrical, mechanical, and procedural aspects of communication. At least, that's the boring definition for it. To be clearer, the *Physical layer* defines standards for the "wire." The wire at one time actually had to be a wire, but now we can define the wire as any media that allows communication. This could include fiber-optic cable and the many types of wireless communication in use today. Later, I will discuss some of standards used at the physical layer of the OSI model.

Layer 2 – Data Link   This layer defines how we put data (1s and 0s) onto the wire. Many methods are in use today, and they have evolved over time. The *Data Link layer* is the only layer that is further divided into two sublayers, the *Logical Link Control (LLC)* layer and the *Media Access Control (MAC)* layer. Each of these sublayers has a role in network communication. The MAC layer examines the physical addresses presented to it and addresses packets that it sends. The LLC layer provides the general path to present the communication to the next layer of the model when appropriate. Later, I will discuss some of the protocols that function at the Data Link layer of the OSI model.

Layer 3 – Network   This layer defines the logical addressing of computers and devices on the network. Logical addresses at the *Network layer* are translated to the physical addresses at the Data Link layer in a way that I will discuss later. The primary protocol used at this layer is *Internet Protocol (IP)*. IP addresses are used to construct the networks on which we rely today. Many other protocols also function at the Network layer, but all relate to logical addressing and the establishment and maintenance of logical address paths. Later, I will discuss the function of many protocols at the Network layer of the OSI model.

Layer 4 – Transport   This layer defines the connection methods for communication between the two devices. Some protocols at the *Transport layer* establish a guaranteed communication link between two devices. Others simply broadcast data to any devices "listening" on the wire. Later, I will differentiate the protocols that function at the Transport layer of the OSI model.

Layer 5 – Session   This layer is primarily responsible for the establishment, maintenance, and termination of computer sessions. That sounds circular, doesn't it? Well, the *Session layer* contains protocols that establish a communication link between two devices. This is sometimes accomplished using three-way handshake, which I will discuss in more detail later in this chapter. The protocols at this layer are not as well known as some of the others, but they are important nonetheless. Later in this chapter, I will discuss the protocols that function at the Session layer.

Layer 6 – Presentation   This layer is responsible for translating the streams of 1s and 0s that were sent over the wire. The *Presentation layer* places information in the data stream that allows the receiving device to determine the intent of the stream. Is it supposed to be a character, part of a picture, a sound, and so on? Presentation layer protocols and standards allow you to use your computer for many purposes—all at once. It also formats, encrypts, and compresses data that is to be sent onto the network.

Layer 7 – Application   The *Application layer* is the closest to you (the user) and the particular program or service you are using. The "application" is not a user application such as Microsoft Word or Excel or even a communication application such as Microsoft Mail or Exchange. Instead, the application is a protocol that the user application or communication application utilizes to begin to put the data into the system and eventually onto the wire. The most common of these Application layer protocols is Hypertext Transfer Protocol (*HTTP*), which is used for browsing the *World Wide Web*. Later in this chapter, I will discuss many Application layer protocols and their use in your network.

TCP/IP model

The *TCP/IP suite* is an entire group of protocols working together to support your network communication. As I mentioned, the TCP/IP suite represents the continual development of protocols, each of which loosely aligns itself to a portion of the OSI model. The DOD defines it as having four layers, as shown in Figure 1.1. Each of the protocols in the TCP/IP suite can be said to function in one or more of these layers. In the following section, I'll discuss the layers of the TCP/IP model as defined by the DOD.

Network Interface Layer   The *Network Interface layer* (also known as the Network Access layer) loosely aligns itself to the Physical and Data Link layers of the OSI model. It therefore represents the methods of putting data out onto the wire and at the same time defines what the wire can be. Later, I will discuss many protocols that are defined at this layer of the TCP/IP protocol suite.

FIGURE 1.1   The TCP/IP protocol suite

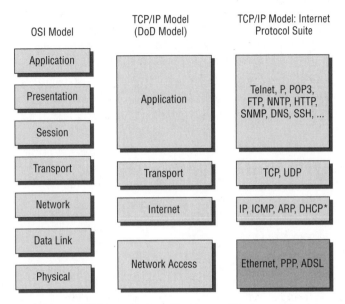

Note: Although DHCP is used to issue IP addresses, it is also considered an Application layer protocol.

Internet Layer   This layer loosely aligns itself with the Network layer of the OSI model. "Inter" means between, so the *Internet layer* defines the logical communication links between two or more computers, such as their IP addresses and the protocols that connect them. You should not confuse the Internet layer of the OSI model with the *Internet*. Think about it this way: the Internet layer of the OSI model provides for "internetworking" of computers to each other, while the largest example of this concept in the world is called the Internet.

Transport Layer   This layer loosely aligns itself to the Transport layer of the OSI model. In the *Transport layer of the TCP/IP protocol suite*, there are only two protocols you need to be concerned with: *Transmission Control Protocol (TCP)* and *User Datagram Protocol (UDP)*. Of these, TCP provides guaranteed connection-oriented communication between devices, while UDP provides a broadcast service or best-effort delivery. Each of these protocols has its purpose. Later, I will discuss in more detail the protocols that function at this layer.

Application Layer   With easily the most protocols of any layer, the Application layer of the TCP/IP protocol suite loosely aligns itself to the Application, Presentation, and Session layers of the OSI model. As you may have guessed, this means it defines the protocols that the user is utilizing, their translation in the network, and the connection methods they will use to communicate. Later in this chapter, I will discuss many of these protocols.

Exam Essentials

Know the purpose of the OSI model and each of its seven layers.   Understand the general purpose for the OSI model of communication and the specific purpose for each of its seven layers.

Know the function of the TCP/IP protocol suite.   Know how the TCP/IP protocol suite loosely aligns itself to the OSI model. Understand which layer(s) of the OSI model relate to each layer of the TCP/IP protocol suite and how they function.

1.2 Classify how applications, devices, and protocols relate to the OSI model layers

In the end, all network devices find each other by their MAC addresses. When it comes to delivering a frame from one host to another, the next MAC address of a computer or a router interface in the path toward the client must be known. Essentially overlaid on top of the MAC address is a logical address that assists you in building complex networks. You should clearly understand that a MAC address is a physical address, whereas an IP address is a logical address.

In the past, we have used primarily one protocol for this logical addressing, IPv4. In the last few years, a new type of addressing, IPv6, has emerged that will allow for the growth of our industry and provide the security and control mechanisms that are needed in today's networks. You should be able to recognize IPv6, IPv4, and MAC addresses, and you should be able to differentiate between the different types of addresses. You should understand the physical or logical addresses used by each network device and be able to differentiate between the different types of communication used by each network device.

MAC addresses

Every device in a network must learn a physical address known as the *MAC address* of another device in order to communicate with it. Since we represent MAC addresses as hexadecimal numbers, it only makes sense to assume that network addresses must be able to read hexadecimal code—but you know what happens when you assume! In reality, network devices can only read binary, so the hexadecimal representation of the MAC address is in fact interpreted by the device as a binary number. Later in this chapter, I will discuss the format of a MAC address.

IP Addresses

You probably wouldn't think you would ever be in danger of running out of a group of things if you had 4 billion of them to start! Well, that is what happened with *IPv4 addresses*. Later, I will discuss the structure of IPv4 addresses, and then you can see what happened. First I'll talk about what the world is going to do next in regard to logical addressing.

IPv6 is the latest logical addressing scheme for networks. Each IPv6 address is a 128-bit binary address represented in hexadecimal numbers. Most companies are not being "forced" into IPv6 as of yet. The latest server and client operating systems (Windows XP, Windows Vista, Windows Server 2003, Windows Server 2008, Windows 7, and so forth) support the protocol, but you don't necessarily have a compelling reason to change as of yet. When you do change, you will need to know a little about hexadecimal addresses to be able to interpret what you are seeing in an IPv6 address. Later in this chapter I will discuss the details, purposes, and properties of both forms of IP addressing.

EUI-64

Just as you wouldn't think that 4 billion IP addresses might not be enough, you would likely never suppose that 2 to the power 48 (281,474,976,710,656) MAC addresses would not be enough. You would likely be right, but just to make sure, the *Extended Unique Identifier 64 (EUI-64)* addresses that are in use in many organizations today provide an address space that far surpasses that of our current *MAC-48* addresses. You will see EUI-64 addresses used more often, essentially replacing MAC-48 addresses, in the coming years, especially when companies begin the transition to IPv6. I will discuss formatting of EUI-64 used in IPv6 addressing in greater detail later in this chapter.

Frames

Do you know how many definitions there are for the word *frame*? I was just researching it to give you a concise definition, and it blew my mind! Anyway, as defined for computer communications, a *frame* is a packet (I will discuss packets next) that has been encoded for transmission over a particular link. In general, you refer to packets at layer 2 of the OSI model (Data Link layer) as frames. Later in this chapter, I will discuss how switches use frames, and the MAC addresses they contain, to segment a network.

Packets

A *packet* is a fundamental unit of information exchange in a computer network. It consists of a header that contains the information about the source as well as the destination of the packet, the data that is to be carried, and a checksum to determine that the packet has arrived safely at its destination and has not been damaged in transit. Packets are defined differently depending on which layer of the OSI model they reside. Table 1.1 shows terms used for packets at various layers of the OSI model.

TABLE 1.1   Packet terminology in OSI model

OSI layer	Packet term
Application	Data
Presentation	Data
Session	Data
Transport	Datagram
Network	Packet
Data Link	Frame
Physical	Bit

Switch

A *switch* is a network device that optimizes traffic flow on your network. A switch works at layer 2 (Data Link); it learns the physical address (MAC address) of all the devices that are connected to it and then uses the MAC address to control traffic flow. Some switches, called *multilayer switches*, also work at layer 3, but here I am focusing on switches that work only at layer 2. Rather than forwarding all data to all the connected ports, a switch can forward data only to the port where the computer with the destination address actually exists. This process automatically segments the network and dramatically decreases the traffic in the segments that are less used. Because of this, switches are often used to connect departments of a company so that communication between two or more departments does not affect other departments that are not involved in the communication. Also, large files can be transferred within the same department without affecting the traffic flow in any of the other departments. Switches can also be used to create virtual local area networks (VLANs) that improve the flexibility of a network design. I will discuss VLANs later in this chapter. Figure 1.2 shows a common switch.

FIGURE 1.2   A switch

Router

Routers are the devices that connect the Internet and make the World Wide Web possible. They use a higher level of intelligence than that of switches. Routers use logical addresses and work at layer 3 (Network) of the OSI model and forward traffic from one network (or subnet) to another. Routers first determine whether the traffic belongs on their network; then they deliver it to the appropriate network hosts while forwarding the traffic that does not belong on their network to another router. Routers determine where to forward traffic by consulting a routing table. An administrator can enter the routing table manually, or the router can learn it by using *routing protocols*.

Multilayer Switch

Whereas a basic switch works solely at layer 2 (Data Link) of the OSI model, a *multilayer switch* can work at both layer 2 and layer 3. Multilayer switches (also called *layer 3 switches*) are essentially switches with a router module installed in them. They are especially useful in networks with VLANs because you can create the VLANs and decide how the VLANs will be routed—all within the same switch. Multilayer switches can be connected to other multi-layer switches and to basic switches to extend VLANs through an organization. I will discuss VLANs in greater depth later in this chapter.

Hub

A hub is a device that has multiple ports into which connections can be made. All devices con-nected to a hub are also connected to each other. A hub does not filter any communication or provide any intelligence in regard to the data stream; it simply lets all the information flow through it and connects anything and everything that is connected to it. Hubs are generally used to connect network segments of computers that are physically close to each other, such as all the computers on one floor of a building or in a computer classroom. There are two major types of hubs: active and passive. An active hub is plugged into a power source so that it can amplify signals as well as connect them. A passive hub does not provide power but provides only connectivity. An example of a passive hub is a patch panel in a network closet. Figure 1.3 shows an active hub.

FIGURE 1.3   A four-port active hub

Encryption devices

In today's world, security is of maximum concern. To provide for greater network security, many organizations, such as the government and military, now use specialized network devices that encrypt (scramble up) data as it flows through the network so that a common user cannot interpret the data. Encryption can also be performed by software protocols, but hardware devices often give network administrators more options and a higher degree of security than software solutions can provide. The precise methods that are used by these types of organizations are far beyond the scope of this book—as I'm sure you can understand!

Cable

Although the "wire" doesn't always have to be a real wire anymore, it often still is. The cables that we use for network communication have evolved as much as the devices that they connect. They are generally classified in categories such as CAT 5 or CAT 6, designating their capabilities for your network. In Chapter 3, "Network Media and Topologies," I will discuss many types of network cables in detail.

NIC

Network interface cards (NICs) are used to connect a computer to the network. A network interface card is like a small computer in itself. Figure 1.4 shows two NICs. Its job is to translate a stream of serial data (one bit at a time) into several streams of parallel data that will be used by the computer. The network interface card also examines every packet on the network cable to determine whether the packet has a destination MAC address that matches its MAC address. If it does not, then the NIC does nothing more with the packet. However, if the address does match, then the NIC will forward the packet to the appropriate port of the computer based on the information contained in the packet.

FIGURE 1.4   Two NICs

Bridge

A *bridge* is a legacy device that is similar to a switch in that it can provide some intelligence to segment a network. Bridges, like switches, can learn the MAC addresses of all the hosts connected to them and use the addresses to control traffic to each of their ports. Bridges, however, are slower than switches, so they have been largely replaced by switches as devices used to segment traffic. You should be aware of these two main types of Ethernet bridges:

Transparent Bridge   A transparent bridge can connect two dissimilar networks, but it is "invisible" to both networks, and it does not provide translation of any kind. For example, if your network contained two Ethernet segments with one Token Ring segment in between, a transparent bridge could connect communication from one of the Ethernet segments through the Token Ring segment to the other Ethernet segment. The Ethernet traffic would not be interpreted by the Token Ring segment.

Translational Bridge   A translational bridge, as you might expect, actually performs a translation between two dissimilar networks. For example, if you wanted to translate data from an Ethernet segment to a Token Ring segment, you could use a translational bridge. By the way, I do realize that the likelihood of your network containing Token Ring is quite remote!

Exam Essentials

Know the basic types of network addressing.   Know the addressing types such as MAC, IPv4, and IPv6. MAC addresses are used with layer 2 devices such as switches, whereas IPv4 and IPv6 addresses are used with layer 3 devices such as routers and multilayer switches.

Know the most common network components.   A network consists of many different components for a reason. Understand the purpose of each common network component and its relationship to the network. Switches segment a network at layer 2 (Data Link), but routers more intelligently segment a network at layer 3 (Network).

1.3 Explain the purpose and properties of IP addressing

IP addresses are the logical addresses that are assigned to each host on a TCP/IP network. A host is generally defined as a NIC or a router interface to which an address is assigned. Basically then, a host is anything with an IP address. By assuring that IP addresses are kept unique within a network, effective communication can be maintained. There are many classes of IP addresses, but some do not fit into a defined class and others that do are reserved for special purposes. In this section, I will discuss the many forms of IP addressing and how they relate to your network.

Classes of addresses

An IPv4 address is a 32-bit binary address represented in what we call *dotted decimal format*. The following is an example of an IPv4 address:

192.168.1.1

In addition to the IP address, a subnet mask is also used with IPv4, which has the effect of "measuring" the address to determine which part of it is the network portion and which part is the host portion. You can think of the network portion as the street on which you live and the host portion as the specific address of your house or apartment. Simply put, where there are 1s in the binary of the subnet mask, the corresponding bits in the IPv4 address are network bits; and where there are 0s in the binary of the subnet mask, the corresponding bits in the IPv4 address are host bits.

A, B, C, D

The early developers of IPv4 established a class-based system of IP addresses that defined five classes of addresses. The engineers wanted to identify the type of class as quickly as possible in the addressing, so they actually did it in the first three bits of the address. Table 1.2 references how this was done and the effect it has on the number of networks and hosts per network. Note that all Class A addresses begin with 000, all Class B addresses begin with 100, all Class C addresses begin with 110, and all Class D addresses begin with 111. Since Class D addresses are used for multicasting and treated in a different way than A, B, or C, the other columns in the table are nonapplicable.

TABLE 1.2   IPv4 classful addressing system

Class	First octet range	Subnet mask	Number of networks	Number of hosts/ network
A	00000001–01111111 1–126 (127 is reserved)	255.0.0.0	126	16,777,214
B	10000000–10111111 128–191	255.255.0.0	16,384	65,534
C	11000000–11011111 192–223	255.255.255.0	2,097,152	254
D	11100000-11101111 224-239	NA	NA	NA

Public vs. Private

Unique IP address assignment on the Internet was originally the responsibility of the *Internet Assigned Numbers Authority (IANA)*, but it has been handed over to other organizations that coordinate with each other to make sure that addresses are unique. The current three major organizations for the entire world are divided geographically as follows:

American Registry for Internet Numbers (ARIN): Serves the North American continent and parts of the Caribbean

Asia Pacific Network Information Centre (APNIC): Serves the Asia Pacific Region

Réseaux IP Européens Network Coordination Centre (RIPE NCC): Serves Europe, the Middle East, and parts of Africa

Addresses that are assigned by these authorities are referred to as *registered*, or *public*, addresses. If you are connecting a computer to the Internet, then you must use an address that has been assigned by one of these authorities. Now I know what you are thinking: "I'm connected to the Internet, and I never contacted any of those organizations." That's probably because you use an address that is provided by your Internet service provider (ISP) that obtained the address from one of these authorities. ISPs have large blocks of IP addresses that they can assign to their clients, thereby giving them a valid and unique IP address to use on the Internet. Some large organizations still go through the process of registering for their own address blocks, but most individuals and smaller organizations simply get whatever addresses they need from their ISP.

Private IP addresses are completely different. To understand a network diagram, you have to be able to see the difference between public and private addresses. Public addresses are said to be routable, whereas private addresses are said to be nonroutable. What does this really mean? Is there something wrong with the bits in the private IP addresses that prevent them from being routed? No, the private addresses are actually nonroutable because they are filtered by the routers that would take you from one network to another on the Internet.

But now you may be asking, "How do they know which addresses to filter?" Well, the original designers of the Internet set aside some groups of IP addresses to be used for private addressing. That way, even if two companies were to choose the same addresses and even if neither of them used a firewall, there still could be no conflict because the addresses would never "see" each other. Table 1.3 lists the addresses that are automatically filtered by routers leading onto the Internet.

TABLE 1.3 Private IP address ranges

Class	Address range	Default subnet mask
A	10.0.0.0–10.255.255.255	255.0.0.0
B	172.16.0.0–172.31.255.255	255.255.0.0
C	192.168.0.0–192.168.255.255	255.255.255.0

As always, the full address is determined by the IP address combined with the subnet mask. The important point to remember here is that these are the addresses that are filtered. In reality, you could use any address that you chose for the private IP addressing schemes of your network. However, if we both decided to use a public address on the inside—for example, 14.1.1.1 for a router—then we could possibly see each other and have an address conflict if everything went wrong with the firewalls and other network protection. In other words, we would not be able to rely on the configured filters throughout the Internet. This is why it is recommended to use the private IP addresses that I have listed, and this is why you should know them.

As you can see in Table 1.2, when the first bit of the address was a 0 and the subnet mask was 255.0.0.0, then the address was a Class A address. There aren't very many Class A addresses, but they sure can have a lot of hosts! These are generally assigned to ISPs, the military, government, and very large corporations.

When the first bit was a 1, the second bit was a 0, and the subnet mask was 255.255.0.0, then the address was a Class B address. There are many more Class B addresses, but they cannot have the tremendous number of hosts as Class A. These are generally assigned to medium-sized to large corporations and smaller governmental entities.

When the first bit was a 1, the second bit was also a 1, the third bit was a 0, and the subnet mask was 255.255.255.0, then the address was a Class C address. There are a great number of Class C addresses, but each one can contain only 254 hosts. These were originally used for small companies and very small government entities.

Classless (CIDR)

Now that you know about the subnet mask, I can talk about classful addressing vs. classless addressing. The first thing to remember is that the names for these can throw you offtrack if you aren't careful. Logically, it might seem that classful would be better than classless. However, this is not always true, and it isn't true either that classless is always better than classful. It depends on what you are trying to accomplish in your network.

Classful addressing takes its name because the first octet of the address determines the subnet mask that will be used, and therefore the subnet mask does not have to be, and is not, advertised by the routers in the routing protocols. In other words, referring to the information in Table 1.2, you will notice that an address that has 1 to 126 in the first octet would be considered a Class A address if it had a subnet mask of 255.0.0.0. With classful addressing, that's its only choice. In other words, with classful addressing, the subnet mask is always assumed to be the one that corresponds with its first octet address.

This has the effect of limiting some network designs that otherwise could have used, for example, networks 172.16.1.0 and 172.16.2.0 with other networks between them. This cannot be done because the classful routing protocols will assume both of the networks to be 172.16.0.0, because of the assumed mask of 255.255.0.0. This will result in a network scheme that will not function properly.

Now let's say you have a routing protocol that actually takes into account the address and subnet mask you assigned to the interface. Wouldn't that be nice? In that case, you could specify the networks 172.16.1.0 and 172.16.2.0 by assigning the subnet mask of 255.255.255.0 to each, rather than the classful subnet mask of 255.255.0.0. (We will discuss subnetting later in this chapter.) If the protocol could advertise the address along with the subnet mask, then you could use these two networks even if you had other networks between them because they would be seen as two unique networks. This type of addressing is used in today's networks because it allows for more complex networking schemes that can make more efficient use of the available IP addresses. This type of routing is referred to as *Classless InterDomain Routing (CIDR)*, and it's used by most ISPs and large organizations to simplify IP addressing and make more efficient use of the addresses they have.

IPv4 vs. IPv6 (formatting)

The following is an IPv6 address on my laptop:

fe80::218:deff:fe08:6e14

That looks pretty weird, doesn't it?

Now I'll talk about what this really says and how you should interpret it.

Each hexadecimal character in the address is actually read by the network device as a binary number with 4 bits. Table 1.4 illustrates the relationship of each decimal, binary, and hexadecimal number and/or character.

TABLE 1.4   Decimal binary and hexadecimal conversion

Decimal	Binary	Hexadecimal
0	0000	0x0
1	0001	0x1
2	0010	0x2
3	0011	0x3
4	0100	0x4
5	0101	0x5
6	0110	0x6
7	0111	0x7
8	1000	0x8

TABLE 1.4 Decimal binary and hexadecimal conversion *(continued)*

Decimal	Binary	Hexadecimal
9	1001	0x9
10	1010	0xA
11	1011	0xB
12	1100	0xC
13	1101	0xD
14	1110	0xE
15	1111	0xF

As you can see from the table, if you were first to convert each of the characters you see in my example address into its binary equivalent, the result would be as follows:

1111 1110 1000 0000 :: 0010 0001 1000 : 1101 1110 1111 1111 : 1111 1110 0000 1000 : 0110 1110 0001 0100

Not so fast, though! Equally important as what you see is what you do not see but you still know must be there. For example, you know that there are a total of 128 bits in this address. Also, you know that each section between a set of colons should actually have 16 bits on its own, so what are you missing?

Well, to begin with, any "leading zeros" can be interpreted by the device easily and can therefore be left out, as you can see in the second section of the previous address. In addition, successive fields of zeros can be represented as ::, but this can be done only once in an address, because otherwise the device wouldn't know how many successive zeros were represented by each ::. If you do a quick count, you will find that you are missing 52 zeros! In other words, although you can represent the IPv6 address in this case as the following hexadecimal number:

fe80::218:deff:fe08:6e14

the device will actually use a 128-bit number that looks like the following:

1111 1110 1000 0000 : 0000 0000 0000 0000 : 0000 0000 0000 0000 : 0000 0000 0000 0000 : 0000 0010 0001 1000 : 1101 1110 1111 1111 : 1111 1110 0000 1000 : 0110 1110 0001 0100

As you can see, this is a huge addressing system:

$$2^{128} = 3.4028367 \times 10^{38}$$

that should allow for an almost limitless supply of addresses. Of course, the last time someone said that, we soon began to run out of addresses!

Well, now that you have seen the wildness of an IPv6 address, you should be glad to talk about the mundane IPv4 addresses. An IPv4 address is a 32-bit binary address represented in what we call *dotted decimal format*. The following is an example of an IPv4 address:

192.168.1.1

As I said before, in addition to the IP address, a subnet mask is also used with IPv4, which has the effect of "measuring" the address to determine which parts of it are the network portion and which parts are the host portion.

Now you may be thinking that IPv4 isn't in the binary form—IPv4 is in the dotted decimal format. Well, the network devices "see" the IPv4 addresses as binary numbers. In fact, 192.168.1.1 ends up looking like the following:

11000000 10101000 00000001 00000001

"How does that happen?" you may ask. Well, I'm glad you asked. The dotted decimal form uses the first 8 bits of binary over and over four times. The bits of the address are then valued based on the following template of values:

128 64 32 16 8 4 2 1 . 128 64 32 16 8 4 2 1 . 128 64 32 16 8 4 2 1 . 128 64 32 16 8 4 2 1

The address would then line up with the template as follows:

1 1   1   1   1   1   1

Everywhere there is not a 1 is a 0.

Later, I will discuss how the subnet mask combines with the IP address to determine which bits will be network bits and which will be host bits. I will also discuss how you can use a custom subnet mask to subnet a network further for more efficient and effective use of IP addresses.

MAC address format

The following is a MAC address on my computer:

00-18-DE-08-6E-14

If you examine this address closely against Table 1.4, you will note that its binary equivalent is the following:

0000 0000 – 0001 1000 – 1101 1110 – 0000 1000 – 0110 1110 – 0001 0100

In other words, the MAC address is actually a 48-bit binary address that is represented as hexadecimal. Figure 1.5 illustrates the structure of a MAC address. The first two bits on the left (high order) represent whether the address is broadcast and whether it is local or remote. The next 22 bits are assigned to vendors that manufacture network devices, such as routers and NICs. This is the organizational unique identifier (OUI). The next 24 bits should be uniquely assigned in regard to the OUI. In other words, if I am HP and I have already used a specific hexadecimal number with one of my OUIs, then I should not use it again. In this way, each NIC has an address that is as unique as a person's fingerprint.

FIGURE 1.5   The structure of a MAC address

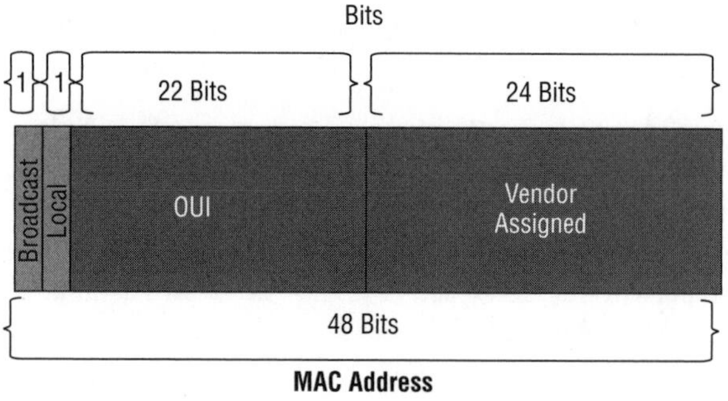

The main point to remember about MAC addresses is that they should be unique within the network in which they are to be used. This means that if one is assigned to a NIC, it should be unique within the whole world, but if a MAC addresses is functioning only on an interface within your LAN, then you should just ensure that it's unique within your LAN. Sometimes administrators may change the MAC address on a router interface, for example, to facilitate a behavior of another protocol. These types of changes are beyond the scope of this book.

Subnetting

Subnetting is a method used to create additional *broadcast domains*. You may wonder why you want additional broadcast domains when broadcasts are typically considered bad; that is, they are something to be avoided whenever possible. Look at it this way: if you have a fixed number of hosts in a network, you can reduce the number of hosts per broadcast domain and therefore reduce the effect of broadcasts on the hosts by increasing the number of broadcast domains. This is because there will be fewer hosts in each of the broadcast domains. In other words, subnetting creates smaller logical networks and thereby reduces the traffic within each logical network.

In addition to reducing the effect of broadcasts, subnetting also allows you to apply security policies in an easy and efficient manner. Each *subnet* can represent a location, role, job, and so on. By applying access control lists and other types of network filtering rules, you can control who gets access to what on a network. This job would be made much more difficult if you could not use subnets.

Now that you know the "why" of subnetting, I'll cover the "how" of subnetting. In plain terms, when you subnet IPv4, you are just reapplying the same sets of rules that were used to create the classful system of IP addressing in the first place. Please refer to Table 1.2 to refresh your memory about these rules.

Are you ready for this now? Actually, we don't strictly follow this classful system anymore, but that doesn't mean you don't need to know it! What we do follow is based on the classful system, but we have customized it to fit our needs using logical addressing methods and new technologies such as NAT, PAT, and proxies, which I will discuss later.

In today's networks, you need to make the most efficient use possible of the IP addressing space that you have been given by ARIN or that you have created for yourself with private IP addressing. To do this, you use custom subnet masks that define the appropriate number of networks and the appropriate number of hosts per network for your particular situation.

You generally start with a classful address that has the capacity to be subnetted further to meet the needs of your network. For example, let's say I have one network defined as 192.168.1.0 with a subnet mask of 255.255.255.0. As I discussed, this subnet mask identifies the network bits and host bits in the network. If you were to convert the dotted decimal subnet mask to binary, you would find twenty-four 1s in a row followed by eight 0s in a row. This means the network portion of the address is the first 24 bits, or 192.168.1. The 0 identifies the beginning of new network, and the addresses after it would be 1 to 254. The last address would be 255; this is not a host address but rather a broadcast address. "What's the difference?" you may ask. Well, if another host wanted to address a packet in such a way that it would be received by all 254 hosts (in this case), then the host would use 192.168.1.255, which is the broadcast address. The broadcast address should be set aside for broadcasts and never be used as a host address.

Now that you have established what you already have, let's say what you have is not what you want. Let's say you want to have 8 subnets with as many hosts as possible in them instead of just one network with 254 hosts. What would you do then? You guessed it—you would subnet the classful network to create the custom networks you need. How would you do this?

You would begin by understanding that you have 8 host bits with which to work. The network bits assigned to you will not be changed, and you will always be moving from the left to the right on your template. The question now is "How many of those 8 host bits do you need to change into subnet bits to create the eight subnets that you need?" (Some people refer to this part as *borrowing*, which is a term I never really liked because I'm not really planning on "giving them back"!) The answer to this question lies in the formula 2^s ≤ # of subnets. In this formula, s is the number of host bits that will be turned into subnet bits, and # of subnets is the number of subnets you need to create.

In this case, 2^s ≤ 8. Solving for s, you find that it must be at least 3. You want the lowest s that works because you also want to maximize the number of host bits that you still have remaining, so s = 3. Now the next question is "Which three?" Well, you are always going to move from the left to the right, so you will start at the left of the remaining 8 bits and take the first 3 bits from the left toward the right. This means that the subnet bits will be the 128, 64, and 32 bits. To make these host bits into subnet bits, you will simply change the corresponding bits in the subnet mask from 0 to 1. When you make this change, the subnet mask will then change to 255.255.255.224 since "128 + 64 + 32 = 224."

The next question on your mind might be "Then what are my 8 subnets?" You can answer this question by determining the increment of the subnets and therefore their numbers and ranges of hosts. The increment is always 256—the last number in the subnet mask that is not a 0. In this case, it's 256 – 224, which equals 32. The first network is always the same as what you started with, but with a new subnet mask. You can express the new subnet mask as 255.255.255.224, or you can express it by using a forward slash at the end of the IP address followed by a number indicating the number of 1s in the subnet mask. In this case, you could express your subnet mask as a /27. This is referred to as *CIDR notation.*

Since all the other networks are determined by the increment, your networks will be as follows:

192.168.1.0/27

192.168.1.32/27

192.168.1.64/27

192.168.1.96/27

192.168.1.128/27

192.168.1.160/27

192.168.1.192/27

192.168.1.224/27

The host ranges and broadcast addresses can then be determined without any further use of the binary. For example, the 0 network will have 30 hosts in it ranging from 1 to 30, and it will have a broadcast address of 31. The 32 network hosts will range from 33 to 62 with a broadcast address of 63, and so on, through the networks.

You can also check your math by understanding that the number of hosts will always be $2^h - 2$, where h is the number of remaining host bits after the subnet bits are determined. In this example, there are five remaining host bits, so the formula will be $2^5 - 2 = 30$. Since this matches the number of hosts as determined by the increment, you know you are on the right track!

Now let's try one that is a little more complicated. Don't worry, I'll walk you right through it, and then you will be able to do it yourself. Let's say you have an IP network of 172.16.0.0 with a subnet mask of 255.255.0.0 and you want to have 60 subnets with as many hosts per subnet as possible. What would the new subnet mask be? How many hosts would you have? What would your networks look like?

You start solving this problem in the same way as the last by noticing where you are beginning in the address, based on the subnet mask. In other words, my first question is always "Where am I?" Since you have a subnet mask here of 255.255.0.0, you are halfway through the address. In other words, you have sixteen 1s followed by sixteen 0s in the subnet mask. The fact that you have sixteen 0s means you have 16 host bits, some of which will be used for subnet bits. The next question is "How many host bits do you need to convert to subnet bits to create the 60 subnets that you need?"

You can answer this question with the same formula as before, $2^s \geq$ # of subnets. In this case, $2^s \geq 60$. Solving for s, you determine that s = 6, since $2^6 = 64$ and that's the first number that is higher than 60. Now the question is "Which six?" Remember that you are always moving from left to right, so the six bits that you will use will be the first six in the third octet starting from the left. This means you will change the corresponding bits in the subnet mask from 0s to 1s. This in turn means that the subnet mask number will change to 255.255.252.0, since 128 + 64 + 32 + 16 + 8 + 4 = 252. In other words, when you change the subnet bits to 1s, the values count and change the subnet mask accordingly.

The next question is "How many hosts could you have per network?" A close look at the template should show you that you have 2 host bits left in the third octet and 8 host bits left in the fourth octet. That's a total of 10 host bits. This means you can have $2^{10} - 2$ hosts per subnet, or 1,022.

Now you might be wondering how you are going to do that and what the addresses are going to look like when you get done. Just as before, the first network is always the same network you started with, but it has the new subnet mask, and the rest of the networks are determined by the increment. In this case, your first network is 172.16.0.0 with a subnet mask of 255.255.252.0. The increment is always 256—the last number in the subnet mask that is not a 0. In this case, the increment is "256 − 252 = 4." This means that the first three networks will be as follows:

172.16.0.0/22

172.16.4.0/22

172.16.8.0/22

Notice that I left some blank space between the network addresses. I like to call that space "thinking room," because you are going to do a lot of thinking in there. It's rather straightforward to see that the first host in the 172.16.0.0 network will be 172.16.0.1, but where do you go from there to get 1,022 hosts? Imagine an old odometer that actually spins out the 10ths of miles. Do you have that in your mind? Now when it gets to nine 10ths, think about what happens. The 10ths will then go back to 0, the number on the left will increment by 1, and then it all starts over again. Right? That's the same thing that happens with the IP addresses, except that it's not 0 to 9 but rather 0 to 255. In this case, when the addresses get to 172.16.0.255, the next number is then 172.16.1.0. Now, here's the kicker: both of those addresses are valid hosts! In fact, there will be a lot of weird-looking numbers that will be valid hosts as well. So, what is the last host in the 172.16.0.0/22 network? The last host is 172.16.3.254, and the broadcast is 172.16.3.255. After that, the 172.16.4.0/22 network starts, which has a broadcast address of 172.16.7.255. Use the "thinking room," and you will see it.

It's extremely important with today's networks that you understand IP addressing and subnetting. The quicker you can determine the subnet on which a host resides, the better you will be at network troubleshooting. I hope this has helped you see IP addresses for what they are without having to convert them to binary numbers. With practice, you will be able to "see" the answers instead of always having to figure them out. I highly recommend you spend some time working on IP address subnetting. One tool that I've found invaluable is the website http://subnetttingquestions.com. It was created in part by Todd Lammle, a fellow Wiley author. This site is free and offers hundreds of questions and answers. Your challenge is to get the same answer as the site has and to do it as quickly as possible.

Multicast vs. unicast vs. broadcast

Three major types of addressing schemes are used on IPv4 networks. These are unicast, multicast, and broadcast. Each type has its own place in the network. In the following sections, I'll discuss each of these types of network addressing schemes:

Unicast   Of the three types of addressing schemes used in IPv4, *unicast* is the most simple and straightforward. A packet (layer 3) or frame (layer 2) is said to have a unicast address if it has one source address and one destination address. If we are discussing packets, then the source and destination addresses are of a layer 3 protocol, likely IP. If we are discussing Ethernet frames, then the source and destination addresses of a layer 2 protocol are MAC addresses. In either case, the devices need to determine only the correct unique destination address to send the packet.

Multicast   *Multicast* addressing can be much more complex than unicast. With multicast addressing there is still only one source address; however, there can be multiple destination addresses. In other words, the frame or packet basically carries a list of destination addresses with it, and each device checks to see whether it is on the list when it sees the data. Multicasting is especially useful for applications that send voice and video through network systems. Multicast addressing uses specialized protocols such as Internet Group Management Protocol (IGMP) to create and carry the "list." The IP addresses carried by IGMP can be mapped to MAC addresses for layer 2 multicasting.

Broadcast   *Broadcast* addressing is similar to just standing in a room yelling out a person's name or an announcement. Anyone in the room who hears you with the name you yelled would be likely to respond, but everyone in the room would be disturbed in the process. On the other hand, if the announcement were actually intended for everyone in the room, then you would have accomplished your goal.

Broadcasting is accomplished by using an address that directs the data to all the members of a network or subnet. Every IPv4 network or subnet has a broadcast address, which is the last numerical address before the next network. In the binary form of a broadcast address, you will notice that all the host bits are 1s. For example, the broadcast address of the network 192.168.1.0/27 is 192.168.1.31. As you can see, the host address portion is 31 in dotted decimal, which is 11111 in binary.

Some services in an IPv4 network work by broadcasts, such as DHCP and even ARP. That said, broadcasts are typically thought of as bad and to be avoided whenever possible. IPv6 uses a different form of addressing referred to as *anycast* to avoid using broadcasts and provide other specialized services. This is beyond the scope of this chapter and not listed as an objective on the current exam.

APIPA

All client computers since Windows 98 are configured by default to obtain their IP address from a *DHCP server*. What if a DHCP server is not available? In that case, they are also configured by default to use an address in the range of 169.254.0.1 to 169.254.255.254. These addresses are called *Automatic Private Internet Protocol Addressing (APIPA)* addresses.

The advantage of using APIPA is that the clients in the same network segment that could not obtain a true IP address from a DHCP server can still communicate with each other. The disadvantage is that the clients can communicate with each other but not with the true network. This can lead to some wild troubleshooting for the unseasoned administrator. The bottom line is that when you see an address that begins with 169.254, you can rest assured that it was not obtained from any DHCP server!

Exam Essentials

Know how to identify an IPv6 address.   An IPv6 address is a 128-bit binary address represented in hexadecimal. Leading 0s and successive fields of 0s may be omitted when representing an IPv6 address. For example: fe80::218:deff:fe08:6e14.

Know how to identify an IPv4 address.   An IPv4 address is a 32-bit binary address that is represented in dotted decimal format. The address is divided into four sections, which each contain 8 bits and are therefore called octets. A subnet mask combines with an IP address to determine which bits are network and which are host. For example: 192.168.1.1 with a subnet mask of 255.255.255.0.

Know how to identify a MAC address.   A MAC address is a 48-bit binary address that is represented in hexadecimal code. MAC addresses are assigned to NICs, routers, switches, and other network equipment and should be unique in the network in which they are to be used. A MAC address must always be determined in order for communication to move from any host on a network to any other host. For example: C0-FF-EE-C0-FF-EE.

Understand different types of IP addresses and their purpose.   Some addresses are unicast, some broadcast, and some multicast and you should know the differences between them. Some addresses are meant for public use, while others are for private use. Network addresses may be subnetted to provide flexibility and enhanced management in a network and understand the general process used to subnet an IPv4 address.

1.4 Explain the purpose and properties of routing and switching

Today's networks are not "your father's network." Networks continue to evolve, and what we want to do on them continues to evolve. We are placing very fast computers on our networks now and expecting to receive reports, email, chat, music, videos, games, and so forth—often all at once! Because of these challenges, network administrators have to rely on newer and better technologies to both control traffic and to provide security for a network. However, the two major components that we use for our network are the same two that we used many years ago, namely, routers and switches. In this section, I will discuss the many protocols that have evolved over time that control and enhance our use of these two main components.

EIGRP

Enhanced Interior Gateway Routing Protocol (EIGRP) is a Cisco proprietary protocol that combines the ease of configuration of distance vector routing protocols such as RIP or RIPv2 (discussed later in this chapter) with the advanced features and fast convergence of link state protocols. It is said to be a distance vector routing protocol with link state attributes. It can also be considered an advanced distance vector routing protocol or a hybrid routing protocol.

EIGRP uses a much more sophisticated metric than RIP or RIPv2. This metric includes the bandwidth of a connection and the delay, which is an experiential factor of how long it takes to pass traffic over the path of the network. It can also be tweaked by an administrator with load and reliability factors. Because of its more sophisticated metric, EIGRP is well suited for small, medium, and even large networks. The only possible disadvantage to EIGRP is that it is Cisco proprietary and therefore operates only on Cisco routers and Cisco layer 3 switches.

OSPF

Open Shortest Path First (OSPF) is by far the most common link state routing protocol in use today. OSPF is so named because it is an "open" protocol. In other words, it's not proprietary, and it uses the Shortest Path First (SPF) algorithm developed by Dijkstra.

The principle advantages of this protocol include that it is quiet on the network—not "chatty" like some of the protocols that preceded it—and that it converges very rapidly when there is a change in the network. In other words, when the tables need to be changed to control network traffic, it makes that happen very fast—usually within a few seconds. Because of these advantages, OSPF can be used on small, medium, and large networks.

RIP

Routing Information Protocol (RIP) is one of the first routing protocols. As you can imagine, being first in regard to technology does not necessarily mean being the best. In fact, RIP is now considered obsolete and is being replaced by more sophisticated routing protocols, such as RIPv2, OSPF, and IS-IS.

The principal reasons for RIP's demise are that it is a "chatty" protocol in which all information that each router knows regarding networks is broadcast every 30 seconds. In addition, RIP uses a "hop count" metric that doesn't take into account the bandwidth of a connection. Finally, RIPv1, commonly referred to as RIP, is classful, which means it does not provide the means to advertise the true subnet mask of a network. In today's varied networks, this type of routing protocol does not have the intelligence needed to route packets efficiently.

RIPv2 solves some of the problems associated with RIPv1 but not all of them. It does not broadcast every 30 seconds but instead uses multicast addressing for its advertisements. This provides for much more efficient use of network bandwidth. In addition, it can be configured to be classless, which means it can carry the true subnet mask of a network and can therefore be used on more complex networks.

RIPv2, however, still uses only a hop count metric. Because of this limitation, it cannot be used effectively in today's networks that provide redundant and sometimes varied speed connections from point to point. It is therefore also considered by today's standards to be a legacy routing protocol.

Link state vs. distance vector vs. hybrid

As I discussed each of the most common routing protocols, I classified them into categories such as link state, distance vector, and hybrid. This is an area of confusion for some, so I want to make very clear the differences between these categories of protocols. You may use one or more of these categories in your network.

Link state identifies and describes one of the most common categories of routing protocols in use today. *Link* means interface, and *state* means the attributes of the interface, in other words, where it is, what is connected to it, how fast it is, and so forth. Link state routing protocols send all this interface information in the form of link state advertisements (LSAs). From these LSAs, the routers will build a map of the network. Each router in the same area will have the same map and will therefore be able to make decisions as to how to forward a packet. The two most common link state routing protocols are OSPF and IS-IS.

Distance vector routing protocols are also exactly what they say they are. Distance, as you know, is "how far." Vector, as you may know, is "which direction." Distance vector routing protocols make decisions by examining these two factors against their routing tables. The most common distance vector routing protocols in use today are RIP and RIPv2. Internet Gateway Routing Protocol (IGRP) was also a distance vector routing protocol, but it is considered "retired" and is no longer in use today.

There is only one hybrid routing protocol with which you must be familiar, EIGRP. It is said to be a hybrid because it is actually a distance vector routing protocol that works like a link state routing protocol. EIGRP is one of the most commonly used routing protocols today, especially on networks that contain exclusively Cisco devices.

Static vs. dynamic

Along with all of this discussion of dynamic routing protocols (such as EIGRP, OSPF, and RIPv2), we should also mention that it's entirely possible for you to configure your own settings in regard to the network tables. The method you use depends on the vendor of the router, but the general principle is the same. Although it would likely not be to your advantage to reconfigure the tables with every network change, there are some times when a specific static configuration might be advantageous. These static configuration tweaks are usually for the purpose of enhancing security, ensuring the reliability of a link, or forcing the system to do something that it otherwise would not do.

Routing metrics

Some routing protocols are much "smarter" than others. By this I don't mean that you are smarter if you use one or the other but that the routing protocol itself makes more intelligent decisions. The data that every routing protocol uses to make decisions is referred to as its *routing metric*. Different routing protocols use different routing metrics. There are four routing metrics used by routing protocols today. These are as follows:

Hop Counts   A *hop* is actually the process of a packet passing through two router interfaces and therefore into a new network or subnet. It's just more fun to say that it "hopped" over the router and into the next network. Routing protocols that only use hop counts, such as RIP and RIPv2, are of limited intelligence because they don't take into account the bandwidth of each link or the traffic currently on it. One hop is equal to any other, regardless of the bandwidth of each option.

MTU, Bandwidth, Delay   Maximum Transmission Unit (MTU) is metric that is carried by EIGRP but not actually used in the calculation of the best route. It can be considered a legacy metric that used to signify the largest size packet that could be sent over the entire route. With today's modern networks, it is no longer needed. The two most common metrics used by EIGRP are bandwidth and delay. Bandwidth is defined as the lowest configured bandwidth of any interface in a proposed route. This is similar to the idea that "The weakest link in a chain determines its strength!" Delay, as I mentioned, is an experiential factor of how long it takes to pass data over the link. These types of metrics offer greater intelligence and usually better routing decisions than hop counts can.

Costs   Whereas EIGRP uses bandwidth and delay to make decisions, link state routing protocols such as OSPF use a metric referred to as *cost*. With OSPF, cost is calculated 10 to the power 8 divided by the bandwidth in bits per second. By this calculation, a connection with a bandwidth of 100Mbps has a cost of 1. Cost is relatively simple metric, but since it is calculated for all possibilities, it can be resource intensive in a complex and dynamic network.

Latency   Latency is a metric that is very similar to delay when used with respect to routing. It defines the amount of time that it takes for a packet to travel from a source to a destination. The difference is that while delay is specifically a routing metric, *latency* is a term that is also used outside of routing, such as in hard drives or memory. The assumption is that something else is waiting for the data to arrive and that the less time it waits, the faster everything else can move.

Next hop

Generally speaking, routers couldn't care less where a packet comes from when they make a routing decision. What they care about is where the packet wants to go. In other words, they are concerned with the destination address in the header of the packet. Based on the destination address, they can determine whether they can deliver the packet themselves or whether they need to send it to another router. If they cannot deliver the packet themselves, then they will consult their routing table to determine the next step. As I mentioned earlier, the routing table will give them the information about the next interface that they can get to, which would be the appropriate place to send the packet. This interface is referred to as the next hop *interface*. This is because going from one network to another is like hopping over a router in the network diagram. As I mentioned, it's really just going through two consecutive interfaces, but isn't it a lot more fun to say "hop"?

Spanning Tree Protocol

In today's networks, switches are often connected with redundant links to provide for fault tolerance and load balancing. Unfortunately, these redundant links can also create physical loops in the network. If these physical loops were allowed to be seen by data traffic as logical loops, the result could be broadcast storms, multiple copies of the same frame sent to hosts, and MAC database instability on devices. To prevent the logical loops from occurring while still maintaining physical redundancy, modern network switches use the *Spanning Tree Protocol (STP)*.

The original STP is defined by the IEEE as 802.1D. Many other faster and more sophisticated spanning tree protocols have been developed over the past 10 years, including Rapid Spanning Tree Protocol (RSTP), Multiple Spanning Tree Protocol (MSTP), and Per-VLAN Spanning Tree Protocol (PVSTP). Each of these protocols has the same goal in mind: to provide multiple viable paths for data fault tolerance and load balancing without creating loops and the problems they cause.

VLAN (802.1q)

A *virtual local area network (VLAN)* is a subnet created using a switch instead of a router. Because of this fact, VLANs have many advantages over subnets created by routers. One of the main advantages of VLANs is that the logical network design does not have to conform to the physical network topology. This gives administrators much more flexibility in network design and in the subsequent changes of that design.

The problem is that subnets created by a router are, by definition, local to the interface from which the subnet was created. In addition, all the hosts off each router interface are in the same subnet. This might be fine if all the hosts in a specific geographic area were always in the same department or security group of the organization, but often this is not the case. This means that an administrator cannot set up security policies for resource use by department and use the subnet address to control the policy, because many departments might be mixed into the same subnet.

VLANs solve this problem by creating the subnets using a switch or even groups of switches. Ports on the switches are assigned to a specific VLAN and therefore in a specific subnet. Now here is the important difference, so pay attention—all ports that are assigned to the same VLAN are logically in the same subnet regardless of where those ports are located in the organization. Because of this fact, the administrator can manage the network and its resources by departments represented by subnets, regardless of where each of the users actually resides. This offers a tremendous advantage to an administrator.

Now, you may be wondering how all the switches know about all the VLANs. Well, the administrator will assign some ports on a switch to carry all the VLAN information to the other switches. These ports, which allow all VLANs to pass through them, are referred to as *trunks*. A VLAN switch that is connected to other VLAN switches will have at least one trunk port. Switches that are central to a topology may have multiple trunk ports. While other trunking protocols exist, the most common trunking protocol by far is *IEEE 802.1q*.

Another advantage of VLANs is that the traffic that is communicated within the interfaces of the VLAN is only on the interfaces of that VLAN and on the trunks. This increases the security in an organization. Furthermore, connecting one VLAN's traffic to another VLAN requires a centrally located (logically) layer 3 device such as a router or a multilayer switch. The administrator can place access lists on this device that will control all traffic between the VLANs. This represents a tremendous improvement over placing separate access lists on all the routers in the organization. Because of these advantages, VLANs are commonly used in many of today's networks.

Port mirroring

Some devices, such as the sensor on an IDS/IPS system, require the ability to monitor all network traffic. Since the VLANs separate the traffic for security reasons, monitoring all traffic sometimes requires getting a copy of network packets from one switch port sent to another switch port, strictly for the purpose of monitoring and logging them. This process, called *port mirroring*, is becoming a more common practice as organizations continue to install more IDS/IPS systems. It is referred to as Switched Port Analyzer (SPAN) on Cisco switches and as Roving Analysis Port (RAP) on HP switches.

Broadcast domain vs. collision domain

In general, routers and other layer 3 devices create additional broadcast domains, while switches create additional collision domains. Now you may be thinking, "Why do I want more of either one of them in my network"? Well, let's take a look at what each one does.

Broadcast domains determine a boundary for messages sent as a broadcast. Many protocols, such a DHCP, use broadcasts to perform their service. This does not negatively affect a network as long as it is controlled in such a way that all broadcasts cannot get to all devices in a large network. Generally speaking, routers and other layer 3 devices stop broadcasts from getting from one network or subnet to another one. This applies whether the subnets were created by router interfaces or by VLANs on a switch. Additional broadcast domains mean less broadcast traffic on each domain and greater control.

Collision domains control which devices can "see" each other through the network. If two devices put data on the network at the same exact time and can sense each other, it results in a collision. Collisions can cause resending of data and slow the network down. (We will discuss collision detection and prevention methods in Chapter 3.) The ironic thing is, the more collision domains that we have, the less the possibility for collisions. This is because there will be fewer devices in each collision domain. Now you may ask, "Why don't we just put each communication into its own collision domain?" Well, in essence that is exactly what modern switch designs do!

IGP vs. EGP

All the routing protocols I've discussed thus far have been Interior Gateway Protocols (IGPs). Border Gateway Protocol (BGP) is an Exterior Gateway Protocol (EGP). Understanding the difference relies upon your knowledge of an *autonomous system*. An autonomous system is a group of devices under the same administrative domain. If a routing protocol works within one autonomous system, it is considered to be an IGP. If it works across autonomous systems, in effect connecting them, then it is considered to be an EGP. That's all there is to it, so don't make it any harder than it really is. The only EGP that you should be concerned with today is BGP; all of the rest are IGPs.

Routing tables

Simply put, routers really do only two things; either they deliver a packet to an intended destination host if that host is on one of the subnets for which they have an active interface or they consult their routing table to determine what to do next. Table 1.5 is a simple illustration of a RIPv2 routing table using hop count. This is actually a "Reader's Digest" version of what you might see in a Cisco router, but you get the point. As you can see, the router that contains this table knows how to get to other networks by virtue of the table. In other words, a packet that comes into this router that is destined for the 10.1.0.0 network will be sent out of a different interface from one that is destined for the 192.168.1.0 network.

TABLE 1.5 RIPv2 hop count

Destination network	Subnet mask	Interface	Metric (hop count)
10.1.0.0	255.255.0.0	S0	1
192.168.1.0	255.255.255.0	S1	1
172.16.0.0	255.255.0.0	S1	2

Convergence (steady state)

Convergence means that everything is in agreement again after change has taken place. In other words, let's say you have a network that is all settled and in a steady state. All routers know the best interface to send a packet out based on the destination address of the packet. Now let's say you add a new interface to a router and thereby create a new path on which traffic could flow. This would cause the routing protocols to acknowledge and examine the new path and determine whether it is a more efficient path than the one they are currently using. In fact, each router that has the intelligence required would need to examine the new path against its current path for each network in its table. It would then make a decision as to whether to make a change. This could temporarily create quite a flurry of activity on a network in regard to routing protocol information exchange. If a router does not have this capability, then you would need to make the changes to the tables manually.

Once all the options are considered and the decisions are made, then the activity will settle down again. A network that has settled back down is said to be have *converged*, so the process of moving through this unsettled state to the settled state is referred to as *convergence*. Some routing protocols offer much faster convergence than others. As I discussed earlier, routing protocols such as EIGRP and OSPF are "smarter" and thus are not normally chatty, but they become very chatty for a short burst of time when something changes on the network. Their ability to move very quickly from an unsettled state to a settled state is referred to as *fast convergence*. This means that a change on an interface that affects the routing tables will have minimal effect on the user data that is traversing the network.

Exam Essentials

Know the most common routing protocols.   Know the most common routing protocols and why each might be used over the other. RIP and RIPv2 are distance vector routing protocols that use hop count as a metric and have limited intelligence of the network. The reason EIGRP and OSPF are the most used protocols is because they have a "smarter" metric that makes decisions based on bandwidth. They also are much less "chatty" and therefore take less overhead and leave more bandwidth for the end users. Remember that all routing protocols except BGP are IGP and that BGP is an EGP.

Understand the concept of VLANs.   VLANs are used in most of today's networks because they enhance flexibility and security. Switches are connected using trunks, which carry all of the VLANs and allow an expansion of the VLAN environment. The most common trunking protocol is IEEE 802.1q.

1.5 Identify common TCP and UDP default ports

As I mentioned, the Transport layer of the TCP/IP protocol suite contains two primary protocols: *TCP* and *UDP*. There are many protocols, most at the Application layer, that use one or the other, or even both, of these protocols as they work their way down the OSI model. The independent sessions that are created are possible because of a logical connection called a *port*.

If people performed only one task at a time with each computer, there might not be a need for ports, but we all know that computers can perform many tasks at one time. Because this is the case, you need a way to identify packets so that they will be processed by the computer in the correct manner. By identifying each packet with a port number, the system assures that the computer will direct the packet to the right area within it where the appropriate processes can be performed.

TCP and UDP port numbers are used to identify packets in regard to the services that they require. You can also filter traffic using these port numbers to restrict only specific types of traffic from a network. You should understand how TCP and UDP ports can be used to facilitate and control traffic. In the following sections, I will discuss the various types of TCP and UDP ports and describe their general use. You should be able to identify the port number that each of the most common network protocols, services, and applications use, as shown in Table 1.6. You should know the port number when given a service as well as the service when given a port number.

TABLE 1.6   The most common TCP and UDP default ports

Service, protocol, or application	Port assignment	Most often used with TCP, UDP, or both
File Transfer Protocol (FTP)	20, 21	TCP
Secure Shell (SSH)	22	TCP
Telnet	23	TCP
Simple Mail Transfer Protocol (SMTP)	25	TCP
Domain Name System (DNS)	53	TCP/UDP
DHCP	67, 68	TCP
Hypertext Transfer Protocol (HTTP)	80	TCP/UDP
Network Time Protocol (NTP)	123	TCP

TABLE 1.6   The most common TCP and UDP default ports *(continued)*

Service, protocol, or application	Port assignment	Most often used with TCP, UDP, or both
Internet Message Access Protocol (IMAP)	143	TCP
Simple Network Management Protocol (SNMP)	161	UDP
RDP	3389	TCP

Exam Essentials

Know the port numbers for the most common protocols.   Be able to identify the port numbers of the most common protocols and whether they are TCP or UDP.

Know the service that the most common protocols perform.   Understand why so many protocols and ports are necessary and the service that each of the protocols performs for a network.

1.6 Explain the function of common networking protocols

Sorry, but it's not enough to just know the port number and the protocol it represents. To truly understand your network and how to manage it, you need to fully understand each protocol, what it does, and how it relates to your network as a whole. Table 1.7 lists all of the most common protocols and their purpose, function, and use in your network. I have also listed each of protocols and given more detailed information about each of them.

TABLE 1.7   The most common protocols

Protocol	Purpose	Function	Use
IP	Addresses and transports data from one network node to another.	A Network layer connectionless protocol, it "fires and forgets." Performs fragmenting and assembling of packets.	IP addresses are assigned to computers and to router interfaces. These addresses are used to transfer a packet into the proper network so it can be delivered to a host.

Protocol	Purpose	Function	Use
TCP	Responsible for flow control and error recovery.	Connection based. Waits for receipt of acknowledgments from the destination that packets have been delivered without errors. Resends packets that are not acknowledged within a specified time frame. Works at the Transport layer of the TCP/IP suite.	Used with protocols that require a guaranteed delivery such as FTP, HTTP, SMTP, and others.
UDP	Broadcasts packets through a network, making a "best effort" to deliver them to the destination.	Connectionless protocol. Works at the Transport layer of the TCP/IP suite.	Used for applications that can provide their own acknowledgments or can be monitored, such as multimedia over the Internet or with noncritical data (such as gaming) where speed is more important.
FTP	Provides the rules of behavior for transferring files through an intranet or over the Internet.	Works at the Application layer of the TCP/IP suite. Provides a protocol as well as an application for transferring files.	Used to browse file structures on a remote computer and to transfer files between computers within intranets and on the Internet.
TFTP	Provides for transferring files within a network.	Connectionless protocol that works at the Application layer. Uses UDP for low overhead without a guarantee of delivery.	Typically used for simple file transfers such as those between a computer and a router or a switch for management purposes.
SMTP	Provides for the delivery of mail messages within a network or between networks.	Works at the Application layer and uses TCP to guarantee delivery of mail to remote hosts.	Typically used to transfer email messages within a network and between networks.
HTTP	Provides for browsing services for the World Wide Web.	Works at the Application layer and provides access to files on web servers through the use of URLs to pages that are formatted web languages such as HTML.	Typically used to browse information on the many servers that interconnect the World Wide Web.

TABLE 1.7   The most common protocols *(continued)*

Protocol	Purpose	Function	Use
HTTPS	Provides for access to resources on the Internet in a secure fashion.	Works at the Application layer and uses SSL to encrypt data traffic so communications on the Internet can remain secure.	Used for Internet communications that must remain secure, such as banking, ecommerce, and medical transactions.
POP3	Allows the storage and retrieval of user email on servers. Allows users to access and download email from servers.	Works at the Application layer. Users can connect to the server and download messages to a client. The messages can then be read of the client.	Used for many email applications. User can check their email boxes and download messages that have been placed in them.
IMAPv4	Allows the storage and retrieval of user email on servers. Allows users to access email on servers and either read the email on the server or download the email to the client to read it.	Works at the Application layer of the TCP/IP suite. Allows a user to read messages on an email server without the need to download the messages off the server.	Typically, this method of email retrieval is convenient for users who travel and therefore might access their email from more than one location. The mail remains on the server until they delete it, so they can gain access to it from multiple locations.
Telnet	Provides a virtual terminal protocol for connecting to a managing server.	Works at the Application layer of the TCP/IP suite. Provides a connection using an authentication method that is performed in clear text. This protocol and application are not considered secure.	Has been used in the past for "dumb terminals" that connected to mainframe computers. Is now used to connect computers to servers, routers, switches, and so on, for remote management.
SSH	Provides the capability to log onto a computer remotely, execute commands, and move files in a secure and encrypted environment.	Works at the Application layer of the TCP/IP suite. Provides for a secure logon and a secure environment in which to execute commands.	Typically used to manage servers from clients and to move sensitive files from one server to another within the same network or between networks.

Protocol	Purpose	Function	Use
ICMP	Provides error checking and reporting functionality.	Works at the Internet layer of the TCP/IP suite. Provides background services that can be used to provide information to an administrator and to request a "quench" of the information flow in the network.	Typically used as part of the ping tool to test network connectivity. Can send back an echo reply when an echo request message is sent to it. Can also send back a message such as "Destination Host Unreachable" and "Time Exceeded" when the connection to the pinged host is not possible.
ARP	Resolves IP addresses to MAC addresses.	Works at the Internet layer of the TCP/IP suite. Includes a cache that is checked first. If the entry is not found in the cache, then ARP uses a broadcast to determine the MAC address of the client.	Typically used by the system as a background service but also includes a utility that can be used for troubleshooting.
RARP	Resolves MAC addresses to IP addresses.	Works at the Internet layer of the TCP/IP suite. It assigns an IP address when presented with a MAC address.	Used with diskless workstations to assign an IP address automatically. Also sometimes used as very rudimentary security for computer authentication.
NTP	Synchronizes time between computers in a network.	Works at the Application layer of TCP/IP suite. Can synchronize time between clients and servers.	Used to synchronize time to assure that authentication protocols such as Kerberos work properly and that applications that require collaboration operate properly.
SIP (VoIP)	Sets up and tears down voice and video calls over the Internet.	Works at the Session layer of the OSI model and the Application layer of the TCP/IP suite.	Typically used for Voice over IP (VoIP) and video communications.

TABLE 1.7 The most common protocols *(continued)*

Protocol	Purpose	Function	Use
RTP (VoIP)	Defines a standardized packet format for delivering audio and video over the Internet.	Works at the Session layer of the OSI model and the Application layer of the TCP/IP suite.	Used to enhance multimedia communications for streaming, video conferencing, and push-to-talk applications.
IGMP	Provides a standard for multicasting on an intranet.	Allows a host to inform its local router, using Host Membership Reports that it wants to receive messages addressed to a specific multicast group.	Used to establish host memberships in multicast groups on a single network.
TLS	A network security protocol that provides for data confidentiality and integrity.	Works through active peer negotiation of authentication and encryption protocols.	Used for secure transmission of data between servers and clients within a network and between networks.
SNMP2/3	Assists network administrators in gathering information about their network.	Consists of a management information database and agents that are network devices. The agents that are in the same community as the database will send information to the database.	SNMP3 is used much more often than SNMP2 because it is much more secure. It uses a secure authentication mechanism and encrypts data as well.
DNS	Resolves hostnames to IP addresses.	Performs a series of steps with one of more DNS servers to resolve a user-friendly hostname to an IP address.	Allows users to address objects on a network or resources on the Internet by their friendly name, while the system can use the IP address to locate the resource.
DHCP	Dynamically assigns IP addresses and other network information to clients on a network.	Used by servers and other devices to dynamically assign IP addresses and other critical network addresses to clients that request them.	Used primarily for clients because servers, routers, and printers are generally assigned a static address.

Transmission Control Protocol (TCP)

TCP is a connection-oriented protocol that works at the Transport layer (layer 4) of the OSI model. It uses IP as its transport protocol and assists IP by providing a guaranteed mechanism for delivery. TCP requires that a session first be established between two computers before communication can take place. TCP also adds features such as flow control, sequencing, and error detection and correction. This guaranteed delivery mechanism is a requirement in order for TCP to operate at all. For this reason, you should understand how TCP operates.

TCP works by a process referred to as a *three-way handshake*. The TCP three-way handshake works as follows:

1. TCP sends a short message called a SYN to the target host.

2. The target hosts opens a connection for the request and sends back an acknowledgment message called a SYN ACK.

3. The host that originated the request sends back another acknowledgment called an ACK, confirming that it has received the SYN ACK message and that the session is ready to be used to transfer data.

A similar process is used to close the session when the data exchange is complete. The entire process provides a reliable protocol. TCP extends its reliability by making sure that every packet it sends is acknowledged. If a packet is not acknowledged within the timeout period, the packet is re-sent automatically by TCP. The only disadvantage of a connection-oriented protocol is that the overhead associated with the acknowledgments tends to slow it down.

File Transfer Protocol (FTP)

FTP, as its name indicates, provides for the transfer of files through a network environment. It can be used within an intranet or through the Internet. FTP is actually more than just a protocol; it is an application as well, and thus FTP works at the Application layer of the OSI model and uses the TCP protocol as a transport mechanism. FTP allows a user to browse a folder structure on another computer (assuming they have been given the permissions to authenticate to the computer) and then to download files from the folders or to upload additional files.

User Datagram Protocol (UDP)

UDP also operates at the Transport layer of the OSI model and uses IP as its transport protocol, but it does not guarantee the delivery of packets. It doesn't guarantee the delivery of packets because UDP does not establish a session. UDP is instead known as a "fire-and-forget" protocol because it assumes that the data sent will reach its destination and does not require acknowledgments. Because of this, UDP is also referred to as a *connectionless* protocol.

Now you might be wondering why anyone would want to use UDP instead of TCP. The advantage of UDP is its low overhead in regard to bandwidth and processing effort. Whereas a TCP header has 11 fields of information that have to be processed, a UDP header has only

4 fields. Applications that can handle their own acknowledgments and that do not require the additional features of the TCP protocol might use the UDP protocol to take advantage of the lower overhead. Multimedia presentations that are broadcast or multicast onto the network often use UDP since they can be monitored to make sure that the packets are being received. Services such as the Domain Name System (DNS) service also take advantage of the lower overhead provided by UDP.

TCP/IP suite

Just for reference and to make sure that we are on the same page, the *TCP/IP suite* includes much more than the protocols of TCP and IP. It's actually a way of identifying all of the protocols on all four layers of the TCP/IP model. In fact, since our focus is on TCP/IP, it really encompasses all of the protocols we are discussing.

Dynamic Host Configuration Protocol (DHCP)

DHCP is actually more of a service than a protocol. When a client comes on to a network, it needs an IP address. You could statically assign every computer in your network, but that would be doing it the hard way. The easier and smarter way would be to use the DHCP protocol (service) to make automatic assignments for you. You can even configure a DHCP server to give a client other information, such as the address of the DNS server.

All Microsoft clients since Windows 98 have their default installation configurations set to obtain an IP address automatically. They are already looking for a DHCP server when they start up. When you include a properly configured DHCP server on your network, you avoid a great number of IP misconfigurations and save yourself a lot of manual labor.

Trivial File Transfer Protocol (TFTP)

TFTP is similar to FTP in that it allows the transfer of files within a network, but that's where the similarity stops. Whereas FTP allows for the browsing of files and folders on a server, TFTP requires that you know the exact name of the file you want to transfer and the exact location where to find the file. Also, whereas FTP uses the connection-oriented TCP protocol, TFTP uses the connectionless UDP protocol. TFTP is most often used for simple downloads such as transferring firmware to a network device, for example, a router or a switch.

Domain Name System (DNS)

DNS is a service and a protocol. It uses relational databases to resolve hostnames of computers and other network clients to their assigned IP addresses. DNS facilitates "friendly naming" of resources on a network and on the Internet so you don't have to remember, for example, the IP address for MSNBC.com. Clients can be statically configured with the addresses of the DNS servers that host the DNS database, or the DHCP server can provide that information to the client.

Hypertext Transfer Protocol (HTTP)

HTTP is the protocol that users utilize to browse the World Wide Web. HTTP clients use a browser to make special requests from an HTTP server (web server) that contains the files they need. The files on the HTTP server are formatted in web languages such as Hypertext Markup Language (HTML) and are located using a uniform resource locator (URL). The URL contains the type of request being generated (`http://`, for example), the DNS name of the server to which the request is being made, and, optionally, the path to the file on the server. For example, if you type **http://support.microsoft.com/** in a browser, you will be directed to the Support pages on Microsoft's servers.

Hypertext Transfer Protocol Secure (HTTPS)

One of the disadvantages of using HTTP is that all the requests are sent in clear text. This means the communication is not secure and therefore unsuited for web applications such as ecommerce or exchanging sensitive or personal information through the Web. For these applications, *HTTPS* provides a more secure solution that uses a Secure Sockets Layer (SSL) to encrypt information that is sent between the client and the server. For HTTPS to operate, both the client and the server must support it. All the most popular browsers now support HTTPS, as do web server products such as Microsoft Internet Information Services (IIS), Apache, and most other web server applications. The URL to access a website using HTTPS and SSL starts with `https://` instead of `http://`. For example, `https://partnering.one.microsoft.com/mcp` is the page that is used to authenticate Microsoft Certified Professionals to Microsoft's private website.

Address Resolution Protocol (ARP)

The *ARP* protocol works at the Network layer of the OSI model and the Internet layer of the TCP/IP suite. It is used to resolve IP addresses to MAC addresses. This is an extremely important function, since the only real physical address that a computer has is its MAC address; therefore, all communication will have to contain a MAC address before it can be delivered to the host. This is accomplished in a series of steps:

1. A computer addresses a packet to another host using an IP address.

2. Routers use the IP address to determine whether the destination address is in their network or on another network.

3. If a router determines that the address is on another network, it forwards the packet to another router based on the information that is contained in its routing table.

4. When the router that is responsible for the network that contains the destination address receives the packet, it checks the ARP cache to determine whether there is an entry that resolves the IP address to a MAC address. If there is an entry, it uses the MAC address contained in the entry to address the packet to its final destination.

5. If there is no entry in the ARP cache, the router resolves the IP address to a MAC address for the destination by using ARP to broadcast onto the local network. It asks the computer with the IP address contained in the destination address of the packet to respond with its MAC address. The router also gives the computer its own MAC address to use for the response.

6. The broadcast is "heard" by all the computers in the local network, but it will be responded to only by the computer that has the correct IP address. All other computers will process the request only to the point that they determine it is not for them.

7. The computer that is configured with the IP address in question responds with its MAC address.

8. The router addresses the packet with the MAC address and delivers it to its final destination.

Session Initiation Protocol (SIP)

SIP is a Session layer protocol that is primarily responsible for setting up and tearing down voice and video calls over the Internet. It also enables IP telephony networks to utilize advanced call features such as SS7.

Real-Time Transport Protocol (RTP)

RTP defines a standardized packet format for delivering audio and video over the Internet. It is frequently used in streaming, video conferencing, and push-to-talk applications.

Secure Shell (SSH)

First developed by SSH Communications Security, Secure Shell is a program used to log into another computer over a network, execute commands, and move files from one computer to another. *SSH* provides strong authentication and secure communications over unsecure channels. It protects networks from attacks such as IP spoofing, IP source routing, and DNS spoofing. The entire login session is encrypted; therefore, it is almost impossible for an outsider to collect passwords. SSH is available for Windows, Unix, Macintosh, and Linux, and it also works with RSA authentication.

Post Office Protocol Version 3 (POP3)

POP3 is one of the protocols that is used to retrieve email from SMTP servers. Using POP3, clients connect to the server, authenticate, and then download their email. Once they have downloaded their email, they can then read it. Typically, the email is then deleted from the server, although some systems hold a copy of the email for a period of time specified by an administrator. One of the drawbacks of POP3 authentication is that it is generally performed in clear text. This means that an attacker could sniff your POP3 password from the network as you enter it.

Network Time Protocol (NTP)

NTP is a protocol that works at the Application layer of the OSI model and synchronizes time between computers in a network. In today's distributed networks, ensuring that the time is synchronized between clients and servers is essential. Authentication protocols, such as the Kerberos protocol used with Microsoft's Active Directory, use keys that are valid only for about five minutes. If a client and a server are not synchronized, the keys could be invalid the very second they are issued. In many of today's networks, an authoritative time source such as the Internet is first used and configured onto a time server (perhaps a domain controller). Then that server uses NTP to synchronize time with other computers in the network. Some computers may be a receiver of the correct time as well as a sender of the time to other computers in the network.

Internet Message Access Protocol version 4 (IMAPv4)

IMAPv4 is another protocol that is used to retrieve email from SMTP servers, but IMAPv4 offers some advantages over POP3. To begin with, IMAPv4 provides a more flexible method of handling email. You can read your email on the email server and then determine what you want to download to your own PC. Since the email can stay in the mailbox on the server, you can retrieve it from any computer that you want to use, provided that the computer has the software installed to allow you to access the server. Microsoft Hotmail is a good example of an IMAPv4 type of service. You can access your Hotmail mail from any browser. You can then read, answer, and forward email without downloading the messages to the computer that you are using. This can be very convenient for users who travel.

Telnet

Telnet is a virtual terminal protocol that has been used for many years. Originally, Telnet was used to connect "dumb terminals" to mainframe computers. It was also the connection method used by earlier Unix systems. Telnet is still in use today to access and control network devices such as routers and switches.

The main problem with Telnet for today's environment is that it is not a secure protocol; everything is transmitted in plain text. For this reason, Telnet is being replaced by more secure methods such as Secure Shell and Microsoft's Remote Desktop Connection, which provide encrypted communication.

Simple Mail Transfer Protocol (SMTP)

SMTP defines how email messages are sent between hosts on a network. You can remember SMTP as "sending mail to people." SMTP works at the Application layer of the OSI model and uses TCP to guarantee error-free delivery of messages to hosts. Since SMTP actually requires that the destination host always be available, mail systems spool the incoming mail into a user's mailbox so that the user can read it at another time. How users read the mail is determined by what protocol they use to access the SMTP server.

Simple Network Management Protocol 2/3 (SNMP 2/3)

The *SNMP* protocol is used to monitor devices on a network. A software component (called an *agent*) runs on the remote device and reports information via SNMP traps to the management systems. These management systems can be configured to record information such as errors on a network or resource information of the computers on a network.

SNMPv2 is an enhancement to the original SNMP (SNMPv1). The management information databases used in SNMPv1 are cumbersome and confusing to an administrator. SNMPv2 provides more user-friendly input and output options for data. SNMPv3 adds security measures for message integrity, authentication, and encryption. The enhancements of *SNMPv3* have made the previous two versions obsolete. The RFC that defines SNMPv3 (RFC-3411) refers to the previous versions as "historic."

Internet Control Message Protocol (ICMP)

The *ICMP* protocol works at the Network layer of the OSI model and the Internet layer of the TCP/IP protocol suite. ICMP provides error checking and reporting functionality. Although ICMP provides many functions, the most commonly known is its ping utility. The ping utility is most often used for troubleshooting. In a typical "ping scenario," an administrator uses a host's command line and the ping utility to send a stream of packets called an *echo request* to another host. When the destination host receives the packets, ICMP sends back a stream of packets referred to as an *echo reply*. This confirms that the connection between the two hosts is configured properly and that the TCP/IP protocol is operational.

ICMP can also send back messages such as "Destination Host Unreachable" or "Time Exceeded." The former is sent when the host cannot be located on the network, and the latter is sent when the packets have exceeded the timeout period specified by TCP. Still another function of ICMP is the sending of source quench messages. These messages are sent by ICMP when the flow of data from the source is larger than that which can be processed properly and quickly by the destination. A source quench message tells the system to slow down and therefore prevents the resending of many data packets.

Internet Group Management Protocol (IGMP)

IGMP is the standard for IP multicasting on intranets. It is used to establish host memberships in multicast groups on a single network. The mechanisms of the protocol allow a host to inform its local router, using Host Membership Reports indicating that it wants to receive messages addressed to a specific multicast group.

Transport Layer Security (TLS)

TLS allows network devices to communicate across a network while avoiding eavesdropping, tampering, and message forgery. It is designed to allow end users to be sure with whom they are communicating. Clients can negotiate the keys that will be used to secure the data to be transferred. TLS is set to supersede its predecessor SSL.

Exam Essentials

Know the purpose of the most common protocols.   Study the table and know the purpose, function, and use of each of the most common protocols.

Know the details of each common protocol and how they relate to your network communication.   Understand the entire nature of each of the most common protocols and how their function relates to your network.

1.7 Summarize DNS concepts and its components

As I mentioned, DNS is a service and a protocol that uses relational databases to resolve hostnames of computers and other network clients to their assigned IP addresses. There are three main components of DNS: DNS servers, DNS records, and Dynamic DNS. In this section, I will discuss each of these components.

DNS servers

DNS servers contain software and configuration that allows them to resolve hostnames to IP addresses for an IP network. They can be a *stand-alone server*, or they can perform other functions in the network, such as being a domain controller as well. They often exchange record databases with other DNS servers through a process called *zone transfer*. In addition, DNS servers can communicate with other DNS servers to discover information that they do not contain. This process is responsible for stitching together the Internet.

DNS records

There are many different types of records used by DNS servers. Each of these types of records has a specific purpose in name resolution.

A record   *Address (A) records* are used to resolve a simple hostname to an IPv4 address.

MX   *Mail exchange (MX)* records specify the mail server responsible for a network and how mail should be routed.

AAAA   An *AAAA* record is the equivalent of an A record, but it is specifically for IPv6.

CNAME   *Canonical name (CNAME)* records are aliases to other records. These make the DNS servers more flexible and adaptable.

PTR   A *pointer record (PTR)* retrieves a resolution for a service or host. The DNS name lookup of that name does not proceed. These records are most often used for reverse lookups (IP address to hostname) for other services.

Dynamic DNS

This is a useful service that allows a computer or device to notify a server to make an entry for it in the DNS database. It can also notify the server of any changes so that the database is automatically kept up-to-date.

Exam Essentials

Know the components that make up DNS.   Know the three main components that make up DNS and basically what they do. Know that the servers use records that can even be input by devices automatically using Dynamic DNS.

Know the types of records used in DNS.   Understand the different types of DNS records and how they are used by the DNS servers and the network as a whole.

1.8 Given a scenario, implement the following network troubleshooting methodology

Generally speaking, troubleshooting is a process of isolation. The best troubleshooters will try to determine what still works and how far it continues to work and then determine exactly where it breaks down. The more you know about the interworking of a network, the better you will be able to determine the weakness or the problem based on its symptoms. There are many different troubleshooting methodologies, but all share the same basic steps. In the following sections, I'll discuss the steps involved in troubleshooting a network.

To facilitate this discussion, I will also present a scenario to which you will apply your troubleshooting methodology. For this scenario, I will use technical information and terminology that I have previously discussed. Specifically, say you have a user who is complaining that she cannot access any intranet or Internet resources. Now, let's apply a troubleshooting methodology to this scenario.

Identify the problem

You go to the user's computer and verify that the user cannot connect to the Internet or any of the network resources. You will now troubleshoot the issue by gathering information and identifying the symptoms of the problem. In addition, you will question users and determine whether anything has changed that could have caused this issue.

Information gathering

You first check to make sure that the network cable is plugged in and that the link light on the network interface card is lit. If it is lit, this indicates that a connection is present. If it is blinking, then it's not only connected but traffic is being passed through the connection. You should always verify the physical connections first, because often that's all you will have to fix—but unfortunately not this time. In this case, you verify that the cable is plugged in and that the link light is lit, so you move on to the next step.

Identify symptoms

By typing `ipconfig /all`, you determine that the computer is set to obtain an address from a DHCP server but the address is 169.254.2.1. Your first thought is, "Hmmm, that looks like an APIPA address, doesn't it?" I wonder how far this problem goes?

Question users

Next you decide to ask around and see whether others are having the same problem. Some users report that they have a connection that seems to be working fine, while others have now lost their connection as well. You go to one of the other computers that recently lost its connection and type `ipconfig`, only to see that it also has an APIPA address of 169.254.5.67. You wonder what's causing this to happen.

Determine if anything has changed

You ask another network administrator, who informs you that only a few servers were due for maintenance last night, but they were supposed to be put back online by this morning. He says he will check into it and get back to you. Could that be the problem?

Establish a theory of probable cause

You reason that if those servers that were down were DHCP servers, then they may not have been available at the time when the users' computers were trying to renew their leases. In that case, the computers would end up with an APIPA address. You decide that this is the most probable cause, but you aren't done yet.

Question the obvious

You are now convinced that the DHCP servers are to blame and that it will be determined that they were not put back online. You run a quick check from one of the affected computers by typing `ipconfig /renew`, but it is not able to renew its address, further confirming your suspicion.

Test the theory to determine cause

You haven't heard from the other administrator, yet your users are still down. You decide that someone may have "dropped the ball." You need to get those DHCP servers up and running, or you need to assign static addresses to those clients for now. In either case, this will require that you escalate the issue and get some results.

Once theory is confirmed, determine next steps to resolve problem

You decide that you will call the senior network administrator and enlist her support to help get the problem fixed. She has the contacts and authority that you do not have. In this way, you will escalate the issue and probably get some fast results.

If theory is not confirmed, re-establish new theory or escalate

If your theory had not proved correct, then you would have needed to go back to "square one" by establishing a new theory and questioning the obvious once again. In this case, you have correctly identified the real problem. Now, it's just a matter of getting it fixed.

Establish a plan of action to resolve the problem and identify potential effects

In this case, if you can just get those DHCP servers back online, then your problem should take care of itself. The operating systems on your client computers should recognize the DHCP servers as soon as they come back online, and they should obtain an address that will allow them a connection to the Internet and the intranet resources. You will verify this with the users who have been affected by taking a quick look at things once the servers are back online.

Implement the solution or escalate as necessary

You call the senior network administrator and tell her your situation. She checks into it and finds that the DHCP servers are not online as they should be. The team was falling behind and did not fully understand the urgency of the situation. The server technicians humbly apologize for their mistake and get the DHCP servers back online.

Verify full system functionality and if applicable implement preventive measures

After you verify with the users that the problem is resolved, you contact the senior network administrator and thank her for her assistance. She asks you to send her an email relating the entire situation and how it all transpired since this morning. Based on what you say about the situation, the senior network administrator will recommend additional training for the server administrators regarding the principles of DHCP, the frequency of lease renewals in your organization, and the effects of not having a DHCP server available to the client computers when needed.

Document findings, actions, and outcomes

You sit down and write that email to the senior network administrator. You focus it not on who was at fault (everyone makes mistakes) but on documenting the actions and/or inactions in regard to the DHCP server and how quickly it led to problems for users in your organization. You also document how it was eventually resolved and the final test that you performed to ensure that all was well again. In addition, you have a server issue log that you will need to update to make this issue easier to identify for another administrator. Now you are ready to move on to your next challenge!

Exam Essentials

Know the steps involved in the troubleshooting methodology.   Understand the basic steps involved in this troubleshooting methodology. Understand the need for and how to document what was done in each step in the troubleshooting methodology.

Understand how to relate the steps to a troubleshooting scenario.   Be able to relate each of the troubleshooting methodology steps to a scenario and answer questions regarding the importance of each step.

1.9 Identify virtual network components

As if it's not difficult enough to keep up with all of the new network components that you can see, now we have to get ready for a new line of components that are invisible! I'm not kidding, many components in today's networks are being virtualized, which means they are created using software components on computers instead of using physical components that you can touch. Before you think this is just a fad that will go away, you should consider that most of the Fortune 100 companies and many military and government installations are already using virtual network components. That's because it allows companies to lower the total cost of ownership and increase the flexibility and security of the datacenter—all at the same time! It is a concept that will only continue to grow. In this section, I will discuss each of the most common virtual components and the new challenges and advantages that they offer; I won't be providing any pictures of these virtual components!

Virtual Switches

A *virtual switch* is a fully functional switch that doesn't exist in a physical sense but instead is composed of software programs and stored in a server. Just because you can't "see" it doesn't mean that you can't use it to control access to your other network components, especially the other virtual ones. The most prominent virtual switch at the time of this writing is the Cisco Nexus 1000v. It can do everything a physical switch can do, but it does it in a virtual datacenter instead of a physical one.

Virtual Desktops

This is an idea that has evolved so much that it seems to have come full circle. First, we had mainframe computers and dumb terminals. All of the real computing was done on the backend (mainframe), while the information was entered into the frontend (terminal). The terminal itself did not have to be very powerful. Then we advanced to PCs that were able to do much, if not all, of the computing right in front of us and only connected to the servers to get more data. The disadvantage of this system was that we had to constantly update the software that we were using on each of the PCs, but the advantage was that most computing could be faster and more customized to what we needed.

What if we could achieve the best of both worlds? What if we could use just about any computer to connect to a desktop that was customized just for us (each of us) and we could then use the computing power of the server to do all of our computing? Furthermore, what if we could connect to this *virtual desktop* from anywhere in the world but the administrator could make all software updates locally at the servers, often to hundreds or thousands of desktops at once? This would allow us to reduce the total cost of ownership while at the same time increasing the security and flexibility of our datacenter. Sound like a dream? Well, companies such as VMware actually specialize in software to assist you in creating these virtual datacenters. In fact, these technologies currently fill the large part of my teaching schedule online as well as in person.

This is the concept of virtual desktop computing. As you can see, it's too good an idea to go away, so you had best learn all about it that you can. While the finer aspects of virtual desktop infrastructure (VDI) are beyond the scope of this book, I highly recommend you find a good Wiley book on the topic!

Virtual Servers

In most large organizations, putting a new physical server into a datacenter involves many steps; often the very first one is just getting permission to issue a purchase order to buy it.

After that comes the procurement, delivery, unpacking, inventory, installation, power, cable, and testing; and that's an abbreviated list. There must be a better way!

Well, what if all of the purchase-order decisions could center around providing a system that could be used to create any server that the organization needs on the fly? What if these servers could be created without any additional hardware or software after the original purchase? What if all of the inventory, installation, power, cable, and testing could be virtually eliminated? Well, pardon the pun, but that is exactly what a *virtual server* and the means to create them can do for an organization. As you can see, this is another idea that is bound to keep growing. I highly recommend you learn about products such as VMware vSphere and Microsoft HyperV. Even though you can't see them, these virtual servers are not going away any time soon.

Virtual PBX

Until now, if you built a new building and then you chose and installed a phone system somewhere in the building, that system would be used to connect all of the lines for the employees, departments, and so on. This was largely a closed-end system in the building that was then connected to the phone company. It was referred to as a *private business exchange* (PBX).

Now, you can opt to instead use a service that is separate from your company. All of the equipment (servers), except for the phones themselves, can exist inside or outside of your building (anywhere in the world really) and can be used to handle calls for all of your lines. This can save your organization on the capital investment of equipment and on the hiring costs of people with the expertise to control it. This is referred to as a *virtual PBX*, and it's one more idea that will only continue to grow.

Onsite vs. Offsite

As I mentioned, all of this virtualization can really be hosted anywhere in the world. That means you can build your virtual datacenters *onsite* and run them yourself, or you can decide to let a third-party host your servers and thereby your virtual desktops, virtual servers, virtual PBX, and so on. In that case, everything would be *offsite*, and you would hold the third-party responsible that your services were maintained. The onsite option might be advantageous, giving you more direct control, if you have the personnel and expertise to handle it yourself. Otherwise, the offsite option might be best if you do not want to dedicate the personnel to the resources. In that case, you will lose a little direct control, but you will potentially save some time.

Network as a Service (NaaS)

Did you ever stop to think that the iPhone or Android *smartphone* that you carry with you is actually much more capable than the computers we used to put a man on the moon? In fact, it's more powerful than the initial computers that we used in the first space shuttles!

As powerful as it is, it's only a fraction as powerful as the servers to which it can connect all over world. Through the latest advances in cloud computing, the entire network of resources that your device needs can be offered virtually. That is the concept behind Network as a Service (NaaS). We now have all of the pieces that we need—the powerful servers and all the services they offer, the computer that you hold in your hand, and the bandwidth required to seamlessly connect the two. As you can see, this is another opportunity that is just beginning and will continue to grow.

Exam Essentials

Know the type of virtual components in today's networks.   Virtual switches are fully functional switches that exist in the form of software instead of hardware. Virtual desktops allow the best of both worlds with a centralized desktop and powerful computing platform that you can access from anywhere. Virtual servers increase the flexibility and control in datacenters, giving the administrator more control to create new servers with less effort. Virtual PBX systems allow for a locally managed "feel" of your phone system, while it can actually be managed from anywhere in the world.

Know the newest services and methods available for modern networks.   You can choose to host your own system, or you can choose to take it all offsite and let a third party provide you with everything that you need to run your business. NaaS is the latest change that provides for powerful computing and information exchange on iPhones, Android devices, and other smartphones.

Review Questions

1. What is name of the unique physical address that is assigned to every network interface card?

   A. IP address

   B. Hostname

   C. MAC address

   D. NetBIOS name

2. How many bits are used to create an IPv4 address?

   A. 8

   B. 6

   C. 32

   D. 64

3. If you have a Class B address with a default subnet mask and you need to create eight
   subnets, then which of the following subnet masks should you use?

   A. 255.255.255.240

   B. 255.255.224.0

   C. 255.255.240.0

   D. 255.240.0.0

4. Which of the following IP addresses are valid only for private IP addressing that is filtered from the Internet? (Choose two.)

   A. 10.1.1.1

   B. 172.17.255.254

   C. 11.1.2.4

   D. 193.168.2.1

5. Which information directory protocol is the standard for file transfer over the Internet?

   A. TCP

   B. UDP

   C. FTP

   D. HTTP

6. Which of the following layers of the OSI model is responsible for logical addressing?

   A. Application

   B. Transport

   C. Data Link

   D. Network

7. Which layer of the TCP/IP protocol suite loosely aligns to three layers of the OSI model?

   A. Transport

   B. Network Interface

   C. Application

   D. Presentation

8. Which of the following is a Session layer protocol that is primarily responsible for setting up and tearing down voice and video calls over the Internet?

   A. SIP

   B. RTP

   C. HTTP

   D. FTP

9. Which of the following is an example of an IPv6 address?

   A. 192.168.1.1

   B. C0-FF-EE-C0-FF-EE

   C. fe80::216:deff:ee09:6d13

   D. ef90::451:defe::ee09:6d13

10. Which of the following subnet masks should you use to obtain 100 subnets from a Class B network?

   A. 255.255.254.0

   B. 255.254.0.0

   C. 255.255.255.128

   D. There isn't enough information to answer the question.

Chapter

2

Domain 2 Network Installation and Configuration

COMPTIA NETWORK+ EXAM OBJECTIVES COVERED IN THIS CHAPTER:

✓ **2.1 Given a scenario, install and configure routers and switches.**

- Routing tables

- NAT

- PAT

- VLAN (trunking)

- Managed vs. unmanaged

- Interface configurations

  - Full duplex

  - Half duplex

  - Port speeds

  - IP addressing

  - MAC filtering

- PoE

- Traffic filtering

- Diagnostics

- VTP configuration

- QoS

- Port mirroring

✓ **2.2 Given a scenario, install and configure a wireless network.**

- WAP placement

- Antenna types

- Interference

- Frequencies

- Channels

- Wireless standards

- SSID (enable/disable)

- Compatibility (802.11 a/b/g/n)

✓ **2.3 Explain the purpose and properties of DHCP.**

- Static vs. dynamic IP addressing

- Reservations

- Scopes

- Leases

- Options (DNS servers, suffixes)

✓ **2.4 Given a scenario, troubleshoot common wireless problems.**

- Interference

- Signal strength

- Configurations

- Incompatibilities

- Incorrect channel

- Latency

- Encryption type

- Bounce

- SSID mismatch

- Incorrect switch placement

✓ **2.5 Given a scenario, troubleshoot common router and switch problems.**

- Switching loop

- Bad cables/improper cable types

- Port configuration

- VLAN assignment

- Mismatched MTU/MTU black hole

- Power failure

- Bad/missing routes

- Bad modules (SFPs, GBICs)

- Wrong subnet mask

- Wrong gateway

- Duplicate IP address

- Wrong DNS

✓ **2.6 Given a set of requirements, plan and implement a basic SOHO network.**

- List of requirements

- Cable length

- Device types/requirements

- Environment limitations

- Equipment limitations

- Compatibility requirements

You can save yourself a lot of future headaches by properly installing and configuring your network and the components that connect to it. The backbone of your network is the collection of routers, switches, and connections between them that allows data to travel from one component to another. Some of these connections may be wired, while others may be wireless. All of the physical connections and equipment must be compatible in order for your network to communicate data effectively.

In addition to the physical connections, it is important to configure your network properly. Networking techniques and protocols such as NAT, PAT, VLAN, PoE, traffic filtering, and QoS will give you options within your network. However, you cannot just do anything you want in the logical or physical installation and configuration of your network. You must follow the general rules, codes, and basic practices that have evolved over the years. I will also discuss the proper installation and configuration of the physical and logical portions of your network.

2.1 Given a scenario, install and configure routers and switches

Even with the variety of new devices that we use today, still the most commonly used are routers and switches. Let's say you were put in charge of installing a network system for a business that provides online video and pictures to its customers. The challenges you would face in regard to router and switch installation would be numerous.

Your tasks might include creating routing tables, NAT, PAT, and VLANs. You might use managed devices that you could configure remotely or unmanaged devices that require very little configuration after their initial installation. You might also need to configure the interfaces with duplex and speed settings as well as IP addresses or MAC address filtering. In addition, specialized options such as PoE, traffic filtering, diagnostics information, VTP, QoS, and port mirroring may also need your attention. In this section, I will discuss each of these concepts and how it would fit into your network installation challenge.

Routing tables

As discussed in Chapter 1, routing protocols that are installed and configured properly on your routers will communicate with each other to create the tables you require. In rare instances, you may also want to add a static route that causes the router to make a different choice or that frees up bandwidth that the routers would otherwise use to communicate routing protocol information. For example, if there were only one main location for all videos once the requests came into your network, then you could create a static route that directs all traffic that is requesting a video to that location with no further need for routing protocol information. In other words, you would enhance the table to make it "smarter" and more efficient. The exact commands you would use to make this change vary by vendor and therefore will not be discussed here, but I will give you a very simple table for greater understanding of this concept. Table 2.1 shows the general purpose of a routing table in determining which interface to use to forward data. For example, if the data had a destination address that begins with 192.16.1.0, the router would use its S1 interface to forward the data.

TABLE 2.1   The General Purpose of a Routing Table

Destination network	Subnet mask	Interface
10.1.0.0	255.255.0.0	S0
192.16.1.0	255.255.255.0	S1
172.16.0.0	255.255.0.0	S1

NAT

Network Address Translation (NAT) is a service that translates one set of IP addresses to another set of IP addresses. NAT is most often used between a private network and the Internet, but it can also be used in other ways such as to translate a group of global internal addresses to a group of global external addresses. NAT can run on a computer, a router, or a specialized device that provides only network address translation. If your organization has recently merged or acquired other organizations, then you might see NAT used between the two IP systems that were set up autonomous to each other and that are very unlikely to just "mesh" perfectly without translation. In this case, the NAT device would contain a table of addresses on one network that are to be translated to addresses on the other network. This table would be a one-to-one mapping of IP address to IP address. Figure 2.1 illustrates NAT.

PAT

Port Address Translation (PAT) is a service that most people actually think of as NAT. When you have two or more computers on the inside of a network that share one external address (usually the outside interface address of the router), the only way to keep their network communication channels separate and organized is by port designation on each packet. PAT changes the source address of a packet as it passes through the router or other device using PAT, appending it with a specific port number. It then keeps a record of the port numbers to which it has assigned packets and the true inside local address of the computers that generated them. In this way, PAT uses ports to provide address translation for many inside source addresses to one outside source address. In other words, PAT is many-to-one in contrast to NAT, which is one-to-one.

FIGURE 2.1   NAT

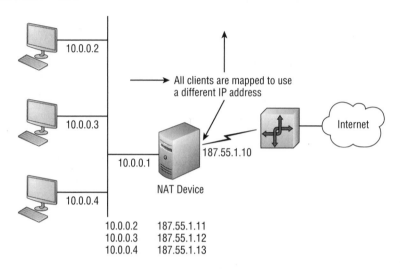

In your scenario, you could use PAT so that employees within your organization could all connect to the Internet using the same registered external IP address, while each employee has a separate internal IP address. Figure 2.2 illustrates PAT.

FIGURE 2.2   PAT

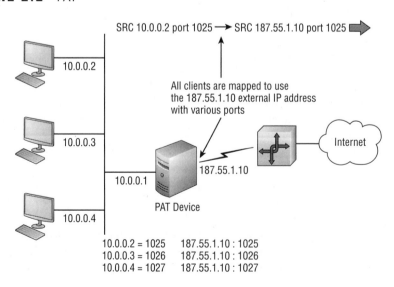

VLAN (trunking)

With conventional networks using only routers for layer 3 and only switches for layer 2, subnets are limited to the physical location in which they reside. This can be constricting to a network administrator if a department spans multiple locations and the administrator wants to manage and set security policies based on subnets related to departments. A *virtual local area network (VLAN)* is the solution to this problem. In a VLAN, switches are used to create layer 2 networks that are equivalent to subnets. These networks can span multiple switches, regardless of the location of the switch, using special links that can carry all of the VLANs. These special links are referred to as *trunks*.

In the example scenario, this would give you the flexibility to design a logical network that does not have to conform to any physical limitations, such as the actual location of the clients. You could manage the security of the entire network as if it were all in the same location, even if it isn't. You could use routers or layer 3 switches to connect the separate layer 3 domains while still maintaining security.

Managed vs. unmanaged

If your network were very simple, you could install routers and switches that required no configuration on your part and basically configured themselves for your needs. In that case, you would be using *unmanaged devices*. However, in the example scenario, there is more to do because your network requires specific configurations on *managed devices*, as I will now discuss.

Interface configurations

Many settings for interfaces on routers and switches will affect the performance and security of your network. Your understanding of settings involving speed, duplex, IP addressing, and MAC filtering will assist you in configuring your interfaces properly.

Full duplex   All communications can be categorized in one of two ways: half duplex or full duplex. The difference centers on whether the communicating parties or devices can "talk" and "listen" at the same time. I will use analogies that include both people and devices to describe these types of communication further.

In *full-duplex* communication, a device can send and receive communication at the same time; in fact, both devices can send and receive communication at the same time. This means the effective throughput is doubled, and communications can be much more efficient. This is typical in most of today's switched networks.

To understand full-duplex communication, think about a telephone. You can talk into the phone and listen to what the other person is saying at the same time—at least most people can. The point is that there are two separate wires that carry the signals, one for the transmit signal and the other for the receive signal. This is the same with network devices; when you use full-duplex communication, you generally just use more wire pairs in the same cable. In your scenario, this type of communication can be achieved only by using a switched environment to provide point-to-point connections to the devices, which I will discuss later in this chapter.

Half duplex   In *half-duplex* communication, a device can either send communication or receive communication, but it cannot do both at the same time. Think "walkie-talkie" to understand this concept. Once you press the button on the walkie-talkie, the speaker is off, and you can't hear anything the other side is saying. That's why you say "over" when you are finished talking and want a response. Half-duplex communications are not as efficient as full duplex, and you would resort to them only if you still had some hubs in your topology, which is unlikely.

Port Speeds   Since networks have evolved for many years, there are various levels of speed and sophistication mixed into networks, often within the same network. Most of the newest NICs can be used at 10Mbps, 100Mbps, and 1000Mbps. Most switches support both 10Mbps and 100Mbps, and an increasing number of switches can also support 1,000Mbps, or even 10,000Mbps. Most switches can also autosense the speed of the NIC that is connected and use different speeds on various ports. As long as your switches are allowed to autosense the port speed, few problems will generally develop that result in a complete lack of communication. If you decide to set the port speed manually, then you should take care to set the same speed on both sides of a link.

IP addressing   The most common addressing protocol in use today is IPv4. This protocol provides a unique IP address for each host on a network. Often, client computers obtain their addresses from DHCP servers. In contrast, you should statically assign servers and router interfaces. An incorrect address on a client will keep that client from being able to communicate on the wire and possibly cause a conflict with another client on the network. On the other hand, an incorrect IP address on a server or router interface can potentially affect many users and even render your network inoperable. For this reason, you should set up DHCP servers carefully and also configure the static addresses assigned to servers and router interfaces carefully.

MAC filtering   As discussed in Chapter 1, every host on a network has a 48-bit hexadecimal Media Access Control (MAC) address. Also, every Ethernet packet contains a source MAC address and a destination MAC address, although sometimes the destination MAC address is a broadcast address such as FF-FF-FF-FF-FF-FF. You can apply *MAC filtering* on your switches working at layer 2 (Data Link) of the OSI model. This focuses on the MAC addresses in the packet and can be configured to let only specific MAC addresses through an interface on the switch. In addition, you can use more sophisticated filters to let only specific addresses into one interface and out of another interface. In other words, the traffic can come in an interface only if it has a destination address for a specific host or group of hosts. MAC filtering is usually applied, where the host computers are connected to the switches. However, you should not use MAC filtering as the only means of security, because MAC addresses can easily be spoofed (faked) with the right software.

PoE

If you have a remote router or wireless access point in a place that is not close to a power outlet, it's possible to power some devices from the electric current provided on standard POTS lines or even general Ethernet current. This feature is referred to as *Power over Ethernet (PoE)*. Many switches, IP telephones, embedded computers, and wireless access points can use this feature for convenient installation.

Traffic filtering

Filtering, in regard to networking, is simply letting some traffic flow through the network while blocking other traffic. What you decide to filter and how you decide to apply a filter will depend on the network on which you are filtering traffic. For example, you might use a very different means of filtering for traffic that is local to your network than you would for traffic that comes from another network or from the Internet. In this scenario, you might consider filtering any protocols that don't assist you in delivering high-quality video content to your customers.

Diagnostics

Once you get the routers and switches up and running, how will you monitor your network to determine whether it is performing as you expected? Many third-party tools can assist you in network diagnostics. Products such as SolarWinds Engineer Toolset or ipMonitor can set up smart monitoring on your system that looks for anything out of the norm. They also offer an array of tools for troubleshooting that include the ability to create a network map. Since we actually think in pictures, a map is a great way to see what is actually going on within your network. Later I will also discuss a protocol called SNMP that can be used to gather information about your network.

VTP configuration

Wouldn't it be nice if the VLAN configuration work that you apply to one of your switches could just be "learned" by the other switches in the network? Well, in essence, that's what *VLAN trunking protocol (VTP)* does for you. VTP is a protocol that is proprietary to Cisco and allows you to create a switch with the role of "server" that you configure with your VLAN information. After that server switch is created, then any "client" switches that are in the same VTP domain will learn the information that you have added to the server switch. In addition, any changes you make to the server switch will be quickly propagated to the client switches. This will save you time and reduce human effort, thereby increasing accuracy.

QoS

In your company within the example scenario, traffic is generated by your office staff for normal clerical operations and by your customers when they request a video from you. Which type of traffic do you think should take precedence? Ideally, you answered that the video traffic should take precedence, because if you don't take care of the customer first, then you won't have a company to worry about for long!

Quality of Service (QoS) is a network technique that divides traffic into categories, usually based on the protocol of the traffic, and then allows for prioritization of each category. Using QoS, you could assure that traffic delivering your online videos has a higher priority than general office traffic. This would make more efficient and effective use of your available bandwidth.

Port mirroring

You may want to use a device, such as an *Intrusion Detection System/Intrusion Prevention System (IDS/IPS)*, to monitor all of your network traffic. Since the VLANs separate the traffic for security reasons, monitoring all traffic sometimes requires getting a copy of network packets from one switch port sent to another switch port, strictly for the purpose of monitoring and logging them. This process, called *port mirroring*, is becoming a more common practice as organizations continue to install more IDSs/IPSs.

Exam Essentials

Know how to manipulate your IP traffic.   Routers use tables that can be built by a routing protocol or can be created manually by the network administrator. You can change the apparent source address of a packet using a protocol such as NAT or PAT. You can use VLANs to separate the logical from the physical in your network and create security and greater flexibility at the same time.

Know what to configure on your interfaces.   Configure most interfaces for full-duplex communication in today's networks, unless you are using a hub, which is not likely. Statically configure the speed of the interface to the highest speed that both sides can handle. Don't rely on autoconfiguration unless you have thoroughly tested it. Configure IP addresses for clients automatically using DHCP, but configure servers and router interfaces statically. Configure MAC filtering to control traffic at layer 2, but don't rely on it for your only security.

Know your more advanced options for configuration.   PoE gives you the option to use regular phone lines or even general Ethernet power to provide power for a switch. Traffic filtering gives you greater control over traffic in your network. Diagnostics tools let you see what's really going on with reports and even network maps. VTP reduces work and increases accuracy in VLAN configuration by letting client switches learn VLAN configuration information from the server switch. QoS lets you prioritize traffic to provide resources for the most important traffic first. Port mirroring lets you monitor traffic that is on multiple ports, even though you are connected to only one.

2.2 Given a scenario, install and configure a wireless network

Wireless networks can be convenient for the user, but they can also require much more configuration for you. When you decide to use wireless connections on your wired network, you don't substitute one set of challenges for another; instead, you simply add a whole new set of wireless challenges to the wired challenges you already face. Some of the challenges of installing a wireless network are WAP placement, antenna types, interference, frequencies, channels, wireless standards, SSID, and compatibility issues. In this section, I will discuss how each of these relate to the correct installation of your wireless network.

WAP placement

You should take into account environmental factors, such as the distance between the client and the *wireless access point (WAP)* as well as the type of construction that is between them. These can affect the power of the intended signal and therefore make any interference from other signals more pronounced. You should take care as to where you place a WAP; be sure there are no other devices in the area that can cause interference and that it is not near any large metal objects. I will discuss much more about issues such as interference, signal strength, and switch placement in Section 2.4 Given a Scenario, Troubleshoot Common Wireless Problems of this chapter and in the next chapter.

Antenna types

Usually, the best place to put a WAP and its antenna is close to the center of your planned wireless network. You can choose from many different types of antennas. Some are omnidirectional, which means they radiate energy with equal strength in all directions. Others are very directional, possibly increasing range but in only one direction. Antennas can even be placed away from the WAP but connected to it with a cable. You might do this if you needed the antenna to be in a location that would not be convenient for the WAP.

If you use multiple WAPs, then you can use more sophisticated means to determine where to best place the WAPs. You can use third-party tools, such as AirMagnet, on a laptop or a tablet PC to survey the site and determine how far your WAPs are transmitting. You can also hire a consultant to conduct a survey for you. Many companies specialize in assisting organizations with their wireless networks and with the correct placement of antennas and WAPs. It's important to place the antennas in the correct place, because an incorrect placement can lead to interference and poor performance.

Interference

Since wireless networks rely upon radio waves to transmit signals, they are subject to interference from many factors. Other wireless devices (such as Bluetooth keyboards, mice, or cell phones) that are close to their frequency can cause a signal bleed and inhibit or even prevent wireless communication. Even microwave ovens, electric motors, and mundane appliances such as refrigerators have been known to affect some wireless networks. Other environmental factors, such as the distance between the client and WAP as well as the type of construction that is between them, can also affect the power of the intended signal and therefore make any interference from other signals more pronounced. You should take care as to where you place a WAP and be sure that there are no other devices in the area that can cause interference. If the interference is on the client side, you may be able to move the client away from the source of the interference.

Frequencies

Setting the channel, in effect, sets the frequency or frequencies that wireless devices will use. I will discuss setting the channel next. It is also possible on some devices to "tweak" those settings and choose a specific frequency. Of course, if you do this on one device, then you must configure the same setting on all the devices that you want to communicate with each other.

Channels

Wireless networks use many different frequencies within a band of frequencies (typically the 2.4GHz or 5GHz band). These frequencies are sometimes combined to provide greater bandwidth for the user. A combination of these frequencies that can be used by the end user is referred to as a *channel*. For the WAP and the clients to communicate, they must be on the same channel. Most likely, your wireless networks will use channel 1, 6, or 11 because these channels are non-overlapping and therefore least likely to interfere with each other when used on devices in the same area.

SSID (enable/disable)

When a wireless device comes up, it will scan for service set identifiers (SSIDs) in its immediate area, which is basically a network name. In your own wireless LAN, you will likely want the devices to find the SSID that you are broadcasting, so you will make sure that it's enabled for broadcast. This is typically not a problem, since your broadcast should be stronger than any neighbor's broadcast, because it is closer. The exception to this rule might be an office building that has many WAPs that are assigned many different SSIDs because they belong to the various tenants in the building. It is then possible that your neighbor's SSID broadcast could be stronger than yours, depending on where the clients are in the building. If users report that they are connected to a WAP but are still not able to see the resources they need or not able to authenticate to the network, you should verify that they are connected to your SSID and not your neighbor's. You can generally just look at the information "tooltip" on the wireless software icon to determine this information.

To enhance your security, you can also choose to set the WAP to disable the broadcasting of the SSID. In that case, users could connect to it only if they were told that it was there and what to type into the wireless configuration. This type of wireless security is not considered very strong and will only keep the most casual "snoopers" off your network. In fact, it may be more trouble than it's worth to disable your broadcast of your SSID because then you will have to tell anyone who wants to use the network where it is and train them how to connect to it. Because of this, it may be more trouble than it's worth; it really just depends on what your organizational policies dictate.

Wireless standards and compatibility

Wireless networks have many standards that have evolved over time, such as 802.11a, 802.11b, 802.11g, and 802.11n. Standards continue to develop that make wireless networks even faster and more powerful. The catch is that some of these standards are backward compatible, while others are not. For example, most devices purchased today can be set to 802.11b/g/n, which means that they can be used to communicate with other devices of all three standards. On the other hand, some devices cannot be configured to be compatible with 802.11a because it uses the 5GHz frequency whereas b and g use only the 2.4 GHz frequency band. You do not have to know the details of OFDM and DSSS; just know that they are competing standards of modulation used in wireless networks and are not truly compatible technologies even though 802.11g/n can and do/use both. You should take care in setting the type of networks that a device can use and make sure the standards on the WAP match the standards on the client or at least are backward compatible. Some devices can use both standards. In the next chapter, I will discuss wireless standards in greater depth, but for now, Table 2.2 lists each standard along with its frequency range and theoretical maximum speed.

TABLE 2.2 Wireless standards

Wireless standard	Modulation	Frequency	Maximum speed
802.11a	OFDM	5GHz	54Mbps
802.11b	DSSS	2.4GHz	11Mbps
802.11g	OFDM/DSSS	2.4GHz	54Mbps
802.11n	OFDM/DSSS	2.4GHz/5GHz	600Mbps

Exam Essentials

Know how to install a wireless network.   Antenna type and antenna placement are very important. Don't place the WAP or its antenna near a large metal object or any other type of interference. Interference can come from other wireless devices such as a Bluetooth mouse, Bluetooth keyboard, or a cordless phone.

Know how to configure a wireless network. Your wireless network will most likely use channel 1, 6, or 11. You can further tweak the channel settings by adjusting the frequency if needed. Assure that your devices are compatible to each other. Remember that 802.11a is not compatible with 802.11b/g, although some devices support both. Configure your WAP not to advertise the SSID if your organizational policies dictate.

2.3 Explain the purpose and properties of DHCP

Dynamic Host Configuration Protocol (DHCP) lets you offload a whole lot of work configuring IP addresses, subnet masks, default gateways, DNS server addresses, and much more to a server that is relatively easy to set up and maintain. Is it for all of your computers on your network? Probably not, but it's most likely the best solution for all of your clients. In this section, I will discuss the properties of DHCP and the options that it provides.

Static vs. dynamic IP addressing

In general, client computers should obtain their IP addresses from a DHCP server whenever possible. This reduces manual effort on the part the administrator and improves accuracy. In contrast, devices such as servers, network printers, plotters, and router interfaces should be statically configured so their addresses do not change. Figure 2.3 shows an example of how to configure a static IP configuration on Windows Server 2008. Figure 2.4 shows an example of the DHCP tool in Windows Server 2008. A DHCP server, should always use a static address and should never obtain an address from another DHCP server.

FIGURE 2.3   A Static IP Configuration on Windows Server 2008

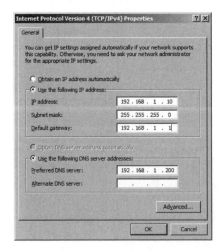

FIGURE 2.4   The DHCP Server Tool In Windows Server 2008

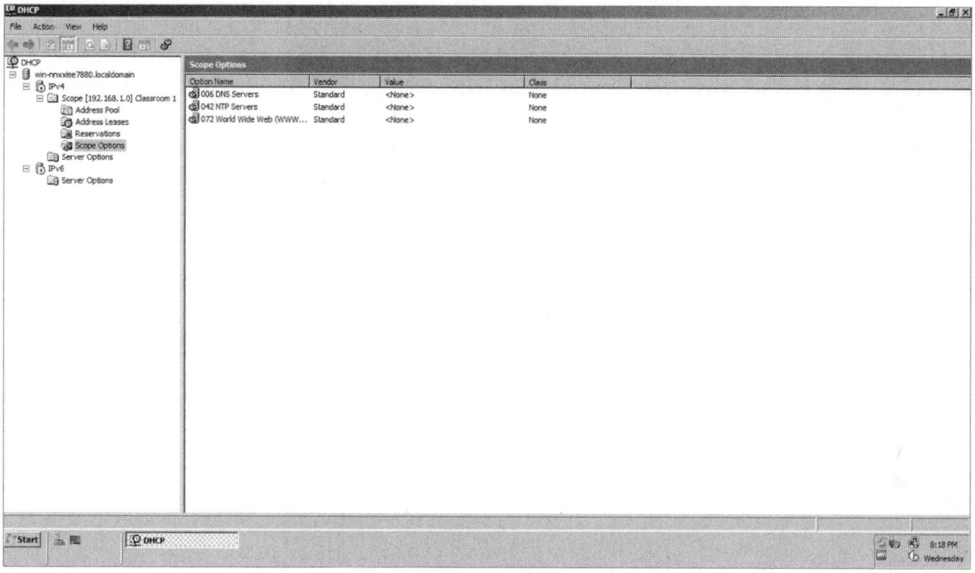

Reservations

Most of your clients will obtain an address from your DHCP server in a rather "random" manner and will hold that address for a period of time as defined by their lease. (I will discuss leases later in this chapter.) You may want some clients to obtain the same address from the DHCP server every time they connect, which is an address that was actually set aside for them based on their MAC address. This type of addressing is referred to as a *reservation*. This is especially handy for clients, printers, plotters, and the like, that are not always connected but that need to have a predictable address when they are connected. By not using a static address for these devices, you can better manage your network because all addresses will be managed from the DHCP server instead of some addressing left "missing" from its lists.

Scopes

A *scope* is a range of addresses that can be assigned to clients. You should set your scopes based on the IP subnets you are using within your organization. You should take care that your scopes do not contain addresses that overlap addresses in other scopes, because this can cause IP address conflicts. The process of configuring scopes on DHCP servers is beyond the scope of this book. Pardon the pun!

Leases

When your client obtains its IP address from the DHCP server, the IP address can be used for a defined period of time that is indicated by its *lease*. On Microsoft DHCP servers, the lease time by default is eight days. Your client will attempt to renew its lease after 50 percent of the time has expired, so if leases are set to the default, then your clients will renew their leases every four days. This will be done by contacting the DHCP server directly. You should increase lease times if you have plenty of addresses to go around for your clients. Conversely, you should decrease lease times if you have fewer IP addresses than clients.

Options (DNS servers, suffixes)

A DHCP server is best known for assigning IP addresses to clients that need them. In reality, though, a DHCP server can assign much more than just IP addresses. When I teach networking classes, I refer to the DHCP server as the "welcome wagon." We don't have them anymore, but long ago small towns had a welcome wagon that came by a new neighbor's home shortly after they moved into the neighborhood and gave them some food, soap, and the like, just to welcome them to the neighborhood and help them get a good start. Your DHCP server can do the same thing for your clients.

To be more specific, you can configure your DHCP server to give your clients a variety of information regarding other servers and services in the network that it just joined. This can include the address of DNS servers and even WINS servers (in case you are still using one) as well as the address of its default gateway to gain access to other networks and to the Internet. All of these settings and more are available to you in the server and scope options of DHCP servers of all kinds. The specific steps for configuring DHCP server and scope options are beyond the scope of this book.

Exam Essentials

Know the main types of IP address configuration. There are two main types of addresses, dynamic and static. Dynamic addresses are obtained by clients from a DHCP server. Static addresses are configured manually by a network administrator. In general, clients should obtain a dynamic IP address from a DHCP server. This saves time and improves accuracy. In general, servers, router interfaces, and printers should be configured with static addresses. This is because other components are configured with their address as a reference, and it generally needs to remain the same.

Know the capabilities of a DHCP server. DHCP servers typically lease addresses to clients for a defined period of time. You can control the length of the lease depending on the abundance or scarcity of IP addresses in your network. Some clients can also have reservations based on the MAC addresses of the clients. DHCP servers can do much more than just assign addresses to clients; they can also give the clients the addresses of other critical servers and important links such as the default gateway.

2.4 Given a scenario, troubleshoot common wireless problems

As I mentioned, when you decide to use wireless connections on your wired network, you don't substitute one set of challenges for another; instead, you simply add a whole new set of wireless challenges to the wired challenges you already face. Some of these wireless challenges include interference, incorrect encryption, incorrect channel, incorrect frequency, SSID mismatch, wireless standard mismatch, distance, bounce, and incorrect antenna placement. Don't worry, though, because in the following sections, I'll discuss how you can address the challenges these issues present.

Interference

As I mentioned, since wireless networks rely upon radio waves to transmit signals, they are subject to interference from many factors. You should take care as to where you place a WAP and be sure that there are no other electrical devices in the area that can cause interference. Certainly anything that produces radio waves (such as a Bluetooth device) can cause interference; however, the interfering object does not have to be a device. Even a large metal object such as a filing cabinet can cause interference if it is too close to a WAP. If you have weak signal at the client, look around the WAP and "see what you see"! In addition, there could be other networks or devices that you do not see that affect your signal. For this reason, you may want to have a professional conduct a thorough wireless survey for your area.

Signal strength

Typically a client will attempt to connect to the network with the highest *signal strength*. Depending on your topology, this can lead to some interesting results. It's possible that your client may attempt to connect to a wireless access point that you did not intend for it to connect to just because of the way the radio waves are transmitted in the area. I've actually seen my laptop connect to a hotel network that was next door to the hotel in which I was staying instead of the hotel where I was staying. It just went right out the window and across the parking lot rather than "down the hall"!

If a user is constantly receiving a weak signal, you should either move the user or move the WAP. Everything that is in between the user and the WAP could be causing the issue. You might consider moving the WAP to a new location that is more central to the users or changing the antenna type. If you are using 802.11b or g, then you might consider using 802.11n, which has a stronger signal than 802.11b or g. As I mentioned, you should also conduct a survey of your environment and assure that your clients, and only your clients, can see your wireless access points.

Configurations

The configuration of a wireless network from the client's perspective should be as automatic as possible, given your security constraints. The more automatic you can make it for the end user, the less headaches you will have! To facilitate this, you should broadcast your SSID so that a user's computer can detect the network and make the connection. If you do not broadcast your SSID then any new users will either to have wireless profile (configured by you) or they will need to configure their computers to "see" and connect to the wireless network. This might require a little training and troubleshooting on your part. You should also communicate any security protocol information and the password that the end users will need in order to connect to and use the wireless network.

Incompatibilities

As I mentioned, wireless networks have many standards that have evolved over time, such as 802.11a, 802.11b, 802.11g, and 802.11n. Standards continue to develop that make wireless networks even faster and more powerful. The catch is that some of these standards are backward compatible, while others are not. For example, most devices purchased today can be set to 802.11b/g/n, which means that they can be used to communicate with other devices of all three standards. On the other hand, only 802.11n devices are backward compatible to 802.11a devices. You should take care in setting the type of networks that a device can use and make sure that the standards on the WAP match the standards on the client or at least are backward compatible. I will discuss wireless standards in detail in the next chapter.

Incorrect channel

Wireless networks use many different frequencies within a band of frequencies (typically the 2.4GHz or 5GHz band). These frequencies are sometimes combined to provide greater bandwidth for the user. A combination of these frequencies that can be used by the end user is referred to as a *channel*. For the WAP and the clients to communicate, they must be on the same channel. Most often, wireless networks use channel 1, 6, or 11.

Latency

Latency, in wireless communication, refers to the period of time that it takes for the data to travel from the transmitting device to the receiving device, sometimes also referred to as *delay*. Many factors can affect latency. We have discussed interference, WAP placement, antenna type, and other devices such as Bluetooth mice and keyboards. All of these can contribute to latency issues in your wireless communications. In addition, security protocols such as WPA2 can increase latency because calculations regarding security must also be made. This is never a good reason not to use security on your wireless network.

Encryption type

Wireless networks can use encryption to secure the communication between two devices. Many forms of encryption are available for wireless networks, from WEP to WPA2 with AES. I will discuss each of these protocols in detail in Chapter 5.

To ensure the greatest degree of security, you should configure your wireless networks with the highest encryption protocol that both the WAP and the clients can support. The main point here is that the WAP and the clients must be configured with the same type of encryption. If the WAP requires higher security than the clients are able to provide (or vice versa), then the clients will not be able to communicate with the WAP.

Bounce

Radio waves don't really bounce off a reflective surface in a very controlled pattern like a laser beam does. Instead, an object between a sender and receiver can cause the radio wave to do very unpredictable things. For example, if you place a WAP next to a file cabinet or other large metal object, the result might be that the wave will radiate out and then bounce right back to the WAP and never really create a strong signal in the environment that you intended. Therefore, if signal bounce is not tightly controlled, your wireless network will not function properly. You can determine the effects of signal bounce by conducting a thorough wireless site survey and paying close attention to what is surrounding your WAPs.

SSID mismatch

When a wireless device comes up, it will scan for *service set identifiers* (SSIDs) in its immediate area. In your own wireless LAN, you will likely want the devices to find the SSID you are broadcasting. This is typically not a problem, since your broadcast should be stronger than any neighbors because it is closer. As I mentioned, the exception to this rule might be an office building that has many WAPs that are assigned many different SSIDs because they belong to the various tenants in the building. It is then possible that your neighbor's ESSID broadcast could be stronger than yours, depending on where the clients are in the building. If users report that they are connected to a WAP but are still not able to see the resources they need or not able to authenticate to the network, you should verify that they are connected to your SSID and not your neighbor's. You can generally just look at the information "tooltip" on the wireless software icon on the user's computer to determine this information.

Incorrect switch placement

The best place to put a WAP (wireless switch) or its antenna is close to the center of the planned wireless network. Some antennas can be placed away from the WAP but connected to it with a cable. You would do this if you needed the antenna to be in a location that would not be convenient for the WAP.

If you use multiple WAPs, then a more sophisticated means may be used to determine where to best place the WAPs. For example, you could use third-party tools, such as AirMagnet, on a laptop or a tablet PC to survey the site and determine how far your WAPs are transmitting. You could also hire a consultant to conduct a survey for you. Many companies specialize in assisting organizations with their wireless networks and with the correct placement of antennas and WAPs. It's important to place the antennas in the correct place, because an incorrect placement can lead to interference and poor performance.

Exam Essentials

Know common wireless configuration errors.   The evolution of wireless technologies can cause compatibility issues if you are not careful, especially between 802.11a and 802.11b/g/n. The most common channels are 1, 6, and 11.

Know common wireless design errors.   Improper placement of a WAP can cause issues with signal strength, bounce, and interference. All of these can cause a latency of the wireless signal and a poor connection.

2.5 Given a scenario, troubleshoot common router and switch problems

Today's networks can be much more complex than networks of the past, but the rationale behind them is still the same: to provide connectivity so that users can share information and resources. When connectivity is affected, the users are brought to a standstill, and productivity quickly declines. Because of this, you need to understand the major issues that can affect network connectivity. In this section, I will discuss the most common router and switch problems and how to troubleshoot them.

Switching loop

Today's networks often connect switches with redundant links to provide for fault tolerance and load balancing. Since a switch will send communication signals out all the ports except for the one that they came in, two or more switches connected with multiple links can cause a loop of communication signals that just keep circulating between the switches. This is referred to as a *switching loop*. Protocols such as the *Spanning Tree Protocol (STP)* prevent switching loops while at the same time maintaining fault tolerance. If the STP should fail, it takes some expertise to reconfigure and repair the network. For this reason, this type of issue should be identified and then escalated.

Bad cables/improper cable types

I will discuss cable types in much more detail in the next chapter, but suffice it to say that it is essential that you use the proper cable for a specified type of network. Using the wrong type of cable can lead to poor performance and intermittent connection issues that are sometimes difficult to troubleshoot. You should also make sure that the cable is actually plugged in and doesn't just look like it is.

Port configuration

Both switches and routers have interfaces that are sometimes referred to as *physical ports*. Depending upon the network topology, design, and purpose, these ports can be configured in a variety of ways. The most common misconfiguration is the speed of the link, but others might include encapsulation type, protocol, duplex, or just whether they are open or shut. Improper port configuration should be one of your primary "suspects" when you are troubleshooting a router or switch.

VLAN assignment

As I mentioned, VLANs on switches allow you to create multiple virtual subnets and at the same time keep a flexible network that is easier to maintain and change when necessary. On the other hand, an improper VLAN assignment on a port will effectively place clients in a subnet that you did not intend for them to enter. This is not only a connectivity problem; it could also create a security issue. You should take great care as to which client computer is connected when you assign a VLAN to an interface.

Mismatched MTU/MTU black hole

Maximum Transmission Unit (MTU) defines the largest size packet that will be expected by a network. In most cases, Ethernet networks use packets that range in size from about 64 bytes to about 1518 bytes. This means that the network protocols expect this size and work their behavior around that expectation.

If the interfaces on the connected devices are not configured with the same MTU, then issues could arise with data being properly and efficiently delivered in your network. An improperly configured router can consistently drop packets it would otherwise forward because the TCP handshake could actually succeed and then connection could hang when the actual data is sent. The effect of this might be that a user cannot get to some websites or even to no website at all. This can affect internal and external connections. A router that is causing this condition is sometimes referred to as a black hole router. You can keep this condition from occurring by assuring that the MTU of the interfaces in your network is properly configured. The precise configuration of MTU on interfaces is beyond the scope of this book.

Power failure

Since these devices run on electricity, obviously the lack of electricity will cause a big problem to say the least. Routers and switches have power supplies that convert the electricity from the power company to power that they can use to operate. You can ensure that your routers and switches get the power that they require by using an uninterruptible power supply (UPS) to provide continuous power when the power company fails. This can be as simple as a battery backup or as complex as a diesel generator. In addition, many devices have redundant power supplies, just in case that all-important element of their design should fail.

Bad/missing routes

As I mentioned, routers use a table of routes to decide how to forward a packet if that packet does not have a destination address in one of the networks directly connected to the router. If these tables are incorrect or are missing information, this can dramatically affect the router's ability to make proper decisions. In most cases, your routing protocols (if properly configured) will automatically provide the information that the routers need. In some cases, you may have to supplement with a static route or two. The bottom line is that if you understand the topology and the function of the routers, then you will be able to troubleshoot the bad or missing routes.

Bad modules (SFPs, GBICs)

Today's devices often contain removable modules that allow them to be configured for custom purposes and to be quickly replaced when they fail. A *small form-factor pluggable (SFP)* is a compact, hot-pluggable transceiver that is used for both telecommunication and data communication. A *gigabit interface converter (GBIC)* is a hot-swappable interface module that is the common standard for Gigabit Ethernet and Fibre Channel. If either of these should fail, it can be quickly replaced with a new module.

Wrong subnet mask

The "other part" of the IPv4 address is the *subnet mask*. In other words, you really don't know what network the address is on unless you also know the subnet mask. It will determine which subnet an address belongs to, and therefore it must be configured properly for network communication to occur. Whenever you are troubleshooting an IP address, you should always check the subnet mask as well. This is because a connection will fail even if you are pinging the right IP address if the subnet mask is not also properly configured.

Wrong gateway

The gateway (also called default gateway) of a computer or switch determines how it will send data to a remote network of any kind. Generally, this is the internal address of the local network's router, because that device provides access to the outside world. You can therefore "narrow down" your search to the gateway when your network connections function well within your subnet but cannot seem to get outside of it. When this is the case, your primary suspects should be the IP default gateways of your switches and computers and the routing tables of your routers.

Duplicate IP address

For your network to function properly, you must provide a unique address for each network interface card and router interface on the network. As long as the addresses are unique, you are on the right track. Sometimes a duplicate address can be placed onto a network because of a manual misconfiguration of a computer, a router interface, or even a DHCP scope. When this happens, you will likely know about it because most of the latest operating systems can detect this issue and bring it to your attention. Figure 2.5 shows the result of a duplicate address on a network. When this happens, you should reassign one of the addresses to make them unique again.

FIGURE 2.5   Duplicate IP address on network

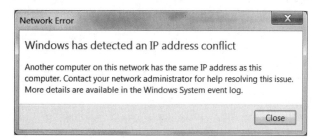

Wrong DNS

As you may remember, DNS is a service that allows a computer or a user to resolve a user-friendly hostname to an IP address. It is an essential service in today's networks because it assists client computers in finding the server computers that they require. It is also an essential component for communication on the Internet. Because of this, an improper configuration of a DNS address on a computer can cause that computer to perform poorly on the local network and to appear to lose its connection with the Internet. If this should happen, you should determine the appropriate address for the DNS server(s) and configure the computer properly.

To determine whether DNS is the problem, you could try pinging the IP addresses of some of your local servers. If you get a reply, then try pinging a known IP address of an Internet server. However, you should keep in mind that some websites such as Microsoft.com have blocked ICMP echo requests. In addition, if many clients have appeared to lose their connections simultaneously, you may also need to reconfigure the DHCP server or scope options for a new DNS server address.

Exam Essentials

Know the basics of logical network configuration and troubleshooting. Spanning Tree Protocol will keep your network from having switching loops if it's properly configured. Port assignments, IP addresses, encapsulation, speed, protocol, and duplex can all affect network communications. VLANs allow you to create multiple subnets on switches. Routers use tables to make routing decisions. If your data is not being forwarded as expected, take a good look at the routing tables.

Know the basics of physical network configuration and troubleshooting. The most common network problems are often physical issues. A bad cable can lead to hours of troubleshooting, as can a bad module, especially if the problem is intermittent. Sometimes it's just a matter of assuring that connections are really plugged in!

2.6 Given a set of requirements plan and implement a basic SOHO network

Today many people work from home or from very small office environments and therefore need only a basic computer and network setup. You should remember that even though a small office/home office (SOHO) network may not be as large as an enterprise network, it still must conform to all of the same standards and protocols. These standards affect both the logical and the physical aspects of the network.

In this section, I will discuss the requirements of a SOHO network. I will also discuss cable lengths, device types, environmental limitations, and compatibility requirements. You will learn that a SOHO network is just a smaller version of an enterprise network.

List of requirements

The list of "requirements" for a *small office/home office (SOHO)* is very short. All you really need are a few computers. Typically you would have fewer than 10 computers, or it would no longer be considered a SOHO environment. The computers that you use should be connected either by cables and a switch or by wireless connections. You would probably want to be connected to the Internet as well, but this is not a requirement. In addition, you would likely connect printers, faxes, scanners, and the like, either with cables or by wireless connections. Finally, you would most likely use TCP/IP as your protocol and IP addressing provided by a DHCP server in one of your devices. You would not necessarily need any server computers, but you might include a file and print server and possibly a domain controller if you wanted to centralize security.

Cable length

If you chose to use cables in your SOHO, then you would be subject to all of the rules and limitations of any larger network. You should not run any twisted-pair cable more than 100 meters (328 feet) from a switch. You can remember this by the phrase "100 meters without repeaters." (A switch is also considered a multiport repeater.) You should also follow the building codes for your area in regard to installing any Ethernet cable through the plenum. The *plenum* is the area in an office building between the ceiling of one floor and the floor of the next. It is typically used for circulation for the building. Using improper cable insulation can cause a fire to "wick" to other parts of the building and also spread toxic gases. Special plenum type cables should be used to prevent this from occurring. These cables are still subject to the "100 meters without repeaters" rule. Your only way around that rule would be to use a fiber-optic cable, which is an expense that is not necessary in a SOHO environment.

Device types/requirements

As mentioned earlier, the devices that you use in a SOHO network are very much the same as those you would use in a larger network, just on a much smaller scale. Devices might include desktops, laptops, routers, switches, printers, faxes, scanners, plotters, and so on. The only requirement in order for it to be considered a network is that the devices are connected to each other in such a way that data can be exchanged and work can be performed; otherwise, it's just a group of unrelated devices.

Environment limitations

If you choose to use a wired network, then you will have few environmental limitations. You would mainly want to assure that any routers and switches are in an area that is protected from flooding or high humidity and cool enough that they can maintain the optimum operating temperature. If you choose to use a wireless network, then you will have to take into account the structure of your building and anything that could cause absorption or reflection of radio waves. You probably don't need expensive wireless survey, but you do want to make sure you can see your data and that your neighbors can't!

Equipment limitations

Devices that you purchase for SOHO networks are generally a scaled-down version of the same type of device you would use for an enterprise network. For example, a router might have the capability to add static routes and specific security configuration, but it will likely be in a graphical user interface (GUI) format so that you can easily understand it with very little training. That said, it will likely not have the flexibility and redundancy of the enterprise-type router and should not be used for larger networks. In other words, you should use SOHO equipment for SOHO environment, but you should generally not use it for a larger enterprise environment.

Compatibility requirements

As I mentioned earlier, in any network there are three components that must be compatible with each other in order for computers to communicate on the network. In this regard, a SOHO network is no different; you must have a compatible media, client or service, and protocol. In regard to the media, I have already discussed your options of wired or wireless. With reference to the client, most businesses use Microsoft operating systems, which include the Microsoft client software. Finally, with respect to the protocol, TCP/IP is the most likely protocol since it provides communications within the network and also facilitates connecting the network to the Internet.

Exam Essentials

Know the components of a SOHO network.   A SOHO network is just a scaled-down network. It may contain a few computers or up to about 10 computers. It might also contain servers, routers, switches, printers, faxes, plotters, and the like, but none of these items is required; a small, unsophisticated device will generally suffice. As with all networks, components must use a common media, client, and protocol. The media could be wireless or wired, the client will likely be built into the OS of the computers, and the protocol will almost always be TCP/IP.

Know the limitations of a SOHO network.   If you choose to use a wired network, then you should run a cable between a switch and a computer for a distance of no greater than 100 meters (328 feet). If you choose to use wireless, then you should configure your computers to connect to your WAP, and you should use wireless security protocols. Typically, the devices (routers and switches) that you will use in a SOHO network are engineered for that purpose only and should not be used in a larger enterprise network.

Review Questions

1. Which of following are true about NAT? (Choose two.)

   A. NAT is a service that translates IP addresses.

   B. NAT is often used to filter MAC addresses.

   C. NAT must be used on a computer to connect to the Internet.

   D. NAT services can be provided by computers, routers, or other devices.

2. Which of the following is a layer 2 network that can be created using a switch?

   A. MAC

   B. WPA

   C. WEP

   D. VLAN

3. Which of the following are true about wireless networks? (Choose two.)

   A. Wireless networks are much easier to maintain than wired networks.

   B. It doesn't matter where you place your antenna or your WAP, as long as it's in your network.

   C. Bluetooth devices such as keyboards and mice can possibly cause interference on a wireless network.

   D. The most common channels for a wireless network are 1, 6, and 11.

4. Which of the following are not true in regard to wireless standards? (Choose two.)

   A. 802.11a and 802.11b are completely compatible.

   B. Most devices purchased today can use 802.11b/g/n.

   C. 802.11a uses OFDM.

   D. 802.11a uses DSSS.

5. Which of the following is true about DHCP?

   A. DHCP can issue IP addresses and only IP addresses to clients.

   B. DHCP servers are also DNS servers.

   C. You can reserve an address for a client based on its MAC address using a DHCP server.

   D. Servers, printers, and routers should always receive their addresses from a DHCP server.

6. A router that is improperly configured so that it consistently drops packets that it should forward is referred to as which of the following?

   A. MTU

   B. WAP

   C. Black hole router

   D. SOHO router

7. Which of the following is true in regard to SOHO networks?

   A. SOHO networks are very large, specialized, high-security networks.

   B. SOHO networks contain the same types of components as enterprise networks but on a much smaller scale.

   C. SOHO networks must always contain at least one server.

   D. SOHO networks must always use wireless connections.

8. If you choose to use twisted-pair Ethernet cables in your network, then what is the greatest distance you should run a cable from the switch to the computer?

   A. 100 feet

   B. 328 meters

   C. 328 feet

   D. 50 meters

9. Which of the following are true about DHCP scopes? (Choose two.)

   A. DHCP scopes define a range of addresses that can be assigned by a DHCP server.

   B. For redundancy, it is best to overlap your DHCP scopes.

   C. Scopes are typically controlled by the MAC address of a computer.

   D. Improper scopes can cause IP address conflicts.

10. Which of the following is a network technique that divides traffic into categories based on the protocol of the traffic and then allows for the prioritization of each category?

   A. WEP

   B. QoS

   C. WPA

   D. PAT

Chapter 3

Network Media and Topologies

COMPTIA NETWORK+ EXAM OBJECTIVES COVERED IN THIS CHAPTER:

✓ **3.1 Categorize standard media types and associated properties.**

- Fiber:
  - Multimode
  - Singlemode
- Copper:
  - UTP
  - STP
  - CAT3
  - CAT5
  - CAT5e
  - CAT6
  - CAT6a
  - Coaxial
  - Crossover
  - T1 Crossover
  - Straight-through
- Plenum vs. non-plenum
- Media converters:
  - Singlemode fiber to Ethernet
  - Multimode fiber to Ethernet
  - Fiber to coaxial
  - Singlemode to multimode fiber

- Distance limitations and speed limitations
- Broadband over powerline

✓ **3.2 Categorize standard connector types based on network media.**

- Fiber:
  - ST
  - SC
  - LC
  - MTRJ
- Copper:
  - RJ-45
  - RJ-11
  - BNC
  - F-connector
  - DB-9 (RS-232)
  - Patch panel
  - 110 block (T568A, T568B)

✓ **3.3 Compare and contrast different wireless standards.**

- 802.11 a/b/g/n standards
- Distance
- Speed
- Latency
- Frequency
- Channels
- MIMO
- Channel bonding

✓ **3.4 Categorize WAN technology types and properties.**

- Types:
- T1/E1
- T3/E3

- DS3
- OCx
- SONET
- SDH
- DWDM
- Satellite
- ISDN
- Cable
- DSL
- Cellular
- WiMAX
- LTE
- HSPA+
- Fiber
- Dialup
- PON
- Frame Relay
- ATMs
- Properties:
  - Circuit switch
  - Packet switch
  - Speed
  - Transmission media
  - Distance

✓ **3.5 Describe different network topologies.**

- MPLS
- Point to Point
- Point to Multipoint
- Ring
- Star

- Mesh
- Bus
- Peer-to-peer
- Client-server
- Hybrid

✓ **3.6 Given a scenario, troubleshoot common physical connectivity problems.**

- Cable Problems:
  - Bad connectors
  - Bad wiring
  - Open short
  - Split cables
  - DB loss
  - TXRX reversed
  - Cable placement
  - EMI/Interference
  - Distance
  - Crosstalk

✓ **3.7 Compare and contrast different LAN technologies.**

- Types:
  - Ethernet
  - 10BaseT
  - 100BaseT
  - 1000BaseT
  - 100BaseTX
  - 100BaseFX
  - 1000BaseX
  - 10GBaseSR
  - 10GBaseLR
  - 10GBaseER

- 10GBaseSW
- 10GBaseLW
- 10GBaseEW
- 10GBBaseT
- Properties:
  - CSMA/CD
  - CSMA/CA
  - Broadcast
  - Collision
  - Bonding
  - Speed
  - Distance

✓ **3.8 Identify components of wiring distribution.**

- IDF
- MDF
- Demarc
- Demarc extension
- Smart jack
- CSU/DSU

Although the basic concept of connecting computers hasn't changed very much since the mid-1980s, the methods used to connect them have changed dramatically. The technologies that are in use now have evolved over the past 30 years to the point where they are today. These technologies will continue to evolve. The components we use in our networks have also evolved because of these technologies.

When you connect computers, your main goal is to provide fast communication with as few errors as possible. You should understand that the type of media and topology you use in your network will largely determine your ability to reach this goal. In addition, you should know that the components you choose for a network will also determine your capability to control network traffic. In this chapter, I will discuss several networking media and topologies and compare the features that they, and the components that use them, bring to your network design to help you control traffic within your network.

For more detailed information on Domain 3's topics, please see *CompTIA Network+ Study Guide, 2nd Edition* (9781118137550) or *CompTIA Network+ Deluxe Study Guide, 2nd Ed* (9781118137543), both published by Sybex.

3.1 Categorize standard media types and associated properties

As networking has evolved, the types of cable and their properties have dramatically changed. We have moved from using cables made only from copper wire to also using cables made from glass fibers. Each of these general categories of cable has its own properties and has many options from which to select. In this section, I will discuss the most common types of cable and their corresponding properties.

Fiber

Fiber-optic cable (fiber) is often used in network backbones to provide high bandwidth for fast, reliable communications. There are two main types of fiber-optic cable: singlemode and multimode. In this section, I will discuss the properties, advantages, and disadvantages of each type.

Multimode

Multimode fiber-optic cable (MMF) uses light to communicate a signal and disperses it into numerous paths (which is why it's *multi*) as it travels through the core and is reflected back via *cladding*, a special material that lines the core and focuses the light back onto it. Multimode fiber provides high bandwidth at high speeds over medium distances (up to about 3,000 feet) but can be inconsistent for very long runs. Because of this, multimode fiber is generally used within a smaller area of a building. Multimode fiber is available in glass or in a plastic version that makes installation easier and increases installation flexibility. As with singlemode fiber, multimode fiber can be used when electrical interference is present, since it is completely immune to it. Figure 3.1 shows the how light is split into multiple paths in a multimode fiber-optic cable.

FIGURE 3.1   Light reflected in a multimode fiber-optic cable

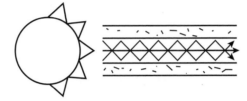

Singlemode

Singlemode fiber-optic cable (SMF) is a high-speed, high-distance media. It consists of a single strand, or sometimes two strands, of glass fiber that carries the signals. The light source that is generally used with singlemode fiber is a laser, although light-emitting diodes (LEDs) may also be used. With singlemode fiber, a single light source is transmitted from end to end and pulsed to create communication. Singlemode fiber is used for long runs because it can transmit data 50 times farther than multimode fiber and at a faster rate. For example, singlemode fiber might be used on an organization's corporate campus between buildings. Since the transmission media is glass, installing singlemode fiber can be a bit tricky. Other layers are protecting the glass core, but the cable still should not be crimped or pinched around any tight corners. It is, however, completely immune to electrical interference since light is used instead of electrical signals. Figure 3.2 illustrates the layers included in singlemode fiber-optic cable.

Copper

Fiber-optic cable is becoming more prevalent, but copper cables are by far the most used in networks today. There are many forms of copper cable and many technologies that have evolved around them.

FIGURE 3.2   Singlemode fiber-optic cable

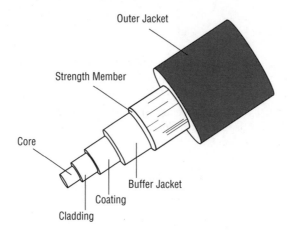

UTP

Unshielded twisted-pair (UTP) cable is the most common type of cable in use today. UTP is used most often because it is far easier to install than STP (which I will discuss next). It is commonly used in the access and distribution areas of a network. The only protection from electrical interference provided by UTP is that the pairs of wires within the cable are twisted, which is usually enough. Figure 3.3 shows a UTP cable.

FIGURE 3.3   A UTP cable

STP

Shielded twisted-pair (STP) resembles UTP except that it includes a foil shield that covers the wires and adds another layer of protection against outside magnetic interference. For this protection to be effective, the connections have to be properly grounded. This adds to the complexity of installations, so most organizations have opted to use fiber-optic cable instead of STP when electromagnetic interference is a problem. Figure 3.4 shows an STP cable.

FIGURE 3.4   An STP cable

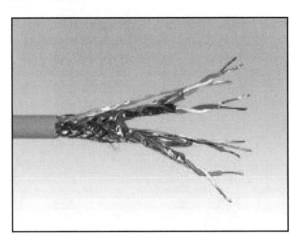

CAT3, 5, 5e, 6, and 6a

The category of a twisted-pair cable indicates the tightness of the twist applied to the wire pairs in the cable. The twist in wire pairs prevents an electrical interference called *crosstalk* from affecting the communication. Crosstalk occurs when a signal bleeds over from one wire to another (even through the insulation of the wire). The tighter the twist, the faster you can transmit information through a cable without suffering from crosstalk. Table 3.1 shows the maximum speed of the main cable categories. Category 5e (enhanced) is the cable type that is currently recommended as a minimum for all new installations.

TABLE 3.1   Cable categories and speeds

	Category 3	Category 5	Category 5e	Category 6	Category 6a
Maximum Speed	10Mbps	100Mbps	1000Mbps	1000Mbps	1000Mbps

You may have noticed that categories 5e, 6, and 6a all have the same maximum speed, so why would you choose one over another? For one thing, compared with category 5e, categories 6 and 6a have more stringent specifications regarding crosstalk and noise. They also require a slightly modified RJ-45 connector to meet the specification and hold the tighter twist.

Coaxial

Coaxial cable consists of an inner core wire and an outer braid of insulating wire. The inner core wire carries the entire signal. Figure 3.5 shows a coaxial cable. In the late 1980s, *coaxial* cable was used as the backbone of network segments and to connect computers to the bus topology that made up the network. The larger coaxial cables that generally made up the backbone were referred to as *thicknet*, while the smaller "drop cables" used to connect the computers were called *thinnet*. Sometimes we used a special device called a *vampire tap* to pierce the coaxial cable and get the signal from the core. Oh, those were the days!

FIGURE 3.5 A coaxial cable

Coaxial cable is rarely used anymore for network backbones or to connect computers, but it is being used today for television connections and to connect cable modems to broadband Internet connections. I will focus our attention on the coaxial cable used for computers today, for which there are basically two standards in general use today: RG-59 and RG-6. Of these, RG-6 offers a thicker core wire for less resistance and better performance.

Crossover

Let's say you wanted to attach a switch to a switch. By this definition, the devices are similar, and therefore you should use a crossover cable instead of a straight-through cable. Suppose you accidentally used a straight-through cable where you should have used a crossover cable; would that work? Well, yes—most modern switches would autosense the difference and "switch the pins" for you. However, for the exam, you should know that straight-through cables are used to connect dissimilar network devices, and crossover cables are used to connect similar devices. Table 3.2 illustrates the most common matchups and which cable to use.

TABLE 3.2 Cable types and uses

Device 1	Device 2	Cable type
PC	Switch	Straight
PC	PC	Crossover
Switch	Router	Straight

Device 1	Device 2	Cable type
Router	Router	Crossover
PC	Router	Crossover

Most of the entries in Table 3.2 are very straightforward; however, the last one is a bit tricky. The reason that a connection between a PC and a router uses a crossover cable is that a PC is very much like a router. In fact, you can create a router from a PC with an additional NIC and the right configuration.

T1 Crossover

A channel service unit/data service unit (CSU/DSU) is a digital interface device used to connect a router to a digital circuit, such as a T1 or T3 line. (I will discuss the CSU/DSU in greater detail later in this chapter.) If you should need to connect one CSU/DSU to another, you would usde a specially pinned cable, referred to as a *T1 crossover cable*. It is pinned in such a way as to let the send circuits on the router connect to the receive circuits on the CSU/DSU, and vice versa.

Straight-through

A *straight (or straight-through) cable* is the most common type of cable used in a network. It is typically referred to as a *patch cable*, because it is used to patch one network device to another. Straight-through cables are generally used to connect network devices that are dissimilar.

For example, in a typical network, a computer is attached to a wall jack using a straight-through cable. The wall jack is attached to a patch panel (for flexibility and redundancy), and then the patch panel is attached to a switch. In essence, a computer attached to a switch uses a straight-through cable. A computer and a switch are very different in regard to how they function on a network and therefore are considered dissimilar.

To assure connectivity throughout your network, the same wiring standard should be used in the cables, the patch panels, and other network connections. There are two competing standards, T568a and T568B, which I will discuss in greater detail later in this chapter.

Plenum vs. non-plenum

The difference between plenum and non-plenum cable involves how each is constructed and where it is authorized for use. Many large multistory buildings are designed to circulate air through the spaces between the ceiling of one story and the floor of the next. As I mentioned in a previous chapter, this area in between floors is referred to as the *plenum*. It is an area that is generally perfect for running cables to connect the many computers in the building.

However, in the event of a fire, the cables in the plenum can become a serious hazard in two ways. First, their insulation can give off a poisonous smoke that would then be circulated throughout the building. Second, they can become a "wick" for the fire and actually help spread it from room to room and floor to floor. Not pretty, huh?

To prevent both of these occurrences, the National Fire Protection Association (NFPA) regulates the use of cables in the plenum to those that it has tested to be safe. A plenum cable is therefore tested to be fire retardant and to create no (or a very small amount of) smoke and poisoned gas when burned. A non-plenum cable does not meet these standards and can therefore be used anywhere except in a plenum. Non-plenum cables are typically less expensive than plenum cables. However, most organizations use plenum cable only in the plenum for obvious reasons.

Media converters

As networking has evolved, the types of cable and their properties have dramatically changed. We have moved from using cables made from copper wire to using cables made from glass fibers. Each of these general categories of cable has its own properties and has many options from which to select. Perhaps one of the best decisions you could make in your network would be to use a combination of these types of cables and technologies. If you do that, then you will need to have media converters at the points where one type of cable and technology connects to another. In this section, I will discuss the most common types of media converters and where you would use each one.

Singlemode fiber to Ethernet

Since you would most likely use singlemode fiber between buildings on a campus, this type of media converter would be used in each building as the fiber-based data signal in the form of light comes into the building to be carried farther through the building in the form of electricity. See Figure 3.6.

FIGURE 3.6   A singlemode fiber to Ethernet converter

Multimode fiber to Ethernet

In some organizations, multimode fiber is used as the backbone within a building. This allows the backbone to carry more data at faster speeds than would be possible using only copper cable. Even when multimode fiber is used in this way, it is unlikely that it will be used all the way to the computers. Typically a multimode fiber to Ethernet converter will be used between the backbone segment and the patch panels that will lead to the wall jacks and finally to the computers themselves.

Fiber to coaxial

In the past, coaxial cable was used as a backbone in some buildings. This is not done very often anymore, but coaxial cables are sometimes used to connect cable modems for the purposes of Internet communications or telecommunications. If you wanted to bring in high-bandwidth communications from a cable provider and then distribute them through-out your network backbone, you would use a fiber-to-coaxial converter (see Figure 3.7).

FIGURE 3.7 A fiber-to-coaxial converter

Singlemode to multimode fiber

As I mentioned earlier, singlemode fiber is typically used between buildings because it can span greater distances, whereas multimode fiber is used within each building because it can have many channels of communication. Therefore, if you use both, the connections between your buildings will use a singlemode to multimode converter. The singlemode fiber will bring in pulses of light in one stream, and the multimode fiber will then divide the signals into multiple channels.

Distance limitations and speed limitations

As you might imagine, the capability of each of these technologies varies greatly from one to the next. For this reason, you will need to choose carefully when you are considering using one technology over another. Two of most important aspects of each type of cable are its maximum speed and maximum distance. Later in this chapter, I will discuss the various LAN and WAN technologies including the maximum distance for each technology.

Broadband over powerline

Broadband over powerline (BPL) is a system that carries data on a conductor wire that is also used for electrical power transmission. In the past, power lines were considered as a suitable media for high-bandwidth communications. Recent advances in technology are now making high-bandwidth communications possible and opening the door for computer communications in SOHO and enterprise networks. You can use a BPL converter to facilitate communications over power lines where other types of communication lines would be difficult or impossible to install.

Exam Essentials

Know the types of fiber-optic cable.   There are two main types of fiber-optic cable: multimode fiber and singlemode fiber. Multimode fiber is typically used within buildings and can disperse the light into multiple paths. Singlemode fiber is typically used between buildings and consists of a single light source that is pulsed.

Know the types of copper cables.   There are three main types of copper cables that are used in today's networks: UTP, STP, and coaxial. UTP cable is the most common type of cable by far. Since they do not have any shielding, they are very easy to install; however, they are not suitable for installations that are close to large magnets, motors, speakers, and the like. STP cables are less commonly used because they are much more difficult to install. They provide a layer of shielding that must be grounded to be effective. They are not used much in today's networks because fiber-optic cables provide a complete immunity to electrical interference. Coaxial cables are still used in today's networks, but in a very different way than they were in the past. They consist of one core wire that carries all of the signal and a braided mesh that acts as a shield. They are primarily used to connect cable modems to the connections from a cable Internet provider.

Know the categories of UTP cables and their purpose.   There any many categories of cables ranging from Category 3 to Category 6a. Generally speaking, the higher the category number, the faster you can push data through it without problems caused by signal bleed called *crosstalk*. You should always use the appropriate category for the task at hand.

Understand the main types of cables and their uses.   Straight, or *straight-through,* cables are used to patch network components together that are not similar to each other such as when connecting a computer to a switch. They are also referred to as *patch* cables. Crossover cables are used to connected similar devices together such as a switch to a switch, router to a router, or even a PC to a router (a PC can perform a routing function so it is similar to a router). A T1 crossover cable is a specialized crossover that is used to connect a CSU/DSU to another CSU/DSU.

Understand the difference between plenum and non-plenum cable.   A plenum is the space in a building that is between the ceiling of one floor and the floor of the next. Since air is generally circulated in this area, the NFPA regulates that only specialized cables can be used that have insulation that doesn't wick fire or give off poisonous gases when it burns. These specialized cables are referred to as *plenum* cables. In all other areas of the network, non-plenum cables can be used.

Understand media converters.   Since we use fiber-optic, copper UTP/STP, and even coaxial cables in the same network, we often need converters. There are many types of converters, and each has a use in the network. Review the definitions of the different media types and their uses, and the place that the converter will be used in the network will be evident for each.

Understand Broadband over powerline.   Broadband over powerline carries data on a conductor wire that is also carrying electrical power transmission. This can facilitate options in SOHO network and even larger enterprise-type networks. You can use this technology in areas where other media would be difficult or even impossible to install.

3.2 Categorize standard connector types on network media

Just as the types of cable that we use have evolved over time, so have the type of connectors. Some connectors have superseded others because of their durability or ease of use. In this section, I will discuss the most common connectors in use today.

Fiber

Depending on whether you are using singlemode or multimode fiber-optic cable and depending on the purpose of your connection, you may choose from many different types of connectors. In this section, I will discuss the most common fiber-optic connectors. You should be familiar with the appearance and general purpose of each type of connector.

ST

The *straight tip (ST)* connector uses a half-twist bayonet type of lock to hold it in place securely. ST connectors are most commonly used with singlemode fiber-optic cable that runs long distances. It resembles a small BNC connector, but it's generally made of hard plastic. Figure 3.8 shows an ST connector.

SC

The *standard connector (SC)* connector is a type of fiber-optic cable connector. It uses a push-pull connector mechanism similar to common audio and video plugs. SC connectors are most often used with multimode fiber-optic cable that is providing a backbone segment for a local area network. Figure 3.9 shows an SC connector.

FIGURE 3.8   An ST connector

FIGURE 3.9   An SC connector

LC

The *local connector (LC)* connector is a fiber connector that is built into the body of an RJ-style jack. The LC connector is perfect for local connections in an organization's telecom room or network closet. Figure 3.10 shows an LC connector.

MTRJ

The mechanical transfer-registered jack (MTRJ) connector is becoming more popular because of its compact size and durability. It contains two fibers next to each other and resembles an RJ-45 connector. It was designed to replace the SC connector and is less than half its size when you consider that it provides two connected fibers instead of just one. Figure 3.11 shows an MT-RJ connector.

FIGURE 3.10 An LC connector

FIGURE 3.11 An MT-RJ connector

Copper

Not all connectors are fiber-optic connectors. In fact, we still use a lot of copper connectors in our networks today. Some copper connectors have "stood the test of time," whereas others are rarely seen anymore, but you might still have to know about them for the exam. In this section, I will discuss the most common types of copper connectors and their general use.

RJ-45

The *RJ-45* connector is the most common of all network connectors. It is used to connect network interface cards (NICs) to hubs and/or switches. RJ-45s can also be used to connect network devices together for communication as well as control. The RJ-45 connector can contain and connect four pairs of wires, although they generally connect only two pairs. Figure 3.12 shows an RJ-45 connector.

RJ-11

Chances are very good that you have held an *RJ-11* connector in your hand, since they are used on all the telephone connections in the United States and most other countries. They can contain and connect two pairs of wires. In regard to computers, you are most likely to use an RJ-11 connector when you attach a modem to a telephone line in the unlikely event you are still using a dial-up connection. I know there are still some out there somewhere! Figure 3.13 shows an RJ-11 connector and jack.

FIGURE 3.12   An RJ-45 connector

FIGURE 3.13   An RJ-11 connector and jack

BNC

Although this type of coaxial connector is rarely used in today's networks, it is still listed as an item to recognize for the exam. Who knows, you might run into one at some point if you "dig up" a very, very old network. The *BNC connector* is pushed in and then locked onto the connection to hold it securely in place while connecting the core wire. Figure 3.14 shows a BNC connector.

FIGURE 3.14   A BNC connector

F-connector

The *F-connector* (Figure 3.15) is a coaxial type connector that is commonly used with cable TV and cable modems. It will most likely be attached to an RG-6 or RG-59 (in older installations) cable and will provide a solid connection to facilitate the carrying of data or television signal.

FIGURE 3.15   An F-connector

DB-9 (RS-232)

The *DB-9* or recommended standard 232 (RS-232) was a cable standard commonly used for serial data signals connecting between data terminal and data communications equipment, such as when connecting a computer's serial port to an external modem. As you can imagine, it is used much less frequently today than it was in the past. Still, you should be able to recognize a DE-9 female connector as one that might be used in an RS-232 connection. These types of connections are being superseded in today's networks by more modern connectors such as USB. Figure 3.16 shows an RS-232 connector.

FIGURE 3.16   A DB-9 (RS-232) connector

Patch panel

A *patch panel* is typically a rack or wall-mounted structure that houses cable connections. A patch cable generally plugs into the front side, while the back holds the punched-down connection of a longer, more permanent cable. The purpose of the patch panel is to offer the administrator a way to change the path of a signal quickly when needed. For example, if a cable inside a wall becomes damaged or fails, a network administrator can "patch around" that cable by simply changing the connection on two patch panels. Figure 3.17 shows a modern patch panel.

FIGURE 3.17   A patch panel

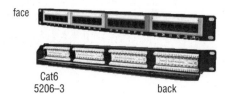

110 block (T568A, T568B)

A newer type of wiring distribution point, called a 110 block, has replaced most telephone wire installations and is also being used for computer networking. On one side of it, wires are punched down, while the other side has RJ-11 (for phone) or RJ-45 (for network) connections. The 110 blocks come in sizes from 25 to more than 500 wire pairs. Some are capable of carrying 1Gpbs connections when used with CAT6 cables. Figure 3.18 shows a 110 block.

FIGURE 3.18   A 110 block wire connector

   The manner in which these wires are arranged is of extreme importance. If you look inside a network cable, you will find four pairs of wires. These wire pairs are twisted together to prevent crosstalk (as I discussed earlier). Then the pairs of twisted wires are also twisted together to help prevent EMI and tapping. You know that the same pins must be used on the same colors throughout a network for receive and transmit, but how do you decide which color wire goes with which pin? The good news is that you don't have to decide—at least not completely. Two wiring standards have surfaced that have been agreed upon by more than 60 vendors including AT&T, 3Com, and Cisco, though there isn't 100 percent agreement in the industry. In other words, over the years some network jacks have been pinned with the T568A standard, and some have used the T568B standard. This can cause confusion if you don't know what you are looking at in your network.

You may be thinking "What's the difference, and why does it matter?" Well, the difference is the position of four wires on one side of the cable—that's it! As you can see in Figure 3.19, pins 4, 5, 7, and 8 are not used at all in either standard. This leaves only the wire pairs to connect to pins 1, 2, 3, and 6. If you connect the green-white, green, orange-white, and orange wires to pins 1, 2, 3, and 6, respectively, on both sides of the cable, then you are said to be using the 568A standard, and you would be creating a straight-through cable that would be used as a regular patch cable for most networks. Note that the reason for this is that most networks use the T568A standard for wall jacks. In essence 568A+568A= straight through and, 568B=568B=straight through, but 568A+568B=crossover. If, on the other hand, you switch from pin 1 to pin 3 and from pin 2 to pin 6 on one side only, then you have created a crossover cable for most networks.

FIGURE 3.19   EIA/TIA T568A and T568B wiring standards

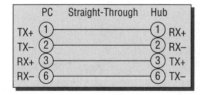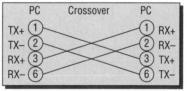

Exam Essentials

Be familiar with the various fiber-optic connectors.   There are multiple fiber-optic connectors that can be used in various locations in your network. Know the main types of connectors and the general build of each one. Also understand where each might be used and why it might be advantageous over other options.

Be familiar with various copper connectors.   There are multiple copper connectors that are used in your network. The most common by far is the RJ-45 connector, which holds four pairs of wires, although only two are generally used. Others include the RJ-11, BNC, DB-9, and F-connector. Know the general build and use of each of these connectors.

Understand patch panels and 110 block connectors.   Wiring distribution not only houses wiring connections but can also provide an administrator with options for reconnects. Know the general build and purpose of each of these.

3.3 Compare and contrast different wireless standards

In Chapter 2, I briefly discussed wireless standards and stated that we would cover them in much more detail in Chapter 3. In this section, I will discuss the most common wireless standards in use in today's networks and the main technology they use. In particular, I will discuss the aspects of distance, speed, latency, frequency, and channels. I will also discuss Multiple Input/Multiple Output (MIMO) and channel bonding.

802.11 a/b/g/n standards

802.11 is the IEEE specification that is used for wireless LAN technology. 802.11 specifies an over-the-air interface between a wireless client and a base station or between two wireless clients. The IEEE accepted the specification in 1997. The original 802.11 standard used a frequency hopping spread spectrum radio (FHSS) signal. There have been many revisions to the standard since then. The following are the major 802.11 standards in use today:

802.11a   802.11a uses *orthogonal frequency division multiplexing (OFDM)* to increase bandwidth. This standard uses the 5GHz radio band and can transmit at up to 54Mbps. It is not widely used today.

802.11b   Uses direct sequence spread spectrum (DSSS) in the 2.4GHz radio band. This standard can transmit at up to 11Mbps with fallback rates of 5.5Mbps, 2Mbps, and 1Mbps. It is quickly being superseded by the newer and faster standards that I'll discuss next.

802.11g   Uses DSSS and OFDM and the 2.4GHz radio band. This standard enhances the 802.11b standard and can transmit at speeds up to 54Mbps. It is one of the most commonly used standards and is backward compatible with 802.11b, since they both can use DSSS and the 2.4GHz band.

802.11n   Uses DSSS and OFDM and the 2.4GHz and the 5Ghz band. This standard enhances the 802.11g standard and can transmit at speeds up to 600Mbps, although most devices in use today support speeds only up to about 300Mbps. This standard is backward compatible with 802.11g and 802.11b and even 802.11a.

Distance

In general, the newer wireless standards can cover greater distances than the older standards, but there is much more to this than "meets the eye." The general distance (also called *range*) of 802.11a/b/g is about 30 meters. 802.11n is a little higher, at about 90 meters. However, these figures should never be taken for granted because they can be affected by the construction of a building, objects around the WAP, or other devices causing interference. You can improve distance (range) of your wireless networks by keeping the WAP and the computers away from large metal objects that can absorb and reflect signals. As you may remember, I already discussed troubleshooting common wireless network issues in Chapter 2.

Latency

In general, latency is the time that it takes for data to travel from a transmitter to a receiver, sometimes also known as *delay*. In wireless communications, latency is very unpredictable to say the least. The reason for this goes back to the fact that wireless communications can be affected by a large number of factors around the WAP and around the computers being used. Latency is not caused by a decrease in the speed of the connection (radio waves always travel at the speed of light) but rather by the fact that additional management frames are used by Carrier Sense Multiple Access with Collision Avoidance (CSMA/CA). Also, CSMA/CA may decide to hold or delay data transmissions.

Frequency

As I mentioned in Chapter 2, you don't usually set the frequency of your wireless devices, at least not directly. You simply choose which type of wireless technology you will use and then select the channel that you will use, or even just accept the default. As I discussed earlier, in general, there are two frequency bands used by 802.11 a/b/g/n. 802.11a uses the 5GHz band. 802.11a/b/g use 2.4GHz band. Finally, 802.11n uses both bands.

You did notice that I said *band*? Well, in this case, the word *band* refers to a range of frequencies that are automatically selected. Some vendors allow you to tweak the advanced settings and select only the frequencies you want. You should, however, be careful if you choose this option because if you set it specifically for one device, then you will need to set it specifically for all the other devices that you want to communicate.

Channels

As I mentioned earlier, wireless networks use many different frequencies within a band of frequencies (typically the 2.4GHz or 5GHz band). These frequencies are sometimes combined to provide greater bandwidth for the user. A combination of these frequencies that can be used by the end user is referred to as a *channel*. Most often, wireless networks use channels 1, 6, and 11. This is generally selected automatically, but you can change the channel if you are receiving interference from another network or wireless device. For the WAP and the clients to communicate, they must be on the same channel.

MIMO

Multiple-input and multiple-output (MIMO) is a technique of using multiple antennas at both the transmitter and receiver to improve communication performance. It is an emerging technology that offers significant increases in speed and distance without a need for more transmission power. MIMO is used with 802.11n and with 4G technologies.

Channel bonding

Channel bonding is a computer networking technique that combines two or more network interfaces on a single computer for increased data throughput. It is used with 802.11g and 802.11n Wi-Fi networking. It is not used with 802.11a or 802.11b wireless networking.

Exam Essentials

Understand 802.11 wireless standards. There are many 802.11 wireless standards that have been developed over the years, including 802.11/a/b/g/n. Each of these standards has its own capabilities and limitations. You should know the frequency, distance, and speed of each standard. Also, 802.11a uses the 5Ghz band, which makes it incompatible with 802.11b/g but still compatible with 802.11n.

Be familiar with the use of channels. Wireless networks operate in a band of frequencies, referred to as a *channel*. The channels most often used are 1, 6, and 11. For your WAP to communicate with your clients, the two must share the same channel.

Be familiar with MIMO and channel bonding. Both MIMO and channel bonding are techniques used to improve the quality of wireless communication. MIMO, used on 802.11n, employs multiple antennas at both the transmitter and the receiver to improve communication performance. Channel bonding, used on 802.11g and 802.11n, combines two or more network interfaces on a single computer for increased data throughput.

3.4 Categorize WAN technology types and properties

Today's organizations use many different types of WAN connections. Your decision to use one connection type over another will largely depend on the properties each connection type offers and the advantages it may provide your organization. In the following sections, I'll discuss the main WAN connection types and their properties.

Types

Most WAN connections are provided by a communications company referred to as a *service provider*. One of the main differences between a WAN and a LAN is that you generally don't own all the connections on a WAN, unless you are the service provider. Because of this, the types of network connections you will encounter in a WAN environment are very different from the connections you are used to in a LAN environment. Most network connection types have evolved over time, offering the right properties to connect a company's computers based on the needs of the company for its connections. I'll discuss WAN connection types such as Frame Relay, T1, T3, DSL, cable modem, ATM, SONET, wireless, and ISDN.

T1/E1

Let's say your company has one location in New York and another in San Diego. For your communications, you would like to have a cable that connects the two locations. You could get a very big truck and a whole lot of cable and just start driving cross-country, carefully spooling out the cable and telling everyone not to bother it. Of course, it still wouldn't work when you got to the end because of the attenuation of copper wire, but that's another story!

This ridiculous example will help you see what service providers have done for you. In essence, they have already rolled out that cable, but they require payment to let you connect to both ends of it. Once you do, that's your connection, and nobody else is on it. The service provider will generally "condition" the line from time to time, testing it and making sure you are getting what you are paying for, but you will be the only one authorized to use it to communicate. Sometimes this division is only logical, but often it is physical as well; in other words, it's your wire and only your wire at many points. Cool, huh?

The most common of these types of connections in the United States has been the *T1*. In Europe, they use a very similar connection called an *E1*. A T1 provides for 1.54Mbps of dedicated bandwidth for the customer. This bandwidth can be used in total or divided up into as many as 24 channels, called DS0s, which are each 64Kbps. An E1 is very similar but offers 32 DS0s instead of 24 for a total of 2.048Mbps. This is accomplished using a device called a CSU/DSU. This gives the customer (you) many options in regard to the dispensation of the bandwidth to network resources. The cost of a T1 or an E1 varies based on the connection points you choose, but it's safe to say you would pay between $500 and $1,000 a month for one T1 line in most locations today. This is why an organization will consider other options before spending the money on a dedicated T1 connection. I should also mention that a T1 is not (by far) the most expensive connection type you can choose.

T3/E3/DS3

Caution, the next couple of options are big bucks! What if you wanted a line like a T1 but much, much larger? Some large companies require high-bandwidth, dedicated connections from one office or data center to another. One way to accomplish this is by using a *T3* line in the United States or an *E3* line in Europe and much of the rest of the world. This type of line provides a tremendous amount of usable bandwidth that can be divided to fit an organization's needs. A T3 provides for 672 DS0s, or the equivalent of 28 T1s or 44.736Mbps! It is sometimes also referred to as a *DS3*. An E3 provides for the equivalent of 512 DS0s, or approximately 17 E1s or 34.368Mbps.

OC-x

If you thought those were fast, you ain't seen nothin' yet! In the term OC-x, the OC stands for "optical carrier," and the x indicates the relative speed of the link. Well, the x just keeps getting bigger and bigger. The original speed of an OC trunk was about 50Mbps, and it was called an OC-1. OC-3 quickly followed with 150Mbps. The standard at the time of this writing is OC-3072, which offers a mind-blowing data rate of 160Gbps—that's with a G! As you might imagine, only very large companies have the need (or the money) for these options.

SONET

How about a protocol that will push data at 150Gbps over fiber links and has to be controlled using atomic clocks? That's what Synchronous Optical Networking (SONET) can do. It's especially useful for networks that span multiple geographic regions because the atomic clock mechanism in it keeps everyone on the same exact millisecond. As you can imagine, this protocol requires expensive equipment and expertise. It is typically used by large communication providers and very large corporations as a transfer mechanism or backbone for data traffic. In regard to speeds, SONET generally provides an STS-1 link of 50Mbps bandwidth and multiples thereof, whereas STS-3 would provide about 150Mbps bandwidth.

SDH

Synchronous Digital Hierarchy (SDH) is a standard that is very similar to SONET. It transfers data over optical fiber using laser light or LED. Its speed and capability are similar to SONET, and its timing is controlled using atomic clocks. SDH was originally defined by the European Telecommunications Standards Institute, whereas SONET was originally defined by the American National Standards Institute. In regard to speeds, SDH defines an STM-0 at 50Mbps bandwidth.

DWDM

Dense Wavelength Division Multiplexing (DWDM) is an optical technology used to increase bandwidth even further over existing fiber-optic backbones. It works by combining and transmitting multiple signals simultaneously at different wavelengths on the same fiber. One fiber is essentially turned into multiple "virtual fibers." Currently, because of DWDM, single fibers have been able to transmit data at speeds up to 400Gbps.

Satellite

Earlier, when I was talking about "coaxial cable that can connect you to the Internet," some of you might have been thinking "What cable? We live out in the countryside and don't have those cables out here!" If that's the case, then your best (and maybe only) option is a satellite hookup. You may also decide to use a satellite hookup because it is the most economical or dependable service in your area. In either case, you will need a dish antenna and a professional installer or instructions on how to find their satellite with your dish antenna. It always makes me laugh when I hear someone say that they put the satellite in the backyard to get the TV signal. That's not the "satellite." The satellite is in geostationary orbit high above the earth, and your little antenna is just going to pick up on its signal from space.

Once you do that, you can then use that signal as a download from the Internet. Now uploading is a bit trickier, since you probably won't have a high-powered transponder. Many satellite communications companies have provided the upload through your regular telephone line dialup connections. Some now provide a DSL line to give you more bandwidth for uploads. Others advertise a two-way satellite system that actually does send some signal back to the satellite from the antenna. These are typically more expensive and harder to install. Satellite communications companies offer data rates that rival those of their biggest competitors, cable and DSL.

ISDN

This is one that I can't believe is still in the exam objectives! It's been so long since we used ISDN that it should just go away, and we shouldn't need to know the details anymore. Oh well, since it's listed on the objectives, I'll go over the most important aspects regarding ISDN BRI and ISDN PRI that you might need to know for the test...and very unlikely for real life.

ISDN BRI is a layer 2 protocol that allows for two communication channels and one control channel. The communication channels are referred to as B (bearer) channels, and the control channel is referred to as a D (delta) channel. Each of the B channels can carry up to 64Kbps of data (that used to be a lot), and the control channel can use 16Kbps for data control. ISDN BRI is sometimes referred to as 2B + D, but this is actually misleading because the B channels are really the only usable bandwidth for data. Thus, an ISDN line can carry a whopping 128Kbps of data! In other words, one T1 is the rough equivalent of 12 ISDN BRI lines. ISDN also employs all kinds of telephone company terminology that identifies the reference points and the devices, but the chance of you having to know that for this exam (or for real life anymore) is so remote that it hardly bears mentioning.

ISDN PRI came out a little later, and it's a very different story than ISDN BRI. An ISDN PRI link is almost the same as a T1 line in regard to its capacity to carry data. It consists of 23 B channels (each with 64Kbps) and 1 D channel (also with 64Kbps). A little quick math should tell you that a single ISDN link will carry 1,472Kbps, which, as you can see, is very close to a T1.

So, why would a company choose an ISDN PRI link over a T1? Actually, it could come down to the availability in an area, the cost, the type of equipment that the company already owns, and the business rationale for the link. Both ISDN PRI and T1 links offer 23 DS0s for a customer's actual bandwidth use. (That's the "dirty little secret" about T1s—you don't get all 1.544Mbps for your use, but you should still know that number for the exam.) Some equipment has ISDN PRI interfaces built in, which allow flexible control of the 23 B channels, so a company can use them for special needs such as video conferences or network-based meetings. ISDN PRI also employs a myriad of telephone company jargon that, thankfully, you will not need to know. Just know that it's 23 B + D and that all channels are 64Kbps DS0s, and you will be fine.

Cable

Cable companies have jumped on the bandwagon and now offer you a path to the Internet that begins with connecting your computer to a special cable modem. That modem is configured by the cable company to be recognized by its central office, also called the *headend* of the cable company. From there, the cable company becomes your Internet service provider (ISP), connecting you to the Internet.

Many small businesses and home users have chosen this option for their Internet connection. The advantages include the fact that most cable companies can provide tremendous bandwidth (10Mbps and faster) downstream and "acceptable" bandwidth (over 1Mbps) upstream. For most users and small businesses, this is all they really need. A potential disadvantage is that you will share bandwidth with others who are in your immediate service area. This means that at peak times your performance could become degraded. This is not the case with the next technology that I will discuss.

ISDN BRI: Then and Now

In the early 1990s, when ISDN BRI was just coming out, I was working at Sprint in Florida. We used to joke that ISDN stood for either "It Still Does Nothing" or "I Still Don't kNow." Sprint wanted about 90 bucks a month for it so that you could combine your Internet service with your telephone services. The problem was that most people at that time were saying "What's an Internet?" You see, the Internet at that point was accessible only by text commands and usually only through a university or a large corporation. It wasn't all that exciting then, except for a few of us "geeks."

By the mid-1990s, though, with the ushering in of the World Wide Web and hypertext browsing, everything had changed. We sold a lot of ISDN BRI during that time until the newer technologies of ADSL and cable modem Internet took its place. Then we still sold it as backup lines to companies that were leasing a T1 or a T3. It was no longer an expensive add-on by that time. Now ISDN BRI is all but gone, but you still need to know the historical information covered in this chapter for the exam.

DSL

Another inexpensive option for small companies and home users, which provides considerable bandwidth for an economical rate, is a *digital subscriber line (DSL)*. The most common of these is the *asymmetric digital subscriber line (ADSL)*. The reason this type of connection can be economical is that the lines it uses are already in place. They are your regular telephone lines. The service provider uses the regular telephone lines and special equipment that multiplexes the signal to provide tremendous bandwidth over that which dialup lines provide.

Now, as you may know, asymmetric means "not the same on both sides" or "not balanced." So, what is not balanced about an ADSL line? The bandwidth is not balanced; in fact, it's not even close. You may have noticed that service providers advertise ADSL using megabits per second for download speed but kilobits per second for upload speed. That's because the upload speed is so much slower that it wouldn't sound that great in megabits per second. For example, one popular carrier offers its Extreme ADSL that has a download speed of 10Mbps and an upload speed of 512Kbps. Sounds pretty good, doesn't? Well, what if I offered it to you with 10Mbps download and only 0.5Mbps upload—how much would you buy then? As you can see, they are both the same, but many people don't catch this fact.

The upload speed of ADSL is generally about ½₀th its download speed. The reason that most people buy it anyway is that they don't really care too much about the upload speed. Most of what they do that is bandwidth intensive is downloading, such as surfing the Internet, watching movies, and pulling down files. Now, if they were building a website or transferring files to an FTP server, that would be a different story altogether. However, most people aren't doing that, so ADSL is fine for them.

For those who want a little more upload speed, a DSL service is available in some areas that provides a balance of upload and download speed. It is referred to as *symmetric digital subscriber line (SDSL)*. Typically, you won't get the fastest download speed with this option, but that is not usually what you are after anyway. If you are considering this option, you are one of the few who really does put large files back onto the Web, such as when building a website or sending files to an FTP server. The additional upload speed will save you considerable time and headaches from watching that agonizingly slow progress indicator line, if you know what I mean!

At the time of this writing, there were many areas that offered SDSL at rates of up to 3Mbps but usually about 1.5Mbps. You might recognize that as about the same as a T1. This is no coincidence since many small businesses consider SDSL to be a less expensive option that gives them essentially what the T1 would have, especially if they are using the bandwidth in its entirety and not dividing the DS0s. Not all areas offer SDSL, but in many areas it can be used to provide bandwidth acceptable to a business and still save money vs. leasing a dedicated T1 line.

What if you want to "have your cake and eat it too"? In other words, what if you want very high bandwidth for both upstream and downstream so that you can watch your movies in HD and upload large files all at the same time? In that case, you will need *very high bitrate digital subscriber line (VDSL)*. Currently, service providers are experimenting with new lines that will provide more than 100Mbps (that's right, I said 100Mbps) for both upstream and downstream simultaneously on regular telephone lines! As you might imagine, this is still an emerging technology, and you had better be prepared to pay for it, at least compared to what you pay now for ADSL or SDSL.

Cellular

This morning when I got to my office computer, the Internet was down. I quickly determined that everything was connected and even tried a restart of my cable modem, but to no avail. I called the provider who said that they were aware of a problem in my area and would have it fixed within a couple of hours. *Hours*! Without Internet? I have a business to run, you know!

Fortunately, I also have a wireless card that fits into any USB port on a computer and then connects to my cellular provider. Mine gives me 7.2Mbps download speed, which is fast enough for a backup line. Because of it, I was able to conduct business rather normally this morning while my primary provider got their issue solved.

The latest 4G technology of these cards can operate at speeds up to 100Mbps, so these types of cards can be used for primary Internet as well as backup lines. There are even some now that allow you to set up your own network and allow a few other users to connect as well. There are two competing standards, Global System for Mobile communications (GSM) and Code-Division Multiple Access. Whether you end up using one or the other of the standards, or even a hybrid of the two, will be determined by the cellular vendor that you choose.

WiMAX

Worldwide Interoperability for Microware Access (WiMAX) is a telecommunications protocol that is sometimes referred to as "Wi-Fi on Steroids." It can be used for a number of applications including broadband connections, but it can also permit usage at much greater distances than Wi-Fi. On a larger scale, such as for an entire community or even a small country, WiMAX is much more cost effective. Identified by the IEEE 802.16 standard, it is being experimented with for "last-mile" connectivity options rather than using cable or DSL. The subscriber uses a WiMAX card that connects to their computer, usually in a USB port. Originally, a few years ago, WiMax could deliver speeds up to 40Mbps, but it can now deliver speeds up to 1Gbps. That's quite an increase in such a short amount of time!

LTE

The Long Term Evolution (LTE) format was first proposed by NTT DoCoMo of Japan and has been adopted as an international standard. At the time of this writing, it is still in the making as far as actually being offered by carriers. When it is released, it will offer over 100Mbps speed on wireless links for phones, PDAs, and computers! It will be the true fourth-generation (4G) standard, although some carriers have "jumped the gun" and are calling enhancements to 3G a 4G standard.

HSPA+

High Speed Packet Access + (HSPA+) is a wireless broadband standard that is used by some vendors for access to the Internet on cell phones and PDAs. Also known as Evolved HSPA, it provides data link rates of approximately 84Mbps down and 22Mbps up. Providers usually offer some service plans at these maximum speeds and others at a slower speed.

Fiber

As I mentioned earlier, fiber-optic cable (fiber) is often used in network backbones to provide high bandwidth for fast, reliable communications. In addition, some companies, such as Verizon, are now offering fiber-optic cable connections to the user's desktop. This technology can deliver Internet speeds up to 150Mbps, but the availability is currently quite limited. It uses an optical network terminal (ONT), which is provided by the vendor and generally offers wired and wireless connections.

Dialup

Also called Plain Old Telephone Service (POTS) or Public Switched Telephone Network (PSTN), *dialup* service offers agonizingly slow (in today's terms) 56Kbps lines.

POTS is a term that telephone company employees assigned to those public switched lines when newer and more "sophisticated" links such as ISDN, T1, T3, and the like began to emerge. The point was that the normal modem-based dialup communications ran on the same lines that everyone had been talking on for almost 100 years! What you should know about dialup are the advantages (yes, there are some) and disadvantages of it vs. the newer technologies that I've covered.

The main advantages of dialup are availability and cost. It is highly available, since almost everyone has a regular telephone line (although that is beginning to change now), and it's available at a relatively low cost when compared to other services. As you may have guessed, the major disadvantage of dialup lines is that they do not support the bandwidth that we need in order to do all of the "fancy stuff" that we want to do on our computers today, such as download movies and large files, surf multiple websites at the same time, and hold video conferences with our peers. Still, some people in the world will hear those screeching tones of the modem handshake when they dial up to their ISP today.

PON

A *Passive Optical Network (PON)* is a point-to-multipoint fiber-to-premises network that allows a single fiber-optic cable to serve multiple premises. The premises can be businesses or homes. As technology advances, more subscribers are using fiber-optic cable to connect the Internet. This is continuing to grow, and more types of PONs are evolving to work with different technologies and with various providers. Many versions of this technology are evolving, and speeds range from less than 1Gbps up to 10Gbps.

Frame Relay

Organizations that have many locations across a wide geographic region and that want to connect each of those locations to each other have many options with today's communications networks. They could connect them all with dedicated lines. This could be very expensive, though, since they would need many dedicated lines. For example, if an organization had just five locations that it wanted to mesh fully with dedicated lines, it would require 15 dedicated lines.

Instead of using dedicated lines, another option available to organizations is to use a network of switches and special routers that spans the globe and can be connected to at any point. These lines take the information from a computer or other host and relay it to its final destination. This type of networking is referred to as *Frame Relay* because the layer 2 frames are actually being relayed across the switches and special routers instead of being sent on dedicated lines. This has been an effective method of communication for many companies over the last 10 to 15 years, but it is gradually being phased out now because of even better communication options.

If you take a Cisco or other type of WAN-based class, you will no doubt learn the details, and a myriad of terminology, about Frame Relay. For the purposes of this course, you should just know that it is a method of using common (nondedicated) lines to communicate network traffic at layer 2 (the Data Link layer) so as to join two hosts within the same subnet. The layer 2 address that it uses, referred to as a *Data Link Connection Identifier (DLCI)*, is generally assigned by the service provider such as AT&T or Sprint. The guaranteed communication rate that the service provider agrees to is the *committed information rate (CIR)*. Thus, the main reason that you might choose Frame Relay over dedicated lines is that you can get an acceptable CIR for your connections for much less money than you would pay to have dedicated lines for each one.

ATMs

I like to joke that *ATM* is a technology that allows you to take money out of your bank! Actually, ATM does not stand for automatic teller machine (at least in this case) but for asynchronous transfer mode. Unfortunately, knowing what the acronym means still doesn't tell you much about what this protocol does. In essence, it's a protocol that was developed after Ethernet, and it provides a much more efficient way of transferring data than does Ethernet.

ATM was originally developed in the mid-1980s to be used for voice, data, and video applications. We needed a more efficient protocol to provide movies and sound for training and for fun. It uses a fixed-length cell of 53 bytes, rather than the variable-length packets that are used by Ethernet. This allows for more efficiency, since the devices never have to fragment and reassemble large packets. The original ATM technology was already much faster than Ethernet; it was able to transfer voice, data, and video signals at up to 500Mbps. It's now even faster and is being used by some telecommunication and Internet providers as a backbone or core layer. ATM, like every other technology, will eventually be replaced by faster successors.

Properties

So, just how do you decide which one of these types of WAN connections is best for your situation? Well, a good place to start is to compare the properties of each type of connection against the needs of the organization in which they will be used. Some of the many properties that you should consider include whether the solution is circuit switched or packet switched, its speed relative to other solutions, the media that is used, and the distance that media can carry the data. In the following sections, I'll discuss each of these important properties of WAN communication.

Circuit switch

The properties of WAN technology types are a description of the events that happen and/or the attributes of the communication. In the case of circuit switch, we are back to our dialup lines. Once you establish a connection on a circuit-switched network, the entire conversation or line of data traffic is sent on those same physical connections until you terminate the connection. If you were to establish a new connection to the same place, you would likely get a very different set of connections that would also "complete your call."

Packet switch

Packet switch networks are very different from circuit switch ones in that each data packet might take a different route to its final destination during the same transmission. The original packet switch network, called X.25, was developed to overcome the challenge of sending reliable communications through an inherently unreliable medium. The unreliable medium at that time was, you guessed it, Ma Bell!

A computer modem's "screeching" must have sounded very different from those original switches than the voice of Alexander Graham Bell saying, "Come here, Watson, I need you."

If one switch weren't getting the job done, X.25 would just take a different path automatically. However, because of the extensive error checking built into X.25, it was inherently very reliable...and very slow!

The newer packet-switched networks include some that I've already discussed in this chapter such as Frame Relay. These networks use sophisticated virtual circuits to avoid errors and thereby improve efficiency and data throughput. They are connection-oriented now, so data doesn't move from one location until it's completely cleared to "land" in the next. This makes for fast and reliable data flow.

Speed

Speed is a little deceptive in that it's a factor of available bandwidth and throughput. In other words, just because you have a T1 doesn't mean you have a fast connection. It depends on how many others are using it and on what you need to do with it. Also, your speed through a network will largely be determined by the available bandwidth on the slowest link that you encounter.

Let's say you were to take a trip all the way across the United States that was mostly on the expressways but you had to climb up and down winding mountain overpasses for the last 500 miles. That last 500 miles would likely take the bulk of your time on the trip, even though it wasn't the greatest distance. The same thing happens when user data comes from one location to another through a very fast backbone: they may have a speed of 10Gbps on the backbone, but as soon as they come into the building and hit your 100Mbps Fast Ethernet switch, their relative speed for the whole connection will be, well, 100Mbps. Maybe there is more to this speed thing than first meets the eye?

Transmission media

This looks like a no-brainer at first glance. Transmission media is the stuff on which the communication is carried. This media could be copper, fiber, or even wireless. The media you choose will depend on your bandwidth needs, security needs, EMI concerns, and the distance you need to send the data before it hits another switch or router. Since I'm talking about the WAN environment, the service provider will have already made these decisions. I will categorize many types of transmission media in the next sections of this chapter.

Distance

Distance is "how far" data is sent. I don't think that's on the exam, but the relative distance of communications on various communications media might "creep in there." Generally speaking, fiber optics are capable of much greater distances because their attenuation rate is nowhere near as high as that of copper connections. This is because the signal being sent is light rather than electricity. In regard to WAN connectivity, the good news is that it's not your problem. The service provider should give you the right links to get you from point A to point B in the most efficient and effective manner. Later in this chapter, I will categorize many types of transmission media in regard to distance and speed.

Exam Essentials

Be able to categorize types of WAN technologies.   Be able to differentiate between Frame-Relay, T1, T3, ADSL, SDSL, VDSL, cable, satellite, OC-x, wireless, ATM, SONET, ISDN, and dialup technologies. Know the major advantages and disadvantages of each and where they are likely to be used.

Be able to categorize WAN properties.   Understand the difference between circuit switch and packet switch. You should be able to categorize WAN properties with regard to speed, transmission media, and distance limitations.

3.5 Describe different network topologies

Basically, a topology is a shape; so, a network topology is the shape of a network. There is, however, a big difference between a physical network topology and a logical network topology. The physical network topology represents how the network looks to your "naked eye." In other words, the physical network topology is the way the components are arranged. The logical network topology represents how information flows through the network, which may not be the same as how it looks to your "naked eye." You should understand the main network topologies and the difference between a physical network topology and a logical one. You should be able to recognize them given a diagram, schematic, or description. In the following paragraphs, I will discuss each network topology in greater detail.

MPLS

Multiprotocol Label Switching (MPLS) is a relatively new mechanism used to create a logical network topology with no dependence on a specific underlying protocol. Instead, it uses labels to make forwarding decisions on packets and thereby offers you a tremendous amount of flexibility in regard to network planning and prioritization of traffic. For example, you could decide to give a specific customer's traffic a higher priority through your network, just because that customer adds more to your "bottom line" than other customers do. The specific configuration of MPLS is beyond the scope of this book.

Point to point

A point-to-point connection is not really so much of a network topology as it is a piece of one. Today's networks generally consist of many point-to-point and various other types of connections. *Point to point* just means that the connection is active only for the sender and the receiver and that there are no other computers or devices involved. In fact, point-to-point connections are said to create communication that is not shared because the only communication is between the sender and the receiver. Point-to-point connections between network devices, such as switches or routers, can provide for very efficient network communication. In fact, you may remember from the earlier discussion that full-duplex communication requires point-to-point connections. Figure 3.20 illustrates a point-to-point connection between two routers.

FIGURE 3.20   A point-to-point connection

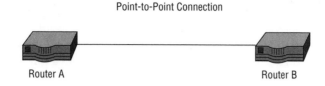

Point-to-Point Connection

Router A   Router B

Point to Multipoint

Point-to-multipoint connections are created when an interface is connected to two or more other interfaces. This is the general effect of a hub on a network in which the data flows into one interface and can flow out of all other interfaces. It can also be seen in router configurations, such as Frame Relay switching (which I will discuss later in the chapter), in which the point-to-multipoint connections are created using subinterfaces (virtual interfaces). Point-to-multipoint Ethernet connections cannot use full-duplex communications because the connections are shared and therefore require the use of CSMA/CD to control the traffic. Point-to-multipoint connections in Frame Relay switching might require the use of special protocols and configuration to control data traffic. Figure 3.21 illustrates point-to-multipoint configurations.

FIGURE 3.21   Point-to-multipoint configurations

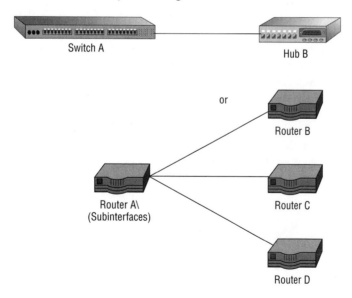

Switch A   Hub B

or

Router B

Router A\
(Subinterfaces)   Router C

Router D

Ring

A ring is a legacy topology that looks exactly like a star topology to the naked eye. The real difference in a ring topology vs. a star topology is the technology that is used. Computers in a ring topology generally used IBM Token Ring technology. Other components can also be arranged in a ring topology and use different technologies. The computers in a ring topology are not generally arranged in a physical ring. In fact, just as with a star topology, they can be next to each other or spread throughout a building. The difference is that the central component that connects them contains the logical ring that facilitates communication on the network using the ring technologies. Figure 3.22 shows a ring topology. Please note that data flows in a very different way, even though the physical topology would be indistinguishable from that of a star topology to the naked eye.

FIGURE 3.22   A ring topology

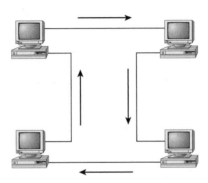

Star

A star topology is a group of computers connected to a central location, such as a hub or a switch. This is the most common topology in use today. The computers may be physically located next to each other or spread throughout an entire building, but the flow of information from among computers must go through the central location. In a star topology, each computer has its own cable or connection to the hub. Since each computer has its own connection, one computer's failing will not affect the other computers in the network. However, if the hub or switch should fail, then all the computers on that hub or switch will be affected. Figure 3.23 is an illustration of a star topology.

FIGURE 3.23   A star topology

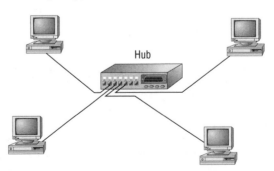

Mesh

The full mesh topology is not often used for networks and is almost never used for individual computers. In a full mesh topology, all the components in the mesh have independent connections to all the other components in the mesh. For example, if there were four computers connected with a full mesh, then the number of connections could be determined by the following formula:

$$[n(n-1)] / 2 = \text{total number of connections}$$

In this example, there would be a total of 12 connectors for 6 connections, and each computer would have to contain 3 network interface cards:

$$[4(4-1)] / 2 = 6$$

Any network with multiple or redundant connections to network components can be considered a mesh topology, but because of the expense involved in building this type of network, they are rarely created for individual computers. A mesh, or even a full mesh, would most likely be found connecting multiple networks in an organization. In fact, the Internet is the best and biggest example of a partial mesh topology. Figure 3.24 shows a full mesh topology with four computers.

Bus

The bus topology was used in earlier networks but is not commonly used today. In a bus topology, all computers are connected to each other by a single cable. Coaxial cable with special connectors called BNC connectors (as shown earlier in Figure 2.8) and T connectors were used. The T connectors provided an independent connection for each computer on the bus. In addition, the bus worked only if both ends of the cable had a special resistor, called a *terminator*, installed. Figure 3.25 shows a bus topology, and Figure 3.26 shows the T connector used to connect the computers to the bus.

FIGURE 3.24　A full mesh topology

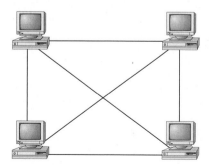

FIGURE 3.25 A bus topology

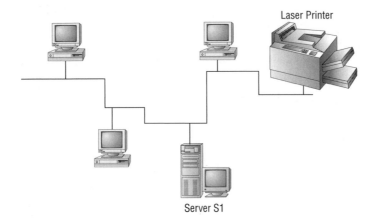

Server S1

FIGURE 3.26 A T connector

Peer-to-peer

Very small business networks and home networks are often peer-to-peer. This means that no dedicated server is involved at all. Each computer acts as both a client and a server. Typically, directory shares or folders are set up on each of the computers, and local accounts on the computers are used to provide some minimal security. Generally, peer-to-peer networks consist of no more than about 10 computers. A network of more than 10 computers creates tremendous confusion because the users might have to know different usernames and passwords to get to the share directories on each computer. Also, what if the other nine computers wanted to use a share directory on the 10th computer all at the same time? The 10th computer's resources would be so overwhelmed with providing the share directory for the others that you might not even be able to use it yourself!

Client-server

In a client-server network, the problem of resource sharing is addressed by using specific high-capacity and high-speed computers to share resources to the client computers. Most of the resources that the clients use are centralized to the very fast server computer. The server computer is typically not used directly by a user. In the most sophisticated networks, these servers are also domain controllers that authenticate a user's access onto the network and control their access to specific resources.

Hybrid

Actually, most networks today are a combination of many topologies. For example, a network will often use a star topology with a partial mesh consisting of some point-to-point and some multipoint connections. This type of hybrid design facilitates customization to the organization's communication needs as well as redundant connections for load balancing and fault tolerance. Figure 3.27 illustrates a hybrid network topology.

FIGURE 3.27   A hybrid configuration

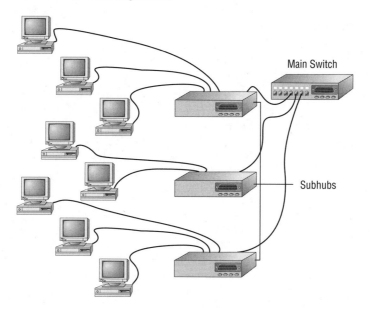

Exam Essentials

Know the difference between a physical topology and a logical topology.   You should know that the physical topology of the network is simply what it looks like or how the components are arranged. The logical topology, on the other hand, represents the flow of information in the network.

Know the main logical network topologies.   You should be able to recognize the MPLS, point-to-point, ring, star, mesh, bus, and hybrid topologies by a diagram, schematic, or description. You should be able to recognize the difference between a peer-to-peer and a client-server network.

3.6 Given a scenario, troubleshoot common physical connectivity problems

Today's networks can be much more complex than networks of the past, but the rationale behind them is still the same: to provide connectivity so that users can share information and resources. When physical connectivity is affected, the users are brought to a standstill, and productivity quickly declines. Although some issues can be very complex and require extensive knowledge of software and configuration, others are as simple as having the right physical pieces connected in the proper way. In this section, I will discuss common physical connectivity problems including bad connectors, bad wiring, open short, split cables, DB loss, TXRX reversed, cable replacement, EMI/Interference, distance, and crosstalk.

Bad connectors

Over time, all connectors can suffer physical fatigue and damage. This is especially true with those that are more fragile, such as some fiber-optic cables. If you are experiencing a complete or even intermittent lack of connectivity, then you should check the connectors to make sure they are not cracked or broken and that the wires or fiber are securely and properly in place. This is one reason that it's important to know what they are supposed to look like, which is why I included all of the figures earlier in this chapter.

Bad wiring

Bad wiring issues can be caused by using the incorrect cable type or even by the improper installation of connectors. You might think that it would be impossible for a cable to allow a connection that lights the link-light but still isn't proper. In fact, that is possible if the person who created the cable did not properly align the wires in the connector. The power and ground could be correct without the transmit and receive being correct as well. In this case, you would get a link-light, but you would not have a connection.

Open short

A short circuit, which is sometimes called an *open short*, is a situation that allows current to flow on a different path than was originally intended in the circuit. In networks, shorts are typically caused by a physical fault in the cable. They can be detected using circuit-testing equipment. Often, the best and fastest remedy will be to use a different cable until the cable that has the short can be repaired or replaced.

Split cables

Sometimes you might want to split a connection into separate directions such as for a coaxial connection to TV and Internet. You should take care to use a high-quality splitter to prevent signal loss. This loss can be measured as I will discuss next.

DB loss

Without getting into the complex math, which you don't need to know, DB loss is an algorithm that is used to calculate the difference between the signal at the source and the signal at the destination. A DB loss of 0 would be perfect but also impossible. There will be some DB loss in every network media, but the idea is to keep the number to a minimum. Depending upon the type of media that you are using, there are tables for acceptable DB loss per 100 feet. Using best practices for each type of connector will keep DB loss within acceptable levels. The exact measurements for DB loss for each media are beyond the scope of this book.

TXRX reversed

Transmit (TX) should connect to receive (RX) for each pair of wires in the network cables, such as patch cables. Earlier in this chapter, when I discussed crossover cables, I mentioned that they are used to connect similar devices. This is because using a normal patch cable to connect similar devices would cause a connection of TX to TX and RX to RX, which would not function properly. This type of reversal can also be caused by the improper connecting of wires on a wall jack or patch panel. Some devices have the capability to autosense the reversal and make the correction, but some devices do not. If you are experiencing this type of problem, it will show itself as a complete lack of connectivity, not an intermittent one.

Cable placement

Proper cable placement in your datacenter or network closet and throughout your building is essential for reliable network communication. Cables should be run either under the raised floor of a datacenter or in the ceiling where they are safe and out of the way but accessible if needed. You should take care to keep them away from power cables, whenever possible, and if you have to cross a power cable, then cross at a 90-degree angle to minimize cross-talk. You should also consider other sources of interference such as EMI, which I will discuss next.

EMI/Interference

Since wires might take on an additional current if placed near any source of magnetism, you have to be careful where you run your communications cables. This property of being affected by external magnetism is referred to as *electromagnetic interference (EMI)*. You can avoid EMI by taking care to keep copper cables away from all powerful magnetic sources. These may include electric motors, speakers, amplifiers, fluorescent light ballasts, microwave ovens, refrigerators, freezers, copy machines, and so on. Anything that could generate a magnetic field should be avoided when positioning a cable.

Distance

Often we decide what cable type to use based on the topology of a network and the distance between its components. This is because some network technologies can run much farther than others without communication errors. All network communications technologies suffer from *attenuation*, which is the degradation of signal because of the medium itself. Attenuation is much more pronounced in some cable types than in others. For example, a good rule of thumb and best practice is that any network using twisted-pair cable should have a maximum segment length of only 100 meters (328 feet). Each cable type has its own limitations because of attenuation, which I will discuss in more detail in the next section.

Crosstalk

Crosstalk is the occurrence of signal bleed between two wires that are carrying a current and are adjacent to each other. It can cause network communications to become slow or to not function at all. Network cable designers minimize crosstalk inside network cables by twisting the wire pairs together, in effect putting them at a 90-degree angle to each other. The tighter the wires are twisted, the less the crosstalk will affect them. Newer cables, such as CAT 6 cable, minimize the effect of crosstalk with a tighter twist, but it still exists and can affect network communications when network speeds are very high. To prevent crosstalk, you should use the appropriate cable for the speed of your network. To completely eliminate it, consider using a fiber-optic cable. Since fiber uses light instead of electricity, it is completely immune to crosstalk.

Exam Essentials

Check the physical connections and cables first.   Network problems are often caused by bad connectors and bad wiring. Check the physical connections before you suspect a more complex problem.

Consider the cable configuration.   Take into account that trying to do too much with the signal without the proper connectors can result in DB loss, which could cause poor performance in all areas. If you decide to split the cable, then use a high-quality cable splitter. Be careful to use the right types of cable and to install wall jacks and patch panels properly to prevent TXRX reversal. This will cause a total lack of connectivity. Use the proper cable for your network speed to prevent crosstalk.

Consider cable placement and distance.   Your network cables should be under the floor, in the ceiling, or in the walls so as to keep them safe from damage. In addition, they should be kept away from electrical cables and away from any large electric motors or magnets to prevent EMI. Finally, you should take into account the proper distance for the type of cable and technology that you are using, such as 100 meters maximum for all twisted-pair cable.

3.7 Compare and contrast different LAN technologies

Today's businesses rely on many types of LAN connections to provide for the transfer of data throughout their networks. The type of LAN connections that you choose will depend on the properties of that specific solution and how they align with the goals of the business.

In the following sections, I'll discuss the main types of LAN connections and their specific properties.

Types

Generally what users have always needed is more speed. Network administrators needed more speed but also the ability to run a link for farther distances without the need for the amplification of signal. This gives them options in regard to network designs and other decisions about which most users are unaware. Over the years, LAN technology types have continued to evolve to meet the needs of users and network administrators. Table 3.3 categorizes many LAN technology types and their major properties of transmission media, speed, and distance.

TABLE 3.3   LAN technology types

Types	Transmission media	Speed	Distance
Ethernet	Copper (first coax then twisted-pair)	10Mbps	100m
10BaseT	Twisted-pair copper	10Mbps	100m
100BaseT	Twisted-pair copper	100Mbps	100m
100BaseTX	Twisted-pair copper	100Mbps	100m
100BaseFX	Multimode fiber	100Mbps	400m
1000BaseT	Twisted-pair copper	1Gbps	100m
1000BaseX	Singlemode fiber	1Gbps	Overall standard for 1Gbps on fiber
10GBaseSR	Multimode fiber	10Gbps	26m–82m
10GBaseLR	Singlemode fiber	10Gbps	25km (about 16 miles)
10GBaseER	Singlemode fiber	10Gbps	40km (about 25 miles)
10GBaseSW	Multimode fiber	10Gbps	26m–82m
10GBaseLW	Singlemode fiber	10Gbps	25km
10GBaseEW	Singlemode fiber	10Gbps	40km
10GBaseT	Twisted-pair cable	10Gbps	100m

You may have noticed that the distance limitations for SW, LW, and EW are the same as for SR, LR, and ER, respectively. That is because they are basically the same standard except that the first group uses SDH frames, whereas the second uses SONET frames.

Properties

The following are the properties of LAN connections:

CSMA/CD   In the past, we had networks that contained devices called *hubs*. Most of these are gone, and you would probably be hard-pressed to find a hub to buy today (maybe on eBay). These hubs created what we called a *shared network*. That meant each computer that communicated in the network had equal access to the same electrical paths as the others. Since the paths could carry only one communication at a time, the computers had to "take turns" accessing the wire.

A protocol called *Carrier Sense Multiple Access with Collision Detection (CSMA/CD)* was developed for this purpose. Each computer using CSMA/CD must sense the "wire" to determine whether current is fluctuating and therefore whether some other computer is using it. If another computer has the wire, then the first computer must wait until the wire is not in use before it can send its data. As you can imagine, if two computers see that the wire is not busy and decide to send at the same millisecond, then the electrical signals will cancel each other out. This is referred to as a *collision*. Once the collision is detected by the protocol, each computer will be given a set time to go based on a back-off algorithm created by the protocol. In this way, the computers will be kept from creating subsequent collisions.

The main problem with using CSMA/CD is that it doesn't work well for networks that are large—like today's networks. Because of this, newer technologies have been developed that do not require the use of CSMA/CD. In most of today's networks, this media access method is effectively disabled due to the wide use of switches instead of hubs.

CSMA/CA   Your LAN can also have wireless communications between computers and devices. When you use wireless, the CSMA/CD protocol cannot be used because the wireless protocols do not provide for any collision detection circuit. Instead, your wireless connections use Carrier Sense Multiple Access with Collision Avoidance (CSMA/CA). The main purpose of this protocol is to assure that the data to be transmitted can be transmitted and received successfully between the two devices. It does this by first listening and then using additional frames to negotiate the network access.

Broadcast   Essentially, there are three types of network communication on IPv4 networks. These are unicast, multicast, and broadcast. Unicast communication consists of a packet that has one source address and one destination address. Multicast communication also has one source address, but it has multiple destination addresses that have to be detected by each host to determine whether the data is for them. Broadcast communications are from one source but go to any destinations in the area where the data is allowed to flow.

A broadcast address at layer 2 will be flooded by switches, in other words, sent out of all the ports except for the one that it came in. Layer 3 broadcasts can be received by all the hosts on a network or subnet. Some network protocols, such as ARP and DHCP, use broadcasts as part of their normal operation. As a network administrator, one of your goals is to keep broadcast traffic to a minimum, with the exception of the broadcast traffic required by the network protocols.

Collision   Generally speaking, a collision domain is part of a network in which collisions could occur if more than one communication were allowed to take place at the same time. In the case of an old network that uses hubs, all the hosts connected to the hub share the same collision domain. A collision then occurs when two or more devices attempt to communicate at the same time in the same collision domain.

The counterintuitive part of this is that when you have more collision domains, you will actually have fewer collisions. When you deploy a network with only switches (no hubs), then each communication is contained in its own collision domain, and there is no possibility for collisions.

Bonding   Let's say you have a couple of 10Gbps interfaces, but what you really need is a 20Gbps link. Could you combine the two physical interfaces into one logical interface? You better bet you could! The process of combining more than one physical interface into one logical interface is called *bonding*. Ether channel links are one type of bonding that allows administrators flexibility and more options in regard to bandwidth allocation.

Speed   Just as with WAN links, the speed of a LAN is a product of available bandwidth. Available bandwidth is what's left over for the users after you take out your overhead to provide the network services. We tend to think that the network is there for our amusement and experimentation, but the truth is that it's really there so "Bob and Mary" can collaborate on a spreadsheet or just check their email. Bob and Mary don't know anything about the network, but they should be able to do their jobs quickly, and the network should be rather transparent for them. Speed is a relative factor, but your job is to provide as much speed as possible with the network connections and equipment available to you.

Distance   This goes full circle back to Table 3.3. Based on the type of transmission media you use, there will be distance limitations for your network segments. Anything with a T in it (100BaseT, for example) will have a distance limitation of 100m before it needs to hit another switch or device to amplify the signal. Fiber optics can span much greater distances because their signal does not attenuate as quickly. You should use the appropriate media to span the distance you need.

Exam Essentials

Be able to categorize LAN technologies.   Be able to categorize the major LAN technologies from 10BaseT through 10GBaseEW in regard to speed, transmission media, and distance.

Know the properties of LAN technologies.   Understand the main properties of LAN technologies, including the CSMA/CD, broadcast communications, collisions, bonding connections, speed differences, and distance limitations.

3.8 Identify components of wiring distribution

Common computer networks have many more components than first meets the eye, that is, unless you are the involved in the initial installation of the network! In that case, you may be involved in purchasing and installing the components that will connect the computers throughout your organization's building. You might also be involved in verifying that all the network components have been installed properly and tested. In the following sections, I'll identify each of these components and the process of verifying their proper installation.

IDF

Often, a wire frame, called an *intermediate distribution frame* (IDF), is located in an equipment or telecommunications room. It is connected to the MDF (discussed next) and is used to provide greater flexibility in regard to the distribution of the communications lines to the building. In other words, it's just one more place where a network administrator or telephone administrator can change their mind and redirect the signal. It is typically a sturdy metal rack that is designed to hold the bulk of cables that are coming from all over the building. The same frame might also hold networking equipment such as routers, switches, and backup drives.

MDF

The main distribution frame (MDF) is a wiring point that is generally used as a reference point for telephone lines. It is installed in the building as part of the prewiring, and the internal lines are connected to it. Then all that's left is to connect the external (telephone company) lines to the other side, and the circuit is complete. These often have protection devices for lightning or other electrical spikes. In addition, they are often used as a central testing point.

Demarc

The point at which the operational control or ownership changes from your company to a service provider is referred to as a demarcation point, or *demarc*. This is often at the MDF in relation to telephone connections and the CSU/DSU (discussed later) in regard to WAN connections. When troubleshooting, network administrators will often test for connectivity on both sides of the demarc to determine whether the problem is internal or external.

Demarc extension

If your offices are in a building with many other tenants, you then have another section of wiring with which to contend. Most office buildings have a central location where the service provider terminates fiber and copper connections. From there, it's either up to the building owner or up to the individual tenants to get the communications cables to the office suites. The length of copper or fiber that is after the demarc but still not up to your office is referred to as a *demarc extension*. Many cabling companies specialize in installing and upgrading these extensions. If you are considering office space, you should verify that these connections are solid and offer you the connectivity and bandwidth you need.

Smart jack

A special network interface is often used between the service provider's network and the internal network. The device provides for code and protocol conversion, making the signal from the service provider usable by the devices on the internal network, such as the CSU/DSU. This device, called a *network interface device* or *smart jack*, often also serves as the demarcation point between the inside wiring and the outside wiring. It often contains the connections and electronic testing equipment to perform local loopback tests and other types of troubleshooting. Figure 3.28 shows an example of a modern smart jack.

FIGURE 3.28   A modern smart jack

CSU/DSU

The channel service unit/data service unit (CSU/DSU) is a digital interface device used to connect a router to a digital circuit, such as a T1 or T3 line. On one side of the device is the WAN, and on the other side is the entrance to the LAN. The CSU/DSU is actually two devices in one, each with a specific purpose. The CSU provides the termination of signal, connection integrity, and line monitoring. The DSU converts the T-carrier line frames into frames that the LAN can interpret. You can generally lease a CSU/DSU from your service provider, or you can buy one of your own. In either case, a CSU/DSU is an indispensable piece of equipment in a network with digital circuit connections.

Exam Essentials

Know the components of wiring distribution.   You should know the purpose for IDFs, MDFs, and other network equipment. You should understand the purpose of CSU/DSU. Finally, you should know that a smart jack at the demarc is often used to isolate whether a network problem is internal or external.

Understand the importance of verifying wiring installation and termination.   You should realize that a network wiring job in a large building can be a complex undertaking. You should understand that many people may be involved and that their relative skill levels will vary greatly. Because of this, a competent network wiring installation will involve extensive testing and documentation.

Review Questions

1. If you needed to run a cable for a distance of 1 mile between two buildings on a campus to provide high-speed communications between them, which of the following media types would be most appropriate?

   A. Coaxial

   B. Multimode fiber

   C. Singlemode fiber

   D. Twisted-pair

2. Which type of cable would be most appropriate to use if you wanted to connect a router directly to a PC?

   A. Straight-through (patch)

   B. Crossover

   C. Rollover

   D. T1-crossover

3. Which of the following fiber connectors is built into the body of an RJ-style jack?

   A. LC

   B. DB-9

   C. SC

   D. ST

4. Which of the following are wireless standards that are compatible with 802.11b? (Choose two.)

   A. 802.11a

   B. 802.11g

   C. 802.11n

   D. 802.11y

5. Which type of WAN connection provides for 24 64Kbps channels for a total of 1.54Mbps bandwidth?

   A. T3

   B. T1

   C. OC3

   D. E1

6. Which technology uses fixed length cells of 53 bytes?

   A. Frame Relay

   B. DSL

   C. ATM

   D. Ethernet

7. Which network topology uses labels to make frame forwarding decisions on packets?

   A. MPLS

   B. Point to Point

   C. Ring

   D. Mesh

8. If you chose to create a full mesh with five computers, how many connections (endpoint to endpoint) would be required?

   A. 30

   B. 5

   C. 10

   D. 8

9. If you have a connection issue that is related to TXRX reversed, which will be the result?

   A. A complete lack of connectivity.

   B. An intermittent lack of connectivity.

   C. You will be able to send but not receive data.

   D. You will be able to receive but not send data.

10. What term refers to the point at which the control and ownership changes from your company to the service provider network?

   A. IDF

   B. Demarc

   C. MDF

   D. CSU/DSU

Chapter 4

Network Management

COMPTIA NETWORK+ EXAM OBJECTIVES COVERED IN THIS CHAPTER:

- ✓ **4.1 Explain the purpose and features of various network appliances.**

    - ▪ Load balancer

    - ▪ Proxy server

    - ▪ Content filter

    - ▪ VPN concentrator

- ✓ **4.2 Given a scenario, use appropriate hardware tools to troubleshoot connectivity issues.**

    - ▪ Cable tester

    - ▪ Cable certifier

    - ▪ Crimper

    - ▪ Butt set

    - ▪ Toner probe

    - ▪ Punch down tool

    - ▪ Protocol analyzer

    - ▪ Loop back plug

    - ▪ TDR

    - ▪ OTDR

    - ▪ Multimeter

    - ▪ Environmental monitor

- ✓ **4.3 Given a scenario, use appropriate software tools to troubleshoot connectivity issues.**

    - ▪ Protocol analyzer

    - ▪ Throughput testers

- Connectivity software

- Ping

- Tracert/traceroute

- Dig

- Ipconfig/ifconfig

- Nslookup

- Arp

- Nbtstat

- Netstat

- Route

✓ **4.4 Given a scenario, use the appropriate network monitoring resource to analyze traffic.**

- SNMP

- SNMPv2

- SNMPv3

- Syslog

- System logs

- History logs

- General logs

- Traffic analysis

- Network sniffer

✓ **4.5 Describe the purpose of configuration and management documentation.**

- Wire schemes

- Network maps

- Documentation

- Cable management

- Asset management

- Baselines

- Change management

✓ **4.6 Explain different methods and rationales for network performance optimization.**

- Methods
  - QoS
  - Traffic shaping
  - Load balancing
  - High availability
  - Caching engines
  - Fault tolerance
  - CARP
- Reasons
  - Latency sensitivity
  - High bandwidth applications (VoIP, video applications, unified communications)
  - Uptime

Once you have your network installed and configured with all of the right components, you will need to monitor and manage those components to get the most out of your network. This will include using specialized hardware and software tools to troubleshoot connectivity issues. To do this effectively, you will need to understand the scope of your network, the components that it contains, and its normal performance characteristics. You will want to establish baselines so that you can determine when your network is underperforming and take the necessary steps to correct the issues. In this chapter, I will discuss these concepts in detail.

For more detailed information on Domain 4's topics, please see *CompTIA Network+ Study Guide, 2nd Edition* (9781118137550) or *CompTIA Network+ Deluxe Study Guide, 2nd Ed* (9781118137543), both published by Sybex.

4.1 Explain the purpose and features of various network appliances

An appliance is a component that has a single purpose or a very small and defined set of purposes. For example, consider the appliances in your house. Your refrigerator keeps your food cold, and your washer/dryer cleans your clothes. If you were to attempt to wash your clothes with your refrigerator, how successful do you think you would be? Each appliance is very good at what it was designed and built to do, but not at much of anything else.

Similarly, for network management, you can use network appliances that are designed and built for a specific purpose. Some of these include load balancers, proxy servers, content filters, and VPN concentrators. In this section, I will discuss each of these network appliances.

Load balancer

In today's networks, the resources that are essential for a user are often stored off the user's computer, sometimes in multiple locations for the same resource. When this is done, the user can gain access to the resources by going to a specific logical location, and the network devices can quickly decide how to obtain the user data and from which physical location to obtain the resource. This all occurs completely unbeknownst to the user. The device that makes all this magic happen is a *load balancer*.

Actually, a load balancer is as much a network role as it is a network appliance. Many devices can be configured to provide a load balancing function. Servers can be configured with multiple NICs and clustered together, routers can be configured with multiple associated interfaces or subinterfaces, and switches (such as the content switch mentioned earlier) can be configured to direct traffic and to change the physical location on each request. This is sometimes referred to as *round robin* since the physical connection just keeps going round and round. These types of load balancing techniques can dramatically improve the speed of the network for the user.

Proxy server

A *proxy* is a person or an agent that performs an action on behalf of someone else. In the legal world, the term is used when an attorney is permitted to sign on behalf of the client. In the information technology (IT) realm, it means relatively the same thing. A *proxy server* is, therefore, a device that makes a connection to another location, most often a website, on behalf of the user.

If an organization wants to centralize access to the Internet to control it and track its usage, it can configure the browsers on the user computers to use the address of the proxy server as a gateway to the Internet.

When the user makes a request on a browser, the proxy server will actually make the request to the Internet on behalf of the user. This allows the organization to control access to the sites users can visit and determine who can visit them and when. Typically, the proxy server will also keep a detailed record of these Internet requests. If a person is being reprimanded or fired for improper Internet use, the HR team often has these reports in hand as Exhibit A!

Also, since the proxy caches the web page, it can be used to speed up access to the page for all users. For example, because a hostname is resolved to an IP address for one user to access a resource, this information can be stored in the proxy and used by other users. A proxy server that provides this type of service is referred to as a *caching proxy*. This type of server is often used to speed access to commonly used Internet and intranet sites.

Content filter

A content filter is a specialized device that can be configured to allow some types of traffic to flow through it while stopping the flow of other types of traffic. This type of content filtering is essential to organizations so that security and productivity can be maintained simultaneously. The biggest difference between the different types of content filters is the level of content they filter. For example, a layer 7 content filter can be configured to be much more selective than a layer 3 filter. In fact, layer 7 content filters can be configured to disallow access to websites that contain data or graphics that are not deemed acceptable by management standards. If a user tries to access a site that contains unacceptable graphics or data, the site will be disallowed not because of an IP address or hostname, or even port address, but because of the nature of the material on the site. This gives you much more granular control over users.

VPN Concentrator

A virtual private network (VPN) is a network connection that is made secure even though it is flowing through an unsecure network, typically the Internet. This is done by using an encapsulation protocol. The encapsulation protocol creates a tunnel between two devices. A device that is sometimes used to create this tunnel is referred to as a VPN concentrator. Most VPN concentrators use either the Point-to-Point Tunneling Protocol (PPTP) or Layer 2 Tunneling Protocol (L2TP) to create the tunnel. The reason that its called a concentrator is that it can handle many VPN connections simultaneously.

Exam Essentials

Know the purpose of various network appliances. A load balancer can create multiple paths for traffic and thereby allow the same session to use multiple physical links. This will result in greater throughput for the session. A proxy server is a device that makes a connection to a website on behalf of a user. It can be used for control and for detailed reporting. Content filters can be used to determine what traffic is allowed to flow into and out of a network. A VPN concentrator creates a secure tunnel between two devices using an encapsulation protocol such as PPTP or L2TP.

4.2 Given a scenario, use the appropriate hardware tools to troubleshoot connectivity issues

Some aspects of network maintenance and troubleshooting require that you get out there with some hardware and do a little manual labor. The term *manual* is actually a stretch here because most of the hardware tools that you will use for your network are actually very sophisticated and don't require much muscle to use. In fact, many of these tools include both software and hardware components. In this section, I will discuss the most common of these hardware tools.

Cable tester

If you buy a patch cable that is made by a cable vendor, there is a very good chance it will be pinned correctly and that the connectors will be securely crimped. On the other hand, if you inherit a patch cable that was made in the field by some other technician, you may not be so lucky. If you cannot make a connection from one device to another and you suspect the cable, the best thing to do for the immediate fix is to try another cable. If the new cable works, then the other cable was probably faulty; maybe it just wasn't created properly in the first place.

Before you throw it away or begin to repair it, you may want to use a *cable tester* to find out whether there is anything wrong with it and, if there is, on which wire or wires the problem is located. A cable tester (Figure 4.1) is a tool with which you connect both ends of the cable to test its connectivity on each of its wires. There are many different types of cable testers, and they vary greatly in design, but most use lights or LCD screens to indicate the connectivity through the cable. They can be very useful when you need to decide whether to continue to use, replace, fix, or discard a cable.

FIGURE 4.1 A cable tester

Cable certifier

With today's modern networks, it's often not good enough just to say that something works and therefore it's set up properly. For example, if you install CAT6 cable, then you expect that it will provide 1000Mbps bandwidth for your data. But the only way that it will do this is if all the wall jacks, patch panels, connectors, and so forth, are installed properly. You could just let the users be the guinea pigs and test it all for you, but the right way is to make sure it's working properly by using a device that can test the network segment to which it's attached and compare the result with what it should be for that type of segment. This device is called a *certifier*. Many different types of certifiers exist, and they are available for copper, fiber, and even wireless networks. Some devices even combine certain aspects of all three types of networks.

Crimper

To attach an RJ-45 connector to the end of a cable, you must strip about an inch of the outer cable insulation without cutting any of the insulation on the eight wires that are inside the cable. You must then press down hard on the right place of the RJ-45 to close the connector around the cable and hold all of the wires "trapped" into place so that the end of the cable sheath is safely tucked inside the connector as well.

To accomplish this feat, you should use a tool that is designed to cut just the outer insulation and leave the other wires untouched; this tool needs to double as an accurate pair of "pliers" that allows you to press on just the right place on the connector. A cable crimper and stripper does just that. There have been many cable crimper and stripper designs over the years. Some tools double as crimping tools/cable strippers. Figure 4.2 shows a crimping tool with a cable stripper integrated into it.

FIGURE 4.2 Cable crimper with stripper

Butt set

Your computer network is closely tied to your telephone network, especially if you are still using modems. For this reason, you may also want to have one of the "old standby" tools in your arsenal that has been used by telephone company line-repair technicians for many years. A butt set (Figure 4.3) looks a phone with a cord and no base, but it's really much more than that. Butt sets have evolved over the years so that they can test all the latest connections. A butt set can connect to and test any pair of phone wires on any modular jack, punch down block, demark block, and so forth. It can also test for dial tone, open line, shorted line, and many other problems.

FIGURE 4.3 A butt set

Toner probe

Another tool that you can use to test the connectivity of wires that run through walls and other obstructions is a *toner probe* (see Figure 4.4). This is a less sophisticated tool that produces a signal (or tone) on one end and then determines whether that signal can still be heard on the other end. The device that produces the signal is called the *tone generator*. There is also another device that is mentioned less often, called the *tone locator*. You can use a tone locator to find the signal in the wire on the other end of the tone generator. This not only verifies connectivity, but it's a great tool for tracing wire connections from the wall outlet to the patch panel when they haven't been labelled properly.

FIGURE 4.4   A toner probe

The tone generator and the tone locator are sometimes referred to as the fox and hound. It is not usually necessary to strip any insulation from the wires in order to locate the tone. The tone locator can usually find the tone through the insulation just by placing it close to the wire. The only real disadvantage of a "fox and hound" is that it generally takes two people to effectively trace and label many wires. Otherwise, one person does a lot running back and forth.

Punch down tool

As I discussed earlier, to increase the flexibility and fault tolerance of a network, most organizations do not use a continuous cable from end to end for each computer connection. Instead, each cable is connected through a series of patch panels. These patch panels provide a method for quickly changing a cable that is part of a computer's connection to the network. Typically, the front side of a patch panel has many RJ-45 connector ports. The back of the panel, however, does not have ports and instead is hardwired with the wires from the cables "punched down" into special connectors that hold them securely in place. This is where the *punch down tool* comes into play.

The process of properly punching down a wire takes a considerable amount of force. You could try to do it without the special tool, but you would probably break the wire or not be able to make the proper connection at all. The punch down tool, shown in Figure 4.5, assists you in applying the right amount of pressure in the right direction. As you push in with the tool, you load up a spring that then releases the proper amount of force to press the wire firmly into the connector while stripping the insulation off the side of the wire to assure a firm connection with the metal connector. With a little practice, you will be able to "punch down" wires with ease.

FIGURE 4.5   A punch down tool

Protocol analyzer

When you first look at the term *protocol analyzer*, you probably think about software and not hardware. In fact, some vendors refer to their packet sniffers as protocol analyzers. However, in its hardware interpretation, a protocol analyzer is a specialized piece of hardware that is made to be carried around to various areas of the network and get information about the traffic in that area. Since the protocol analyzer can be physically moved to the network it will analyze, it can get the most accurate and reliable information possible.

At first glance, a protocol analyzer might look very much like a laptop, but if you look closer, you might see a difference in the keyboard as well as the types of connecting ports on it. You might also notice a more rugged design. Companies such as Network Instruments and MetricTest specialize in this type of product.

Loop back plug

A loopback plug connects "transmit to receive" and "receive to transmit," but it does so on the same connection. This causes the device to see its output as input from the network by "looping back" the data. Because of this, the software that needs a live network will be fooled into thinking it has found one. Loopback plugs can also be used to test whether a network interface card is sending a signal and whether an interface on a switch is actively sending data. Figure 4.6 shows the wiring diagram of a typical loopback plug.

FIGURE 4.6 A loopback plug

TDR

A *time domain reflectometer (TDR)* (Figure 4.7), as its name implies, is a pretty sophisticated piece of network-troubleshooting equipment. It sends a low-level electromagnetic pulse and listens for any reflection of that pulse (similar to radar). In fact, it's like radar for finding breaks or even weaknesses (bad splices or connections) in copper network cables. If you are troubleshooting a problem with a copper cable, a TDR can tell you exactly how far the problem is from where you are testing. That way, if the wire is buried or is in a wall, you will know that you should probably just try to use a different cable (if one is available). On the other hand, if the problem is accessible, then you may be able to fix it. Either way, knowing exactly where the problem exists is half the battle.

FIGURE 4.7   A TDR

OTDR

If a TDR can be called sophisticated, then an *optical time domain reflectometer (OTDR)* (Figure 4.8) is positively out of the space age! An OTDR performs the same function as a TDR but does it with light on fiber-optic cables. Whereas most of the cables that you test with a TDR will be shorter than 100 meters long, you can test cables that are several kilometers long with an OTDR. An OTDR can also detect the fiber cable length and therefore tell you exactly where a break is in the fiber. It can also make you aware of bad splices or connections along the entire route of the fiber cable. For these reasons, OTDRs are an indispensable tool for working with today's long and sophisticated fiber-optic cable runs.

FIGURE 4.8   An OTDR

Multimeter

Now that I have discussed the expensive and sophisticated tools, let's return to the basics while using a little ingenuity as well. You can test the continuity of the wires in a cable and determine whether there is current on the wire with a plain old multimeter. Actually, there was a day when a multimeter was as fancy a tool as there was, because we used a different tool to check continuity than we did voltage. Now a *multimeter* is a staple tool for anyone who is involved in networking or electronics of any kind.

Most of today's multimeters, as shown in Figure 4.9, can provide you with a digital readout of a myriad of tests, including continuity, resistance, voltage, current, and so on. You simply set the multimeter for what you need. Some troubleshooting might require taking two measurements, one of known good connectivity and the other of what you are troubleshooting, and then comparing the two. It might not be as automatic as some of the other more sophisticated tools, but a multimeter can give you many answers if you know just how to ask the right questions.

FIGURE 4.9   A multimeter

Environmental monitor

One of the nicer things about being involved in IT in a large organization is that you generally get the coolest room in the building, at least in regard to temperature. It's extremely important to keep servers, routers, switches, and other network equipment cooled down and humidity controlled while they are running. The recommended temperature range for a data center is between 68 and 75 degrees Fahrenheit, and the recommended relative humidity is 50 to 60 percent. Staying in this range will improve the reliability and longevity of the components; in other words, it saves the company money too!

Since this is very important, most companies don't trust the environment of a data center to the thermostat on the wall. Instead, more sophisticated and sensitive temperature and humidity monitors are used throughout the data center to ensure that the correct environment is being maintained. These monitors may inform the administrator of a problem or may also be tied into the cooling systems in their respective areas.

Exam Essentials

Know the hardware tools for troubleshooting connectivity issues.   A cable tester is a tool to which you connect both ends of a cable in order to test the connectivity of the wires. A cable certifier can be used to determine whether the cable will effectively carry a specified load. A crimper is a tool used to correctly install connectors, such as RJ-45 and RJ-11 connectors. A butt set is an old tool that has been used for years by line-repair technicians to test lines. A toner probe can be used to locate the correct wire pair from the wall jack to the patch panel. A punch down tool is used to securely connect wires to a patch panel. A protocol analyzer can be a specialized piece of hardware that allows you to get information about your network. A loopback plug is a specially designed connector that causes the device to see its own output as input, thereby assisting you in testing the device. A time domain reflectometer sends electromagnetic pulses down a copper wire and listens for the reflected signal. In this way, it can determine the location of weaknesses or even breaks. An optical time domain reflectometer does the same thing with fiber optic cable, but it uses light. A multimeter allows you to test the continuity of wires as well as get information about voltage, amperage, and resistance on any circuit. Finally, an environmental monitor is a device that senses and controls temperature and humidity; often used in network operations centers. .

4.3 Given a scenario, use the appropriate software tools to troubleshoot connectivity issues

There are a great many software tools and utilities to choose from that will assist you in troubleshooting connectivity issues. In fact, many troubleshooting utilities are built into the most popular operating systems. Some of these utilities are based on the command line and are not obvious to the end user. As a network administrator, your knowledge of the existence and proper use of these tools will set you apart from your peers. In the following sections, I will discuss and illustrate the proper use of the most common troubleshooting utilities.

Protocol analyzer

A software-based protocol analyzer is like a powerful electron microscope and interpreter for network traffic. It allows the network administrator to examine the information within the packets carefully and thereby make more informed decisions about the network. For example, an administrator may use a protocol analyzer to find a failing network interface card that is putting out a constant stream of data onto the network, sometimes referred to as a *chatty NIC*. The administrator would be able to find the specific NIC based on the source MAC address, which could be found in the packet sniffer's output (as shown in Figure 4.10) for each packet. This is only a small example of how you might use a protocol analyzer. Other uses include scanning the network for intrusion attempts, obtaining the IP source and destination addresses, and even examining the data itself, provided that it is not encrypted.

Throughput testers

In general, throughput is the amount of data that a network can pass in a given period of time. You might think that you could just take a large file and transfer it while timing how long it takes and then dividing the file size by the time. In reality, though, this would not take into account the overhead mechanisms built into the protocol such as acknowledgments and TCP window size. For this reason, you might want to use dedicated software such as Netcps, IxChariot, or Iperf, which considers these factors and gives you a more accurate throughput measurement.

FIGURE 4.10   A protocol analyzer output

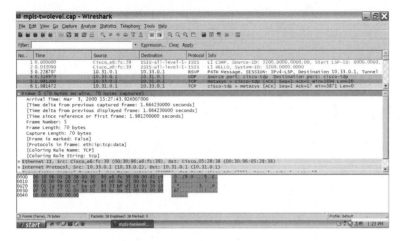

Connectivity software

Many companies now produce software for network connectivity and testing. This software might include protocol analyzers or network sniffers, which we have discussed previously, or terminal emulators and remote desktop software. Its purpose may be specific to the company that produced it, or it could be used for a wider range of purposes. For example, OmniCom Technologies, WolfVision, and IBM all offer connectivity software options.

Ping

The *ping* tool, which stands for Packet InterNet Groper, is one of the most common utilities used by network administrators. It is primarily used to verify general network connectivity, but it can also be used to test name resolution in a network. The ping tool includes switches that allow you to customize your test. You should know how the ping tool operates and its most common uses in network troubleshooting.

You initiate a ping request simply by typing the word **ping** at a command prompt followed by a space and then the IP address or hostname of the host to which you would like to test connectivity. An echo request packet is sent by the ICMP protocol, and an echo reply is sent back by the responding host. You can also use many options with ping to make a request more specific, as shown in Figure 4.11.

Tracert/traceroute

Suppose you use the ping tool and find that you have a problem with connectivity in your network. Now let's suppose your network is a complex configuration of switches and routers that carry information to all the hosts within it. Furthermore, suppose that the computer you are pinging is located on the other side of your network and that you have to transmit through multiple routers to get to the subnet of the destination computer. If you do not get a reply, then how could you possibly know where the communication is breaking down? The answer is that you cannot—at least not with the ping tool.

FIGURE 4.11 The ping tool

```
Command Prompt                                                    _ □ ×

C:\Documents and Settings\Bill  Ferguson.XP1>ping /?

Usage: ping [-t] [-a] [-n count] [-l size] [-f] [-i TTL] [-v TOS]
            [-r count] [-s count] [[-j host-list] | [-k host-list]]
            [-w timeout] target_name

Options:
    -t              Ping the specified host until stopped.
                    To see statistics and continue - type Control-Break;
                    To stop - type Control-C.
    -a              Resolve addresses to hostnames.
    -n count        Number of echo requests to send.
    -l size         Send buffer size.
    -f              Set Don't Fragment flag in packet.
    -i TTL          Time To Live.
    -v TOS          Type Of Service.
    -r count        Record route for count hops.
    -s count        Timestamp for count hops.
    -j host-list    Loose source route along host-list.
    -k host-list    Strict source route along host-list.
    -w timeout      Timeout in milliseconds to wait for each reply.

C:\Documents and Settings\Bill  Ferguson.XP1>
```

The *traceroute* tool (also called the tracert tool) is a network utility that uses ICMP to create a list of routers through which a packet is transmitted. Using the traceroute tool, you can determine not only that the connection cannot be made to a computer but also which router could not forward the packet to the next subnet. In other words, you can isolate a network failure to a specific location in your network.

The terms *traceroute* and *tracert* are sometimes used interchangeably, but they are not actually the same; traceroute is the generic term for this type of tool, which can be used by Novell, Cisco, and other types of TCP/IP hosts, while tracert is specific to Microsoft clients and servers in a TCP/IP network.

You initiate the tracert tool on a Microsoft client by typing **tracert** at the command prompt followed by a space and then the IP address or hostname of the computer to which you want to test connectivity. You can find a complete list of tracert commands by typing **tracert /?**. Figure 4.12 is an example or tracert output.

FIGURE 4.12 The tracert tool in Microsoft

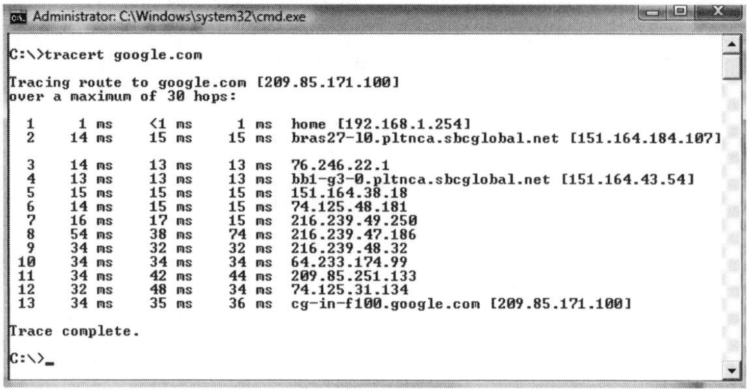

```
Administrator: C:\Windows\system32\cmd.exe

C:\>tracert google.com

Tracing route to google.com [209.85.171.100]
over a maximum of 30 hops:

  1     1 ms    <1 ms     1 ms  home [192.168.1.254]
  2    14 ms    15 ms    15 ms  bras27-10.pltnca.sbcglobal.net [151.164.184.107]

  3    14 ms    13 ms    13 ms  76.246.22.1
  4    13 ms    13 ms    13 ms  bb1-g3-0.pltnca.sbcglobal.net [151.164.43.54]
  5    15 ms    15 ms    15 ms  151.164.38.18
  6    14 ms    15 ms    15 ms  74.125.48.181
  7    16 ms    17 ms    15 ms  216.239.49.250
  8    54 ms    38 ms    74 ms  216.239.47.186
  9    34 ms    32 ms    32 ms  216.239.48.32
 10    34 ms    34 ms    34 ms  64.233.174.99
 11    34 ms    42 ms    44 ms  209.85.251.133
 12    32 ms    48 ms    34 ms  74.125.31.134
 13    34 ms    35 ms    36 ms  cg-in-f100.google.com [209.85.171.100]

Trace complete.

C:\>_
```

Dig

Domain Information Groper (Dig) is a flexible tool for interrogating DNS servers. Some administrators choose Dig over nslookup because of its ease of use and clarity of output. It can be used with all forms of DNS servers including Microsoft, Linux, and even legacy Berkeley Internet Name Daemon (BIND) servers. You can begin to use dig by typing **dig** on the command line. To get more information about dig, type **dig /?.**

Ipconfig/ifconfig

The *ipconfig* tool displays network configuration values and refreshes addresses configured by DHCP servers on Microsoft computers. You can also use it for a wide range of other troubleshooting scenarios. The *ifconfig* tool is the same sort of command that is used by Unix and Linux systems. You should know the purpose and main functionality of both of these commands, which I'll cover in the following two sections.

Ipconfig

When you type **ipconfig** at the command line without any switches, it displays the IP address, subnet mask, and default gateway of all the network adapters on a computer. You can use it as a very quick method of verifying a basic IP configuration. By adding switches, you can get much more information about the configuration, and you can control other network parameters such as the DNS resolver cache on a computer. In addition, you can release and renew IP addresses that are assigned by a DHCP server provided that the computer is configured to obtain an IP address automatically.

The ipconfig tool is a very powerful troubleshooting tool as well. For example, if you examine the ipconfig output and find that the IP address begins with 169.254, then you should immediately recognize that as an Automatic Private IP Address (APIPA) and know that the computer is configured to obtain its IP address from a DHCP server, but that a

DHCP server was not available. On the other hand, an IP address of 0.0.0.0 would indicate that an administrator has released the IP address from a DHCP server and has not renewed an address. Table 4.1 explains the additional options available when you type **ipconfig**.

TABLE 4.1   Common ipconfig commands

Ipconfig option	Purpose
ipconfig /all	Displays the full TCP/IP configuration for all adapters. (Adapters include physical interfaces as well as dial-up connections.) This option also displays the DNS servers that the computers are using to resolve hostnames to IP addresses.
ipconfig /renew	Releases and renews the IP address on an adapter. (The computer must be configured to obtain an IP address automatically.)
ipconfig /release	Releases an IP address that was obtained automatically but does not renew an address. This is a useful tool when moving a computer from one subnet to another.
ipconfig /flushdns	Flushes the DNS client resolver cache. This can be a useful tool when you're troubleshooting name resolution problems.
ipconfig /displaydns	Displays the contents of the DNS client resolver cache. It includes entries that are preloaded from the Hosts file as well as recently obtained resource records.
ipconfig / registerdns	Initiates manual dynamic registration for the DNS names and IP addresses that are configured on a computer. It's especially useful when troubleshooting DNS name resolution problems.

Ifconfig

The ifconfig tool (shown in Figure 4.13) is used in Unix and Linux operating systems to configure interfaces and view information about configured interfaces. Note that the syntax of the ifconfig tool is very different from ipconfig. You should know the general uses of the command.

Nslookup

DNS is an essential component in most networks today. The nslookup utility allows you to troubleshoot problems related to DNS. You can use nslookup to research information about a DNS server or to set a DNS configuration on the server. You can use nslookup in either noninteractive or interactive mode. You should know the difference between these two methods of use.

FIGURE 4.13 The ifconfig tool

```
eth0       Link encap:Ethernet  HWaddr 00:13:46:E5:AA:BB
           inet addr:124.33.121.150  Bcast:255.255.255.255  Mask:255.255.254.0
           UP BROADCAST RUNNING MULTICAST  MTU:1500  Metric:1
           RX packets:562070 errors:0 dropped:0 overruns:0 frame:0
           TX packets:17450 errors:0 dropped:0 overruns:0 carrier:0
           collisions:0 txqueuelen:1000
           RX bytes:50757226 (48.4 MiB)  TX bytes:3820874 (3.6 MiB)
           Interrupt:5 Memory:e7004000-0

eth1       Link encap:Ethernet  HWaddr 00:13:46:E5:CC:DD
           inet addr: 10.42.42.1    Bcast: 10.42.42.255  Mask:255.255.255.0
           UP BROADCAST RUNNING MULTICAST  MTU:1500  Metric:1
           RX packets:19419 errors:0 dropped:0 overruns:0 frame:0
           TX packets:27901 errors:0 dropped:0 overruns:0 carrier:0
           collisions:0 txqueuelen:1000
           RX bytes:3960038 (3.7 MiB)  TX bytes:17347260 (16.5 MiB)
           Interrupt:10 Memory:e7000000-0

lo         Link encap:Local Loopback
           inet addr:127.0.0.1  Mask:255.0.0.0
           UP LOOPBACK RUNNING  MTU:16436  Metric:1
           RX packets:0 errors:0 dropped:0 overruns:0 frame:0
           TX packets:0 errors:0 dropped:0 overruns:0 carrier:0
           collisions:0 txqueuelen:0
           RX bytes:0 (0.0 B)  TX bytes:0 (0.0 B)
```

To use nslookup in noninteractive mode, simply type the command you want to initiate. Alternatively, at the command prompt, you can enter interactive mode to determine what to type. To do this, type **nslookup**, press Enter, and then type **?** to see a list of all the commands you can execute. Determine the command you want to use and then type **exit** to get out of interactive mode. You can use many commands with nslookup. It's not necessary that you know all of them (thank goodness!), but you should know that they all relate to hostname resolution in one way or another and that the tool is generally used on large domain-based networks.

To use nslookup in interactive mode, type **nslookup**, and then press Enter. You can then execute multiple nslookup queries and commands from within the nslookup utility. To exit the utility, simply type **exit**. The commands in interactive mode are the same as those in noninteractive mode, except that you don't have to type **nslookup** before each command. Figure 4.14 shows the nslookup tool in interactive mode.

Arp

Arp is a service that works in the background and resolves IP addresses to MAC addresses so that packets can be delivered to their destination. As you may recall, each computer keeps an arp cache of entries that have been recently resolved (within the past 10 minutes). First the computer checks the arp cache; then, if the entry is not in the cache, arp will be used to broadcast into the local network and request that the computer with a specific IP address respond with its MAC address so that the packet can be addressed and delivered.

Since the packets cannot be delivered until the MAC address is discovered, arp is a crucial component in the system. Because of this, you should know how to identify problems that might be caused by an errant arp cache. In addition, you should know how to troubleshoot the arp cache when necessary.

FIGURE 4.14   The nslookup tool in interactive mode

```
C:\Windows\system32>nslookup
Default Server:  google-public-dns-a.google.com
Address:  8.8.8.8

> server 8.8.4.4
Default Server:  google-public-dns-b.google.com
Address:  8.8.4.4

> www.yahoo.com
Server:  google-public-dns-b.google.com
Address:  8.8.4.4

Non-authoritative answer:
Name:    any-fp.wa1.b.yahoo.com
Addresses:  72.30.2.43
            98.137.149.56
Aliases:  www.yahoo.com
          fp.wg1.b.yahoo.com

> exit
```

You can access the arp tool and the syntax for its use by typing the following at a command prompt:

arp /?

The two general types of entries found in an arp cache are dynamic and static, as shown in Figure 4.15. Your knowledge of both types of entries is essential to understanding how arp operates and therefore how to troubleshoot it. You should be able to distinguish between dynamic and static entries in an arp cache. Static entries are indicated with an s, whereas dynamic entries are indicated with a d.

Dynamic entries are automatically added to the cache every time ARP resolves an IP address to a MAC address. The lifetime of these entries varies between operating systems but is generally no more than about 10 minutes, unless they are used within the 10 minutes, in which case the clock starts again. Dynamic entries typically do not cause problems. They are clearly marked as dynamic.

FIGURE 4.15   The arp tool

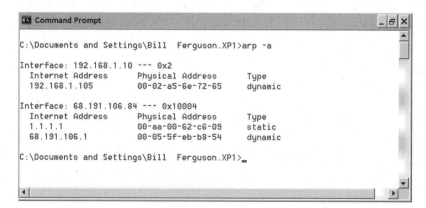

```
Command Prompt                                                    _ □ ×

C:\Documents and Settings\Bill  Ferguson.XP1>arp -a

Interface: 192.168.1.10 --- 0x2
  Internet Address      Physical Address      Type
  192.168.1.105         00-02-a5-6e-72-65     dynamic

Interface: 68.191.106.84 --- 0x10004
  Internet Address      Physical Address      Type
  1.1.1.1               00-aa-00-62-c6-09     static
  68.191.106.1          00-05-5f-eb-b8-54     dynamic

C:\Documents and Settings\Bill  Ferguson.XP1>_
```

Static entries, on the other hand, are very different from dynamic entries. Static entries must be added by an administrator and, once added, become a permanent entry in the cache unless they are deleted. For example, if you wanted to add a static entry to an arp cache for a computer with an IP address of 192.168.1.10 and a MAC address of 00-aa-00-62-c6-09, you would type the following at the command prompt:

```
arp -s 192.168.1.10      00-aa-00-62-c6-09
```

Now, before you start adding static entries to all your computers, you should know that they have advantages and disadvantages. There is only one reason to add a static entry to an arp cache: faster IP to MAC address resolution between two computers on the same network. Adding a static entry might increase performance, but this is very doubtful on today's modern networks. In addition, adding a static entry to resolve an IP address to a MAC address does not affect the name resolution time to resolve the hostname to an IP address, done by DNS, which usually must occur first.

Although the advantages of adding a static entry are ambiguous, the disadvantages are very real. Adding a static entry to an arp cache ties a specific MAC address to a specific IP address. This might be fine as long as you don't change the NIC on the computer identifying the entry. If the NIC should fail and be replaced by another NIC, the static entry for the IP address will override the dynamic entry that would otherwise be created in the cache. In other words, since the IP address of the computer will already be listed in the static entry, another IP address and MAC address (the dynamic entry) will not be added. Of course, the new NIC would have a different MAC address, so the arp cache would be incorrect. Consequently, computers with the static entry would not be able to communicate with the computer containing the new NIC.

To troubleshoot the problem, you should remove the static entry from the arp cache. You can remove the static entry for the previous example by typing the following at a command prompt:

```
arp -d 192.168.1.10      00-aa-00-62-c6-09
```

You can also use a wildcard (*) in place of the IP address and MAC address to delete all hosts from the arp cache.

Nbtstat

NetBIOS over TCP/IP (NetBT) resolves NetBIOS names to IP addresses. TCP/IP provides many options for NetBIOS name resolution, including cache lookup, Windows Internet Name Services (WINS) server query, broadcast, DNS server query, and Lmhosts and Hosts file lookup. Although the operating systems and applications created in the last 10 years use hostname resolution and not NetBIOS name resolution, you may still have a legacy application (prior to Windows 2000) that uses NetBIOS name resolution. In that case, your knowledge of the nbtstat utility will help you troubleshoot name resolution problems. In addition, you can use this tool to remove or correct a preloaded entry in the NetBIOS name cache.

The nbtstat utility has a fairly complex syntax that allows you to customize a query. You can also keep it simple and just use the beginning of the syntax to obtain a broader range of output. You can view the syntax of nbtstat and the options available by simply typing **nbtstat** at a command prompt and pressing Enter. Table 4.2 describes the most common options used with nbtstat.

TABLE 4.2 Common nbtstat options

Nbtstat option	Display
nbtstat -n	Displays names registered locally by the system
nbtstat -c	Displays NetBIOS name cache entries
nbtstat -R	Purges the NetBIOS name cache and reloads it from the Lmhosts file
nbtstat -RR	Releases NetBIOS names registered with the WINS server and then renews their registration
nbtstat -a name	Performs a NetBIOS adapter status command against the computer specified by name and displays the local NetBIOS name table for the computer and the MAC address of the computer
nbtstat -S	Lists the current NetBIOS sessions and their status, including statistics

Netstat

Suppose you are troubleshooting an application for a user and you know the application uses a specific protocol and therefore a specific port or ports, for example, FTP and ports 20 and 21. If the user's computer is having a problem running the application, you might want to make sure that computer is active and listening on the appropriate ports. This is the type of scenario that might require your use of the netstat tool.

You can use the netstat tool to display protocol statistics and current TCP/IP connections, as shown in Figure 4.16. The netstat tool has many options that you can use to customize the output for your situation. Table 4.3 lists the options available in netstat and the general function of each option. You can list the syntax and all the options by typing the following at the command prompt:

netstat /?

When you use it with no options, netstat simply displays active TCP/IP connections.

FIGURE 4.16 The netstat tool

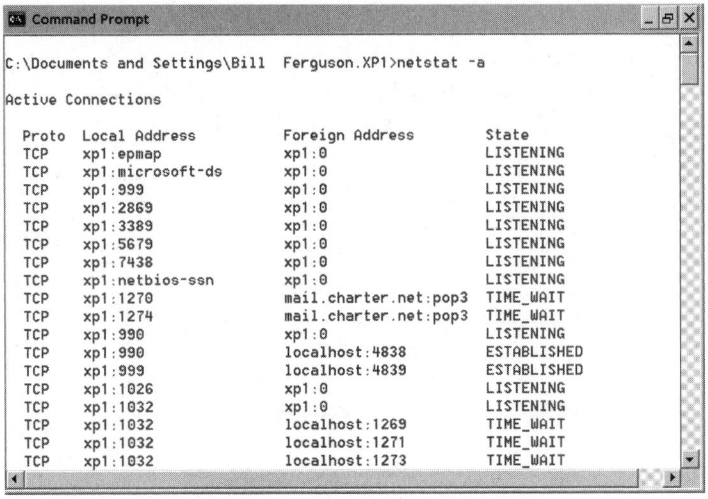

```
Command Prompt                                              _ ☐ ×

C:\Documents and Settings\Bill  Ferguson.XP1>netstat -a

Active Connections

  Proto  Local Address          Foreign Address        State
  TCP    xp1:epmap              xp1:0                  LISTENING
  TCP    xp1:microsoft-ds       xp1:0                  LISTENING
  TCP    xp1:999                xp1:0                  LISTENING
  TCP    xp1:2869               xp1:0                  LISTENING
  TCP    xp1:3389               xp1:0                  LISTENING
  TCP    xp1:5679               xp1:0                  LISTENING
  TCP    xp1:7438               xp1:0                  LISTENING
  TCP    xp1:netbios-ssn        xp1:0                  LISTENING
  TCP    xp1:1270               mail.charter.net:pop3  TIME_WAIT
  TCP    xp1:1274               mail.charter.net:pop3  TIME_WAIT
  TCP    xp1:990                xp1:0                  LISTENING
  TCP    xp1:990                localhost:4838         ESTABLISHED
  TCP    xp1:999                localhost:4839         ESTABLISHED
  TCP    xp1:1026               xp1:0                  LISTENING
  TCP    xp1:1032               xp1:0                  LISTENING
  TCP    xp1:1032               localhost:1269         TIME_WAIT
  TCP    xp1:1032               localhost:1271         TIME_WAIT
  TCP    xp1:1032               localhost:1273         TIME_WAIT
```

TABLE 4.3 Common netstat options

Netstat option	Display
netstat -a	Displays all connections
netstat -r	Creates a routing table of the computer and all active connections
netstat -o	Processes IDs so you can view the owner of the port for each connection
netstat -e	Displays Ethernet statistics, such as packet discards and errors
netstat -s	Displays per-protocol statistics, such as detailed TCP and UDP statistics
netstat -n	Does not convert addresses and port numbers to names but instead shows them as IP addresses

Route

You can use the route tool on Windows and clients to set up static routes on the client itself. By building a table in the client device, it will, in effect, be a router for some traffic that it receives. This might be useful if the device is also being used to provide access to a cable modem or DSL router that has a connection to the Internet. Figure 4.17 shows Route options. You can also add or delete routes from the table using the switches provided. Table 4.4 shows the most common switches used with the route tool.

TABLE 4.4 Common route options

Route option	Display
route print	Displays the current routes known by the client, including the local loopback and broadcast
route add	Can be used to add a route to the existing table if needed
route change	Can be used to change an existing route when needed
route delete	Can be used to permanently delete a route from the table when no longer needed
route /?	Displays route help to see more detailed information and syntax

FIGURE 4.17   The route tool

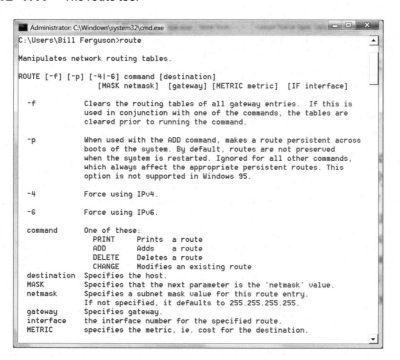

Exam Essentials

Be able to identify and apply the appropriate tool for a given troubleshooting scenario.
Protocol analyzers are best if you need to see "inside" a packet and determine the protocol, source and destination addresses, port, and so on. Throughput testers are appropriate if you suspect that the network bandwidth might not be sufficient to meet your needs. Connectivity software is available from many third parties to assist you in further analysis of issues that are specific to your organization or industry. Ping is a tool that allows you to verify connectivity between two devices. It works by sending echo request packets and receiving echo reply packets. If you do not receive a reply with ping, tracert/traceroute is a tool that assists you in determining the last router that was able to process the packets. You can use this information along with your network diagram to isolate the issue. Dig is a tool for interrogating DNS. Ipconfig and ifconfig are tools that are used to obtain information about a current connection. Ipconfig is used for Windows software; ifconfig is used for Unix and Linux. Nslookup is another tool that you can use to troubleshoot common issues with DNS name resolution. Arp is a protocol that resolves IP addresses to physical (MAC) addresses. Arp is also the command you use to get information about the arp protocol. Nbtstat is a legacy protocol that provides NetBIOS name information. You would likely use it only if you have hosts with operating systems or applications that were created prior to the year 2000. Netstat is useful to determine which ports are open and active. Finally, route is a command that you can use to set up static routes. This can in effect make a computer perform a routing function.

4.4 Given a scenario, use the appropriate network monitoring resource to analyze traffic

As a network administrator, it's important that you know the devices that are connected in your network, their general capabilities, and what they are actually doing at any given moment. If you have been managing a network for a long while, this will generally be the case; but suppose you were "thrown in" to the position of network administrator in a network of which you had no prior knowledge. There would be many network monitoring tools from which you could choose to gather information about your network and to determine what had already occurred there before you were responsible. In this section, I will discuss the various network monitoring tools you could use.

In particular, I will discuss protocols such as SNMP, SNMPv2, and SNMPv3. All of these assist you in obtaining information about the components of your network, but one might be better to use than another. In addition, I will discuss a variety of tools that can assist you in compiling logs that give you a "big picture" of your network and its devices as well as detailed information where needed. Finally, I will discuss tools for traffic analysis and network sniffers that will help you "stay on top" of your network in the future.

SNMP

Simple Network Management Protocol (SNMP) is a protocol that has been used by network administrators for more than 20 years to get information about the devices in their network. If you were using SNMP, you would be able to start getting the "big picture" of what is out there on your network. The general principle behind SNMP is that network components (such as computers, routers, and switches) can be installed with agent software that causes them to report information back to a central server installed with *Management Information Base (MIB)* software. The agents and MIB they report to are all said to be in the same *community*. You can configure agents to gather and report specified information such as type of device, processors, RAM, hard drive space, software installations, and so on, to the MIB that shares the same community name with the agents. This reporting of the agent is referred to as a *trap*. The commands that you use are generally *get requests* and *set requests*.

This might all sound like a great idea to help you learn about your network, but if you were to choose the first version of SNMP, there might be a problem. The problem with earlier versions of SNMP was that the information that was being gathered for the network administrator could also be read by an attacker. To address this issue, later versions of SNMP employ security measures such as encryption methods and integrity algorithms. Now let's examine a more secure version of SNMP.

SNMPv2

SNMPv2 revises and improves the original SNMP. It includes enhancements in performance, security, and confidentiality of the network data. It remains backward compatible with the original version. Should you choose this version, you would be more secure than with SNMP, but why stop here?

SNMPv3

Secure Network Management Protocol version 3 (SNMPv3) was developed in December 1997 to address even more security issues. It uses a secure authentication mechanism and encrypts data packets in transit. It also employs a message integrity algorithm to assure that the information that is sent to the administrator is accurate and has not been changed in transit. As you can see, this would be your best bet in today's security-conscious network. You could get the information that you need to understand your network better, while at the same time prevent the attackers from gaining information that you would rather they didn't have.

Syslog

Now that you are beginning to understand your new network, take a look at what has occurred there in the past and also set in place a method of recording specific information for the future. You might want to consider using syslog, the de facto standard for logging, especially if you are using Linux or Unix. Syslog allows you to collect information about the operation of many different devices and application packages. You can also use it to establish a baseline of normal traffic and compare the baseline at a later date when you feel that something unusual is happening, such as an attack or misconfiguration. If you are not using Linux or Unix, then you have many other options that I will discuss later.

System logs, History logs, and General logs

One thing that computers and network devices are very good at doing is keeping track of exactly what they are doing and what they've already done. With the proper configuration, most devices can give you a wealth of information about how they have been used, what changes have been made to their configuration, when these changes were made, and who made them. You can generally create system logs, history logs, and general (event) logs on servers, PCs, and network equipment such as routers and switches.

System logs are generally used with servers to determine what services are available to the users and what system resources are being used to provide the services. History logs, as you might imagine, keep track of events that have already happened and changes that have already been made to a system. They are sometimes very useful in isolating the source of a problem that was introduced by a change or another network event. General (event) logs can be used to track changes to configurations; security auditing; and the starting, refusing to start, and stopping of services. Windows servers combine many of these logs in a tool called Event Viewer, which allows you to view and manage the System, Application, and Security logs. In your situation, you should examine the Event Viewer to see whether anything looks "out of place," paying special attention to red "alert" messages. Figure 4.18 shows the Windows Logs in Event Viewer on Windows Server 2008.

Traffic analysis

Traffic analysis is the process of intercepting and examining messages in order to deduce information from patterns in communication. Generally speaking, the more information that you intercept and examine, the more you can infer from the messages. This is true even if the messages are encrypted and cannot be decrypted. This can be done in the context of military intelligence or counter intelligence and is a general security concern. Dedicated software programs such as i2, Visual Anaytics, Memex, Orion Scientific, and others, can be used to perform traffic analysis techniques.

Now that you are in charge, you may want to install appliances or software that will analyze traffic and learn normal traffic patterns. You could then use these to determine any anomalies and ensure that you stay alert to any future attacks on your network.

FIGURE 4.18   Windows Logs on Windows Server 2008

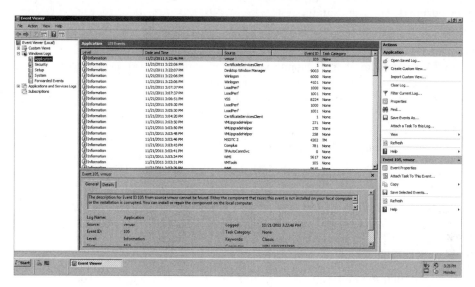

Network sniffer

Many third parties have developed sophisticated equipment to perform other network tests such as connectivity, load, and throughput tests. These products use both hardware and software to analyze the network performance and make recommendations for improvement. Companies such as Fluke Networks (www.fluke.com) specialize in equipment and software to test and evaluate networks. You might consider using these types of devices to examine your network and identify any weaknesses or abnormalities that could affect network communication.

Exam Essentials

Know the main purpose and types of SNMP software.   The main purpose of SNMP software is to gather information about computers and devices on your network. This is accomplished using devices with agent software and a central device that collects the data into a Management Information Base. SNMP (SNMPv1) is functional but lacks the security of the later types of SNMP. SNMPv2 improves upon security and confidentiality of data, but it's still not as secure as SNMPv3. Developed in December 1997, SNMPv3 is a secure protocol that assists you in gathering information about your network in a confidential manner.

Know the types of logs that you can use to collect and analyze traffic.   Syslog is the de facto standard, especially for Linux and Unix installations. It is flexible and can assist you in obtaining information about devices and software in your network. Windows clients and servers use system logs, history logs, and other general logs to gather information for trouble-shooting purposes. You can examine system logs for information about your network and compare baselines against the current log to detect attacks or just misconfiguration.

Be familiar with traffic analysis and network sniffer tools.   Traffic analysis tools enable you to capture and examine traffic data to deduce information from patterns of communication. By examining a pattern of communication and comparing it to patterns of communication on a "normal day" based on your baseline, you can uncover anomalies that might be an attack or a misconfiguration. Network sniffer tools are hardware components that have a high degree of intelligence because of the software that they use. You can use them to perform network connectivity, load, and throughput tests.

4.5 Describe the purpose of configuration management documentation

It has been said that the best map in the world won't do you any good if you don't know where you are! Over the past 30 years or so, the tools to help you to "see" your network better have improved tremendously. We tend to think and understand things in pictures, so a picture is indeed "worth a thousand words." I remember when the picture was on a whiteboard...or even a chalkboard! Now, you can use programs such as Microsoft Visio or CiscoWorks to gain visibility as never before.

The technologies may have made things easier, but whether you use the latest tools or the "old standbys," the purpose of having accurate configuration management documentation is the same as ever: to help you make better decisions about your network. In this section, I will focus on the tools you can use to "see" your network more clearly. In particular, I will discuss wire schemes, network maps, documentation, cable management, asset management, and baselines.

Wire schemes

One day maybe most networking will be wireless, but for now this is not the case. In fact, most networks have thousands of feet of wiring that works its way around a building. I'm using the word *wiring* here in a loose sense, because the backbone of a network often consists of fiber-optic cable. Still, the network administrator must understand where all the wiring is connected and therefore what the options are in regard to fault-tolerant connections and changes to the network design.

To facilitate this knowledge, most companies keep detailed wiring schematics that show how cables are wired throughout an organization, what is connected to each one, and where there are cables that can be used for growth. The network administrator must keep these wiring schematics up-to-date when changes are made to the network. It is also a very good practice to label the wires themselves whenever it is not completely obvious where they are connected.

Network maps

There is a big difference between the physical shape of a network and the logical shape of a network. The physical shape is what the network looks like to the "naked eye," but the logical shape defines the path that a packet takes to get from one part of a network to another. Since these concepts are so different, the diagrams that represent them will also be very different.

A physical *network map* might describe where you have routers, switches, servers, client workstations, and other network equipment and what cables are being used to connect devices. It might look very much like a wiring schematic, except that the emphasis will be on the devices at the ends of the wires rather than the multitude of wires connecting them. Detailed information about the devices currently being used, such as IP addresses, in service date, capabilities, and so on, could also be listed. This type of diagram could be used for planning the network or eventually replacing outdated equipment that is hampering network performance.

A logical network map, which describes the path the traffic takes to get from one router or switch to another, might be used for troubleshooting. Often network designers use multiple paths through various network devices to load balance a network and provide fault-tolerant routes when needed. This type of diagram will usually list the IP addresses and subnet information of the devices and will take into account the configuration of devices such as VLANs on switches or access lists on routers. If traffic is suddenly not able to get from one part of a network to another, then a diagram showing the exact path that the traffic is supposed to take would be of great value to a person troubleshooting the problem.

Documentation

You should always keep documentation as up-to-date as possible. This may not be as easy as it sounds. Any replacement or upgrade of network equipment could well require an update to a physical network diagram. Any change in configuration on a router or a switch, such as a new router interface or a new VLAN, will require a change in the logical network diagram. To track these changes and their documentation, many companies use job logs that list the change that was made, when it was made, and when it was documented. Microsoft, as well as other companies, offers software to facilitate this process. Some organizations assign a team member the job of ensuring that the documentation is kept up-to-date. Everyone still has a responsibility for logging their own changes, but one person is primarily responsible for the entire process. This can reduce headaches and "finger-pointing."

Cable management

The IT industry has special concerns in regard to the many cables that are used throughout a building. The cables are individually not large or bulky but can become bulky when many cables are combined. The cables must be physically secured, which is generally accomplished using cable ties, cable trays, cable ladders, and cable baskets through the route of the cables. At the same time, the cables and cable ends must be accessible so that network administrators can terminate them to patch panels (discussed earlier) to allow for easy changes if a cable should be damaged or inoperable. Finally, in most organizations, cables are labeled or special colors are used to indicate the type of cable and make ongoing cable management easier.

Asset management

Asset management is not just a technical term but instead refers to a system whereby things of any value are monitored and maintained. As you can imagine, there are many "things of value" associated with your network and network systems. In fact, most of the components that I've discussed have considerable value. IT asset management includes standards and processes for the procurement, maintenance, life cycle management, updating, and eventual disposal of equipment such as routers, switches, servers, appliances, and the like.

Baselines

If you go to a doctor and your temperature is 104 degrees Fahrenheit, what does that indicate? You have a fever, right? How do know that you have a fever? When I said 104 degrees, you compared that to 98.6 degrees, which is the normal temperature for a healthy human being. Well, there are also normal readings for a network, but they aren't as simple as 98.6 degrees Fahrenheit. In fact, they may be customized to a type of network or even to your specific network.

There are four lifeblood resources to any network or any devices on the network: processor, memory, disk subsystem, and network subsystem. A serious weakness in any of the network resources can easily spread and affect the other resources. When a lack of a resource causes this type of problem, this is generally referred to as a bottleneck. How do you prevent bottlenecks? You must understand what your network looks like in regard to these resources when it is healthy so that you can determine what to change when it is not. A record of measurements taken by network diagnostics and system-monitoring equipment when the network is healthy is referred to as a *baseline* of the network. You should have a baseline of your network because although your network may be similar to other networks, no two networks are exactly alike. Typically, baselines are stored in log files that are accessible to the network administrator when needed for comparison.

Change management

Each organization will determine its own policies for designing, configuring, and managing their own network. These policies and procedures should be created by the network teams who know the system best and should be "signed off" on by a high-level management person, such as an executive of the company. They should reflect the overall goals of the company in regard to network connectivity, disaster recovery, fault tolerance, security, and so on. Each company will need to decide what is important to them. Only after the policies and procedures are in place can the correct configurations be initiated and administered by the networking teams.

Exam Essentials

Understand various network documents.   You should understand the use of a wire scheme, physical diagram, logical diagram, baseline, and network documentation.

Understand the need to update network documentation.   You should understand the frequent and consistent need to update network documents such as wire schemes, logical and physical diagrams, and baselines. You should know that logs are often used to track changes to the network and when the change was recorded in each of the documents.

4.6 Explain different methods and rationales for network performance optimization

The main role of a network is to make its resources available to the end user. End users generally don't know how the network functions, and they don't want to know. All they need is to get their documents and emails so that they can do their job. On the other hand, you must be aware of the latest networking technologies so that you can continue to make the resources transparently available to end users. To facilitate this, you can employ many methods to make the network more efficient. In the following sections, I'll discuss the most common of these methods and the specific reasons for their use.

Methods

One of the main jobs of a network administrator is to create and preserve available bandwidth. This is the bandwidth available to the users after the network administrator factors in the overhead of running the network. In other words, a 1Gbps connection does not really give the users 1Gbps but instead gives them a share of the bandwidth that remains after the overhead of the network is considered. Administrators use many technologies to keep overhead to a minimum and assure that each type of user traffic gets the share of available bandwidth it requires. In the following sections, I'll discuss the most common of these technologies.

QoS

Quality of service (QoS) refers to the ability to provide different types of traffic flow with different types of service through the network. In other words, some types of traffic can receive priority and custom queuing through the network. This type of service is especially useful for video and voice applications that must maintain a consistent data flow in order to function properly. With good QoS, even a congested network can handle these types of applications.

Traffic shaping

Traffic shaping is controlling computer network traffic to optimize performance and/or reduce latency. This technology works to slow down some traffic flows that do not need all the bandwidth in the path they are using. In this way, it increases the available bandwidth for other traffic flows that need it. Traffic shaping uses bandwidth throttling, which is typically applied to specific connections on the network edges. Traffic shaping can also be applied to specific devices at the network interface card.

Load balancing

Today's networks often have multiple connections from a source to a destination. One of the reasons for this type of configuration is *load balancing*. When more than one path exists from a source to a destination, you can use each of the multiple paths to, in essence, "spread out" the traffic flows, thereby maximizing your available bandwidth on each connection. This is generally accomplished using routers or multilayer switches. Some of the most common types of traffic that are load balanced in today's networks include websites, FTP, DNS, and Internet Relay Chat.

High availability

High availability is a system design protocol that sets a limit on unplanned downtime during a given period of time. Organizations that manage significant amounts of money or even human lives will generally strive for very high availability for their computer systems and network connections. In some organizations, for example, one of the goals is to provide *five nines* uptime, which means that the system must be available 99.999 percent of the time. In other words, there can be no more than 0.001 percent of unplanned downtime. Since there are exactly 525,600 minutes in a year, this equates to 5.26 minutes per year ($525,600 \times .00001$)!

Unplanned downtime is due to a network failure. Another type of downtime, referred to as *planned downtime*, includes maintaining and upgrading the network during periods of low traffic.

Caching engines

Computers and people tend to do the same things over and over. The principle of a cache is to store the resources that a device or a user needs to enable them to perform a task much faster in later attempts than the first time the task was performed. For example, if many users are accessing a popular website, a caching engine can be used to keep the links and data for the website at a location that is faster for the users to speed up their performance. Caching engines can also be used for files and resources internal to an organization so that the users can get to them while still conserving available bandwidth. This service typically requires no user configuration and is transparent to the user.

Fault tolerance

Earlier, we mentioned that one of the reasons for redundant connections is load balancing. Another reason for redundant connections is fault tolerance. Fault tolerance, in regard to network connections, is the ability to lose one connection without losing the connectivity that a user requires. It is generally accomplished using routers or multilayer switches, which provide multiple connections from a source to a destination. In this case, if one connection fails, the other connections are still available to user traffic. This in turn increases the high availability of the network resources.

CARP

You can use Common Address Redundancy Protocol (CARP) to reduce the effect of a computer failing while providing a critical service. This is because another computer that has the same address can also be used for the service. This not only provides for fault tolerance, but it can also be used for load balancing. For example, if a single computer is running a packet filter and it fails, it will effectively block all communication downstream of it. If there are two computers that are using CARP to provide the same service simultaneously and one computer fails, then the users will not be affected because the traffic will be redirected to the other computer.

Reasons

In an uncongested network, none of the strategies previously discussed would be necessary. In today's networks, however, powerful PCs are often used to download pictures, videos, and other large files. Because of this load, the biggest and best networks can still suffer from congestion. This can be because of latency sensitivity, high-bandwidth applications, and large uptime requirements. In the following sections, I'll discuss each of these reasons.

Latency sensitivity

Latency is defined as the time delay between the moment when a process is initiated and the moment when one of its effects becomes detectable. In regard to networking, latency sensitivity refers to the susceptibility of an application or service to the speed or consistency of a network connection. In other words, some applications that people use on a network are not as sensitive as others to latency because they do not require a real-time or even an interactive connection to the user. Other applications and services require a high degree of consistent user interaction and are therefore considered to have high latency sensitivity.

High bandwidth applications (VoIP, video applications, unified communications)

Many applications that people use today require a tremendous amount of bandwidth relative to the applications used in the past. The types of applications that we use have evolved. Very early programs used batch processing that simply requested a list or set of information from a server and then waited for a response. Then we progressed to interactive applications that had to be able to give the user quick answers so that they could make the next decision. Nowadays, many of the applications that we use are considered real time, which is to say that the user is watching, listening to, and interacting with the application itself. These include, but are not limited to, VoIP and video-streaming applications. I will discuss each of these emerging technologies in this section.

If you think about it, it's all come full circle. We started with the telephone in the late 1800s, which used only voice. This technology remained in place for quite a while. Then we began to add computers to the telephone lines in the late 1970s. After this, many new communication lines were developed (such as T1, Frame Relay, ATM, SONET, and so on) to enhance the communication between computers. These new types of communication lines have become very sophisticated and powerful. Now, we have decided that we can achieve great speed and quality advantages for telephones by putting those voice connections onto the sophisticated lines that were first developed for computers. VoIP provides a merging of voice, data, and video technology that allows easy collaboration of information between people for business and personal use. Obviously, it requires a network that supports its bandwidth requirements.

I can remember sitting down with my mom and dad at 6 p.m. every night to find out what was going in the world by watching the news on one of our three channels! We didn't have a clue what had happened that day until the news told us at that time. We also got only one chance to take it all in, because we certainly had no way to record it. Today, we can all watch the videos of anything we choose whenever we want over the Internet. We can find out about what's going on in the world in a matter of minutes and sometimes even watch as it happens on our own computers. Video applications come in many forms, and the vendors' names are not important. The most important thing for you to understand is that these applications are real time in regard to the way they are watched by the user and therefore require a tremendous amount of bandwidth to operate effectively.

Uptime

As I mentioned earlier, *uptime* for a network is a measure of the amount of time that a network system is available to the user. It is often used as a measure of network stability and reliability. The greater the uptime, the better the network is for the users. Many businesses strive for 99.999 percent uptime of the network and its essential components.

Uptime can also be defined as the amount of time that a specific component has been up and has not been restarted. This is a very different definition than that for a network, because with network uptime, higher is always better. On the other hand, an extremely high uptime for a specific server might indicate negligence, since updates and patches often require a reboot that will reset uptime for that device.

Exam Essentials

Be familiar with methods of optimizing network performance.   QoS allows you to identify specific traffic flows and prioritize where needed. Traffic shaping optimizes performance and reduces latency by redistributing available bandwidth. Load balancing uses multiple paths for the same traffic flow to maximize available bandwidth. High availability is a system design protocol that sets a limit on unplanned downtime during a given period of time. Caching engines can be used to access files faster after they are used for the first time. Fault tolerance, in regard to networking, is the ability to lose one connection without losing the connectivity that a user requires. Finally, CARP allows you to run the same critical service on two different computers or devices that share the same IP address so that the loss of one device will not mean the loss of the service and connection for the users.

Understand reasons for network performance optimization.   Latency sensitivity is the susceptibility of an application or service to the speed or consistency of a network connection. Many of the applications that we use today, such as VoIP and video applications, are interactive and therefore are considered high-bandwidth applications that may have special needs in regard to methods of optimization. Uptime is generally considered as the amount of time that a network or resource is available to the user; however, the same term can also be used to designate the amount of time since a resource was restarted.

Review Questions

1. Which of following could be considered a network appliance? (Choose two.)

   A. Router

   B. Switch

   C. Load balancer

   D. Content filter

2. Which type of tool would you be most likely to use to test and even communicate on telephone lines?

   A. Butt set

   B. Crimper

   C. Toner probe

   D. Protocol analyzer

3. Which of the following can give you information about the location of a copper network cable break?

   A. TDR

   B. OTDR

   C. Protocol analyzer

   D. Environmental monitor

4. Which of the following best describes throughput?

   A. The size of a pipe between the receiver and sender

   B. The average size of a file to be transferred

   C. The amount of data that a network can pass in a given period of time

   D. The amount of time it takes to pass data from sender to receiver

5. Which tool is primarily used to establish connectivity between two devices?

   A. Ping

   B. Ipconfig

   C. Nslookup

   D. DHCP

6. Which of the following can be used to display protocol statistics such as active ports?

    A. Netstat

    B. Nbtstat

    C. Ping

    D. Dig

7. Which of the following are true regarding SNMP, SNMPv2, and SNMPv3? (Choose all that apply.)

    A. All SNMP versions allow you to gather information about your network devices.

    B. SNMPv2 is more secure than SNMPv3.

    C. SNMPv3 is more secure than SNMPv2.

    D. All versions of SNMP are inherently secure.

8. Which service allows you to manage different types of traffic and establish priorities between them?

    A. Traffic shaping

    B. High availability

    C. QoS

    D. Caching engines

9. Which of the following provides for failover redundancy on critical connections using a "group of redundancy"?

    A. Fault tolerance

    B. CARP

    C. Caching engines

    D. Baselines

10. Which types of traffic would generally be considered high bandwidth? (Choose two.)

    A. VoIP

    B. Printer sharing

    C. Network management

    D. Video

Chapter 5

Domain 5 Network Security

COMPTIA NETWORK+ EXAM OBJECTIVES COVERED IN THIS CHAPTER:

✓ **5.1 Given a scenario, implement wireless security measures.**

- Encryption protocols:
  - WEP
  - WPA
  - WPA2
  - WPA Enterprise
- MAC address filtering
- Device placement
- Signal strength

✓ **5.2 Explain the methods of network access security.**

- ACL:
  - MAC filtering
  - IP filtering
  - Port filtering
- Tunneling and encryption:
  - SSL VPN
  - VPN
  - L2TP
  - PPTP
  - IPSec
  - ISAKMP
  - TLS

- TLS 1.2
- Site-to-site and client-to-site
- Remote Access:
  - RAS
  - RDP
  - PPPoE
  - PPP
  - ICA
  - SSH

✓ **5.3 Explain methods of user authentication.**

- PKI
- Kerberos
- AAA (RADIUS, TACACS+)
- Network access control (802.1x, posture assessment)
- CHAP
- MS-CHAP
- EAP
- Two-factor authentication
- Multifactor authentication
- Single sign-on

✓ **5.4 Explain common threats, vulnerabilities, and mitigation techniques.**

- Wireless:
  - War driving
  - War chalking
  - WEP cracking
  - WPA cracking
  - Evil twin
  - Rogue access point

- Attacks:
  - DoS
  - DDoS
  - Man in the middle
  - Social engineering
  - Virus
  - Worms
  - Buffer overflow
  - Packet sniffing
  - FTP bounce
  - Smurf
- Mitigation techniques:
  - Training and awareness
  - Patch management
  - Policies and procedures
  - Incident response

✓ **5.5 Given a scenario, install and configure a basic firewall.**

- Types:
  - Software and hardware firewalls
- Port security
- Stateful inspection vs. packet filtering
- Firewall rules:
  - Block/allow
  - Implicit deny
  - ACL
- NAT/PAT
- DMZ

✓ **5.6 Categorize different types of network security appli-ances and methods.**

- IDS and IPS:
  - Behavior based
  - Signature based

- Network based
- Host based
- Vulnerability scanners:
  - NESSUS
  - NMAP
- Methods:
  - Honeypots
  - Honeynets

One thing that you should never believe is that we network computers to improve security. In truth we network computers to share resources and then we have to address a myriad of security issues and threats. We address these network security issues and threats using both hardware and software. Also, many protocols have evolved over the past 20 years or so that are specifically designed to mitigate network security threats. In the following sections, I'll discuss specialized hardware devices, software, and protocols that are used to address network security threats.

For more detailed information on Domain 5's topics, please see *CompTIA Network+ Study Guide, 2nd Ed* (9781118137550), or *CompTIA Network+ Deluxe Study Guide, 2nd Ed* (9781118137543), both published by Sybex.

5.1 Given a scenario, implement appropriate wireless security measures

When wireless networks were in their infancy, the words *wireless* and *security* really didn't belong in the same sentence. In fact, some organizations chose to put security second so they could experience the freedom and general "cool factor" of wireless networking. Even some of the early security protocols that were developed for wireless networks didn't really offer much in the way of security. Now, with advancements in technology, it's possible to secure your wireless network from most intruders. It's also still possible to set up an unsecure network for temporary purposes, such as at some of the training centers where I teach. The main thing that you want to avoid is setting up an unsecure network that you think is secure. In this section, I will discuss your options in regard to wireless security protocols and configuration and the impact on you when choosing each of these options.

Encryption Protocols

Encryption is not a new concept; it's a very old one that goes back to the days of the Pharaoh in Egypt. The basic idea with encryption is that the message can be coded in such a way that it can be read only by a person or entity who possesses that right decoder, or *key*. There are many types of encryption algorithms in use today, but there is a small subset of them that are most commonly used for wireless communication. In this section, I will discuss the most commonly used wireless encryption methods.

WEP

One of the first attempts at wireless security was *Wired Equivalent Privacy (WEP)*, which attempted to secure the very first wireless connections. WEP attempted to secure the connections by encrypting only the data transfer, but WEP was found not to be equivalent to wired security because the security mechanisms that were used to establish the encryption were not encrypted. It used a key length that was originally 64-bit and then later upgraded to 128-bit. WEP also operates only at the lower layers of the OSI model and therefore cannot offer end-to-end security for applications. Because of these shortcomings, many people have chosen newer and more sophisticated methods of securing wireless communications; however, some unknowing people are still using this unsecure protocol, and it can still be selected on a lot of wireless devices even to this day. The bottom line is that WEP may keep a curious snooper out, but any hacker worth his salt won't have a hard time cracking WEP security.

WPA

Wi-Fi Protected Access (WPA) was designed to improve upon WEP as a means of securing wireless communications. It can usually be installed as an upgrade on systems that currently use WEP. WPA offers two distinct advantages over WEP:

- Improved data encryption through the *Temporal Key Integrity Protocol (TKIP)*, which scrambles the keys using a hashing algorithm. TKIP also provides an integrity-checking feature that ensures that the 128-bit per packet keys haven't been tampered with or altered. TKIP is no longer considered secure.

- User authentication through the use of the *Extensible Authentication Protocol (EAP)* and user certificates. This ensures that only authorized users are given access to the network.

WPA2

Wi-Fi Protected Access version 2 (WPA2) further improves on WPA, offering additional advantages such as the following:

- Can use the Advanced Encryption Standard (AES) mode of encryption for much stronger security and longer security keys.

- Implements CCMP, which is based on the 802.11i standard and offers an enhanced data cryptographic encapsulation mechanism that replaces TKIP completely with a security method that is much stronger. It has been mandatory on Wi-Fi certified devices since 2006.

WPA Enterprise

WPA Enterprise is a wireless protocol that enhances security using IEEE 802.1x and a separate authentication server. It provides for user account and certificate-based authentication.

You should consider using it if your organization is of medium to large size. It will serve to enhance security by allowing you to centralize your security policies. Later in this chapter, I will discuss the authentication services that you can use for WPA Enterprise.

MAC address filtering

As you know, every host on a network has a 48-bit media access control address (MAC address) that is usually expressed in hexadecimal. In addition, every Ethernet packet contains a source MAC address and a destination MAC address, although sometimes the destination MAC address is a broadcast address such as FF-FF-FF-FF-FF-FF. MAC filtering can be applied to your wireless access point and configured to let only specific MAC addresses through an interface on the wireless access point (WAP). In other words, the user can connect to the WAP only if the user's MAC address is configured as an accepted address. This might seem like a great idea at first, but you should never use it as your only wireless security, that is, if you really want a secure wireless network. The reason that you should not use it as your only means of security is that, with the right software, the acceptable MAC addresses can easily be determined and spoofed!

Device placement

In Chapter 2, I discussed device placement in relation to performance. You may remember that I stated that performance would probably be enhanced by placing the WAPs as close to the center of the communications area as possible. The reason that this is effective is that the radio waves radiate out in all directions (with an omnidirectional antenna), and therefore you can cover the area more effectively and give computers more area in which they can connect if you work from the center.

As it turns out, this technique will also slightly improve the security of your wireless network but in a very different way. By placing the WAPs close to the center of your communications area, you can also control the perimeter of the communications area more effectively. In other words, you can limit the instances in which your wireless area goes farther than you had intended. Of course, to know for sure whether it's in your parking lot or your neighbor's building, you should check it yourself or, better yet, have a professional do a site survey. This should be considered only in addition to other security methods, since, on its own, it's a very weak method of securing your network.

Signal strength

Typically, you don't control the signal strength of your wireless network on an ongoing basis. At least, there is no "signal strength dial" that you turn one way or the other. If you use the latest wireless technologies, such as 802.11n, they will broadcast with more signal strength than the earlier technologies. Of course, in relation to security, that additional strength might not be what you need. To shape the signals, you could use directional antennas that allow devices to connect to each other but do not radiate in all directions. Also, in many ways the placement of your WAPs will affect the signal strength of your broadcast.

Exam Essentials

Understand encryption protocols.   There are many different wireless encryption protocols from which you can choose. Some, such as WEP and WPA, are no longer considered secure and should not be used if security is your goal. WPA2 is considered a secure protocol and should be used whenever possible.

Understand MAC address filtering.   MAC address filtering controls who can connect to a WAP based on their MAC address. Because MAC addresses can easily be spoofed, it should never be used as your only form of wireless security. It can be used in conjunction with stronger forms such as WPA2.

Understand device placement and signal strength.   Device placement and signal strength can go hand in hand. You can alter your signal patterns by placing WAP close to the center of the wireless network area or by using specialized directional antennas. A key to keeping a wireless network secure is limiting it to the area in which you are using it.

5.2 Explain the methods of network access security

One thing that you should never believe is that people network computers to improve security. In truth, we network computers to share resources, and then we have to address a myriad of security issues and threats. We address these network security issues and threats using both hardware and software configuration. Also, many protocols have evolved over the past 30 years or so that are specifically designed to mitigate network security threats. In the following sections, I'll discuss access lists, tunneling and encryption, and remote access protocols.

ACL

Generally speaking, an *access control list (ACL)* is a method of identifying traffic and then making decisions based on the attributes of that traffic. The attributes considered might be the source IP address, destination IP address, source MAC address, destination MAC address, protocol, or even specific port information in the header of the packet. What is identified and filtered will largely depend upon the type of device on which the list is configured. For example, ACLs on switches are very different from ACLs on routers. In the following sections, I'll discuss each of these types of ACLs and the filtering they provide.

MAC filtering

As I discussed earlier in this chapter, every host on a network has a 48-bit hexadecimal MAC address, and every Ethernet packet contains a source MAC address and a destination MAC address. *MAC filtering*, applied on switches working at layer 2 (Data Link) of the OSI model, focuses on these addresses in the packet and can be configured to let only specific MAC addresses through an interface on the switch. In addition, more sophisticated filters can let only specific addresses into one interface and out of another interface. In other words, the traffic can come in an interface only if it has a destination address for a specific host or group of hosts. MAC filtering is usually applied at the access layer of a computer network, where the host computers are connected to the switches. Whether your network is wired or wireless, MAC address filtering is generally not used as the only means of security, because MAC addresses can easily be spoofed with the right software.

IP filtering

The source IP address and destination IP address of the packet are contained in the IP header of a packet, sometimes referred to as *layer 3* (Network) addresses. *IP filtering*, usually associated with routers, is a process of configuring the devices to pass through only the desired IP traffic but block everything else. This is the most effective way to filter, since anything that is forgotten will not be passed through. Another method of filtering is to let all traffic pass through except what is specifically configured to be blocked. The problem with this method is that any traffic that is forgotten will be passed through; therefore, this method is much less secure.

As I mentioned, IP filtering is most often associated with routers, but most devices have configuration options and settings for IP filtering. It can be applied in layer 3 switches, which are switches that have a router module within them, or in a number of firewall devices, such as a Cisco PIX firewall. In fact, even Windows XP clients have the option to filter IP addresses in their advanced network settings, although this is recommended only for a specific client with a specific reason. Otherwise, filtering at the router or firewall should be used.

Port filtering

Ports are numbers contained within a packet that indicate the purpose of a packet and thereby allow a computer to do many different things at once over the wire. When you are browsing, checking your email, and receiving some files through the Internet all at once, you are taking advantage of ports.

TCP/IP has 65,536 ports available. As you can imagine, some ports are used much more than others. Ports are divided into three main groups, or designations:

Well-Known Ports   These port numbers range from 0 to 1023. They are the most commonly used ports and have been used for the longest period of time. When CompTIA states that you should know the definition of well-known ports, it's referring to the ports in this group. You can refer to Chapter 1, Table 1.6, for a list of the most common well-known protocols and their ports.

Registered Ports   These port numbers range from 1024 to 49151. Registered ports are used by applications or services that need to have consistent port assignments. These ports, like the well-known ports, are agreed upon by most organizations for standardization of use.

Dynamic or Private Ports   These port addresses range from 49152 to 65535. These ports are not assigned to any particular protocol or service and can therefore be used for any service or application.

It is common for applications to establish a connection on a well-known port and then move to a dynamic port for the rest of the conversation. It's important that you understand port numbers, because you may be configuring them for communication purposes as well as to provide *port filtering* and therefore prevent the communication of specified applications or services.

Tunneling and encryption

For most companies with multiple locations, the prospect of installing dedicated leased lines, such as T1s or T3s, to each of their locations is cost prohibitive and unnecessary. It's unnecessary with today's networks because it's possible to use the Internet as a secure connection between the locations. *Tunneling* is a process of encapsulating one protocol within another so as to provide a secure communication through an unsecure medium, typically the Internet. The processes and protocols used to create tunnels have changed over the past 15 years, and some tunnels are therefore more secure than others. Some tunneling protocols also encrypt the data contained in the packets, while others do not. In the following sections, I'll discuss the protocols used for tunneling and the security they provide.

SSL VPN

The Secure Sockets Layer (SSL) protocol uses cryptography to provide secure authentication and communication privacy over the Internet. It is typically used for e-commerce. When used in conjunction with a VPN on a site that is allowing e-commerce, the advantage SSL offers is that many of the filters are already configured. In other words, if a site wants to allow e-commerce using SSL, then the ports for SSL already must be allowed through any firewalls or other network filters. This means that an SSL-based VPN might be much easier to configure than one that requires that a new protocol and its ports be allowed through the firewalls of the network.

VPN

As mentioned, a virtual private network (VPN) is a network that is not really private, since it runs through an unsecure network. However, a VPN is made "virtually" private using an encapsulation protocol, also called a *tunneling protocol*. You can accomplish this using SSL and cryptography. There are also other protocols that are specifically designed to provide a tunnel that encapsulates a well-known protocol, for example, IP, with a secure protocol only known by the sender and receiver.

L2TP

Layer 2 Tunneling Protocol (L2TP) is one of the most common tunneling protocols in use today. The only Microsoft clients that support L2TP are Windows 2000 Professional and newer. Windows 2000 Server and newer servers also support L2TP.

L2TP uses IP/Sec to authenticate the client in a two-phase process. First it authenticates the computer, and then it authenticates the user. Authenticating the computer helps prevent a man-in-the-middle attack, where the data is first intercepted by another computer and then forwarded to the intended receiver. LT2P can also authenticate the end of the tunnel with an IP address so that it doesn't send data to an unintended receiver. L2TP works by using digital certificates, which means the computers that use L2TP must support digital certificates.

PPTP

Point-to-Point Tunneling Protocol (PPTP) is a protocol used to create a secure tunnel between two points on a network over which other protocols such as Point-to-Point Protocol can be used. This tunneling functionality provides the basis for many VPNs. Although PPTP is a widely used tunneling protocol, other tunneling protocols, such as L2TP, provide even greater security. PPTP also cannot authenticate the end of the tunnel and thereby prevent a man-in-the-middle attack, but L2TP can. Because of these disadvantages of PPTP, it has been largely replaced by L2TP.

IPSec

Internet Protocol Security (IPSec) is a framework of protocols designed to authenticate connections and encrypt data during communication between two computers. It operates at the Network layer of the OSI model and provides security for protocols that operate at the higher layers of the OSI model. Because of this, you can use IPSec to secure practically all TCP/IP-related communications, including tunnels.

The function of IPSec is to ensure that data on network is safe from being viewed, accessed, or modified by anyone except the intended receiver. IPSec can be used to provide security within networks as well as between networks. To be more specific, IPSec has three main security services:

Data Verification   This ensures that the data received is actually from the source from which it appears to have originated.

Protection from Data Tampering   This ensures that the data has not been changed in any way during the transmission between the sending computer and the receiving computer.

Privacy of Transactions   This ensures that the data that is sent is readable only by the intended receiver.

There are two main modes of IPSec: transport mode and tunnel mode. Transport mode is used to send and receive encrypted data within the same network. Tunnel mode is used to send encrypted data between networks. It includes an encryption mechanism as well as an authentication mechanism. The only Microsoft clients that can use IPSec are Windows 2000 Professional and newer. Windows 2000 Server and newer servers can also use IPSec.

ISAKMP

Many of the protocols that we use to secure communication and establish tunnels require the exchange of keys. To keep the communications regarding these keys secure and prevent attacks, such as a replay attack or denial-of-service attack, we use a protocol that provides for the secure creation and management of the keys. The protocol that we use is referred to as Internet Security Association and Key Management Protocol (ISAKMP). This protocol is used in conjunction with Internet Key Exchange (IKE) and sometimes with Kerberized Internet Negotiation of Keys (KINK).

TLS

TLS allows network devices to communicate across a network while avoiding eavesdropping, tampering, and message forgery. It is designed to allow end users to be sure with whom they are communicating. Clients can negotiate the keys that will be used to secure the data to be transferred. TLS is set to supersede its predecessor Secure Sockets Layer.

TLS 1.2

Introduced in August of 2008, the latest revision of TLS, which is named TLS 1.2, provides many security enhancements over that of the original protocol. These include the use of a longer key and a more sophisticated hashing algorithm as well as stronger encryption algorithms for the authentication phase. Because of these enhancements, the earlier versions of TLS have been rendered obsolete.

Site-to-site and client-to-site

The tunneling protocols that I've discussed, and sometimes combinations of them, can be used to establish two main types of tunneling. These are commonly referred to as site-to-site and client-to-site. Site-to-site tunneling is generally used to send and receive encrypted data within the same network or company. Organizations can use specific hardware and software to build a tunnel that only they can use. In contrast, client-to-site tunneling is used to establish secure communications between networks, organizations, and individuals. Protocols such as those we've spoken of above are used to establish authentication of the user or organization as well as encryption of the data they will send.

Remote Access

Generally speaking, remote access means that your user is not on a device that is connected within the LAN of your organization but is connected outside your LAN instead. The user may be connecting from home or from a hotel, but, in either case, the place from which they are connecting is not part of your organization. With remote access your goals are twofold. Your first goal is to provide the user with a user experience as close as possible to what they would have if they were connected within the LAN. Your second goal, though not second in importance, is to maintain the security of your system. This means you need a method by which the user can authenticate to the network, and then you need a method by which the user can securely transmit sensitive data. In the following sections, I'll discuss the tools and protocols that can assist you in meeting these goals.

RAS

Remote Access Service (RAS) is a remote access solution that is included with Microsoft Windows Server products. Its main function is to give users the same access to the network from a remote location as if they were actually sitting at their desks, although sometimes the access is much slower. RAS is implemented in Windows NT Server as RAS and in Windows 2000 Server, Windows Server 2003, and Windows Server 2008 as Routing and Remote Access Server (RRAS), but both product implementations offer the same basic functionality—remote access connectivity to a LAN environment. RAS servers can provide dial-up connections using modems as well as VPN connections using WAN miniports. Figure 5.1 shows an RRAS server on Windows Server 2008.

FIGURE 5.1 An RRAS server on Windows Server 2008

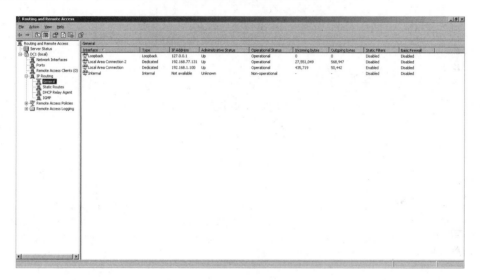

RAS is also capable of providing security using the tunneling protocols of which I've spoken, such as PPTP and L2TP, although L2TP is available only on Windows 2000 and newer servers. RAS and RRAS servers support remote connectivity to all the major client operating systems in use today.

RDP

Remote Desktop Protocol (RDP) is a protocol used by Microsoft to establish remote display and remote control capabilities between servers and clients on a Microsoft network. It is the protocol on which Windows Terminal Services operates. Originally, Terminal Services offered two options during installation: Remote Administration and Application Server. In later versions of Terminal Services (Windows Server 2003), only Application Server is offered. This is because Remote Desktop Connection, which also uses the RDP protocol, is now included with the Windows XP Professional and Vista client software and

Windows Server 2003 and Windows Server 2008 server software. Figure 5.2 illustrates a Remote Desktop Connection tool in Windows Server 2008.

FIGURE 5.2 The Remote Desktop Connection tool

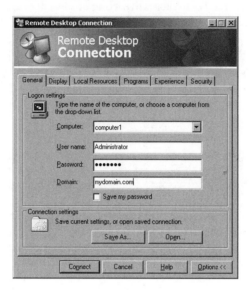

PPPoE

Point-to-Point Protocol over Ethernet (PPPoE) is a protocol that has become popular because of the growing number of people who use cable modems and DSL connections to access the Internet. PPPoE is a specification for connecting users on a LAN to the Internet through a common broadband medium such as a cable modem or DSL line. Its main function is to encapsulate PPP frames inside Ethernet frames. All the users on the LAN can share one common connection to the Internet. PPPoE can also be implemented with wireless devices that connect multiple users in a wireless LAN to the Internet.

PPP

Point-to-Point Protocol (PPP) is the standard remote access protocol used today. It provides for authentication mechanisms, error checking, and multiple protocol support. You can choose from among several authentication options, including Password Authentication Protocol (PAP), Challenge Handshake Authentication Protocol (CHAP), and Extensible Authentication Protocol (EAP). (I will discuss each of these protocols in greater detail later in this chapter.)

The PPP protocol establishes a session with this three-step process:

1. Framing rules are established between the client and the server. These include the size of the frames allowed as well as the data rates that can be used.

2. The client is authenticated by the server using the configured authentication protocol.

3. Network control protocols (NCPs) configure the remote client for the correct LAN protocols, TCP/IP, and so on.

After these three steps are successfully completed, the server and client can begin to exchange data.

ICA

Independent Computing Architecture (ICA) is a proprietary protocol designed by Citrix for application server systems. It defines a specification for passing data between servers and clients but is not bound to any platform. ICA is commonly used on Citrix WinFrame and Citrix Presentation Server. It can be used on Windows, Mac, Linux, and even Unix clients as terminals, which are referred to as *thin clients*. These systems work best when only data is needed and do not function well in environments that require large graphics, movies, or live content such as streaming video or audio. Their communication can be secured using an application-independent tunneling protocol such as L2TP with IPSec.

SSH

First developed by SSH Communications Security Ltd., Secure Shell (SSH) is a program that allows you to log in to another computer over a network, execute commands, and move files from one computer to another. SSH provides strong authentication and secure communications over unsecure channels. It protects networks from attacks such as IP spoofing, IP source routing, and DNS spoofing. The entire login session is encrypted; therefore, it is almost impossible for an outsider to collect passwords. SSH is available for Windows, Unix, Macintosh, and Linux, and it also works with RSA authentication. SSH operates at the Application and Session layers (layer 7 and layer 5) of the OSI model.

Exam Essentials

Understand MAC filtering vs. IP filtering.   MAC filtering works on switches at layer 2 (Data Link) of the OSI model and uses the destination MAC addresses of frames to make filtering decisions. IP filtering works on routers, works on layer 3 switches, and can even be configured on individual clients and servers. It can use the layer 3 (Network) source and destination addresses (generally IP addresses) to make filtering decisions on packets.

Understand the various forms of tunneling.   Tunneling is a process of encapsulating one protocol within another and is typically used for secure data transfer through an unsecure network. You should know that there are various forms of tunneling including SSL VPN, VPN, L2TP, and PPTP. Each has its own advantages and disadvantages. For example, a VPN using SSL might be advantageous if SSL is already being used, since the correct filters would already be in place. In addition, L2TP is much more secure than PPTP but requires the latest clients and servers.

Understand IPSec.   IPSec is a framework of protocols that is designed to provide secure authentication and secure data transfer between two computers. It works at the Network layer of the OSI model and can be used to secure practically all TCP/IP-related communications including tunnels. It has three main security services: data verification, protection from tampering, and privacy of transactions. The only Microsoft clients that can use IPSec are Windows 2000 Professional and newer. Windows 2000 Server and newer servers can also use IPSec.

Understand remote access.   You should be familiar with remote access services such as RAS and RRAS. In addition, you should understand remote access protocols such as RDP, PPoE, PPP, ICA, and SSH. You should understand the appropriate use of each protocol and the difference between remote control protocols, such as RDP, and remote access protocols, such as PPP and PPPoE. You should understand the difference between site-to-site tunneling and client-to-site tunneling and how each implementation is used.

5.3 Explain the methods of user authentication

Authentication is a process by which people prove their identities. For example, you have to use a driver's license or some other form of picture ID to prove that you are who you say you are when you check in for a flight. In person, this is not typically difficult, but over a network it can become much more complicated.

User authentication is a process by which users prove their identity over the network. This is generally accomplished in one of three methods, or a combination of them, also called *factors*. The three factors by which users prove their identity are as follows:

- Something they know
- Something they have
- Something they are

Something a user *knows* could be a password or the personal identification number (PIN) that corresponds to their smart card. Something a user *has* could be a smart card or a cryptographic key. Something a user *is* would relate to biometric authentication, such as a fingerprint, voiceprint, cornea or iris scan, or a hand geometry print. You can also combine these factors to create even greater security.

Each of these factors of authentication uses different protocols. It's important that you understand your options in regard to each type of user authentication. In the following sections, I'll discuss the most common methods of user authentication.

PKI

Public Key Infrastructure (PKI) is a method of user authentication that falls into the "something I have" category. If the user possesses the right key (a series of mathematical computations), then the user can prove their identity and gain access to a resource. If the user does not have the right key, then they cannot gain access to the resource. The keys are stored in an electronic document called a *certificate*. An important part of PKI is the process of tracking the certificates themselves and to whom they are issued. The servers and services that verify a user's identity and track the certificate are called *certificate servers.*

You can use your own certificate server to track the certificates that you issue within your own organization. If you need to prove your identity to others, you can also use a third-party company, such as VeriSign, that specializes in verifying identities and issuing the appropriate certificates and keys. Most organizations use a certificate hierarchy whereby they trust someone because someone else trusts them.

PKI works by using a pair of keys called the *public key* and the *private key*. The public key identifies the user and can be used to encrypt data that will be sent to the user so that only the user can decrypt it. The public key does not decrypt data. Since it does not decrypt data, it can be freely distributed without a concern as to whether it will be stolen or intercepted. It's kind of like a key that only locks your house but will not unlock it. You wouldn't be worried if more people had a key that would only lock your house, would you?

The private key is the other key in the key pair and is very different from the public key. The private key is held only by the user and is not shared with anyone. It is stored by the user's operating system and automatically used by the operating system and by PKI-enabled applications. The private key simply decrypts anything that the public key has encrypted. In fact, it is the only key that can decrypt what the public key in its key pair has encrypted.

To put this into practice, let's say you wanted to send me an encrypted email. First, you would need for me to send you my public key. Using my email software, I would send you an email that contains my public key and gives you an opportunity to store it for use. You would then create your email and use my public key to encrypt the email. You would then send me the encrypted email, which I would then decrypt and open with my private key. The email software will actually handle the use of the keys for us; all we have to do is get the process started by selecting to use encrypted email between us. This is just one example, and there are many other uses of PKI for user authentication, encryption, and identity verification of the sender of a message.

Kerberos

Kerberos is an authentication protocol that was developed by MIT and named for the mythical three-headed dog that guards the gates of Hades over the River Styx. It is commonly used in LANs, and it is the default authentication protocol for Windows Active Directory and for Novell NDS systems. Kerberos was specifically designed to prevent *replay attacks* whereby a user records the process of authentication of a device to a resource and then "plays back" the appropriate pieces, thereby gaining access.

To prevent replay attacks, Kerberos uses a system of keys that expire as soon as they are used or after a definable period of time (usually five minutes). When users first log on, they receive a special token called a *ticket-granting ticket* (TGT). When they need access to a resource, their system will present the TGT to a server called a *key distribution center*

(KDC), which is usually also a domain controller. The KDC will then give the user's computer either a key to access the resource or another TGT to access the next KDC that is in the path toward the resource. In a large network with multiple domains, this process may be repeated several times just to get access to the resource. In all cases, the TGTs and the keys obtained from them expire as soon as they are used and cannot be used again. Now you can see why they named it after the three-headed dog that guards the gates of Hades!

Kerberos works well when all the users are part of a network and are therefore authenticated by the domain controller. If the user is not from within the network, then special provisions can be made to make the user recognized by the network and therefore able to use Kerberos for authentication. These provisions will vary depending on the operating system, but it's often simpler to just use PKI for accounts that are not part of the network.

AAA

Authentication, authorization, and accounting (AAA), pronounced "triple A," is an overall term that defines the goals of an organization in regard to its data and resources. As I mentioned earlier, *authentication* is a process of users proving their identity. It essence, you are asking "Who are you?" Authorization is the process of determining what resources a user has access to once authenticated. Here you are asking "What are you allowed to do?" Finally, *accounting* is a process of tracking the resources the user has connected to and the resources they've used. It can be understood to ask "What did you do?" Many services and protocols have been developed that conform to AAA concepts. Two of the most common services that are used with remote access are RADIUS and TACACS+. I will discuss each of these services in the next sections.

RADIUS

Remote Authentication Dial-In User Service (RADIUS) is a service that provides a centralized system for authentication, authorization, and accounting. Remote access servers become clients of another server referred to as a RADIUS server. The authentication of the users is then actually performed by the RADIUS server based on certificates, Kerberos, or some other type of authentication. RADIUS uses UDP to broadcast the communication between the remote access servers (RASs) and the RADIUS server. The RAS becomes a go-between that opens the door, or doesn't, for the client computer to come in and use the resource. Also, because all requests are centralized through the RADIUS server, accounting for those requests is also centralized. RADIUS is supported on all the latest Microsoft Server systems such as Windows 2000 Server, Windows Server 2003, and Windows Server 2008. When RADIUS is used with wireless networks, IEEE 802.1x, and WPA, the result is WPA for Enterprise, which we discussed earlier in this chapter.

TACACS+

Terminal Access Controller Access Control System+ (TACACS+) is a service that is similar to RADIUS but uses TCP to communicate between the RAS and the TACACS+ server. It was developed by Cisco Systems to address the need for a more scalable AAA solution. The fact that it uses TCP (a connection-oriented protocol) instead of UDP (a connectionless protocol) offers several advantages, namely, that the RAS server receives an acknowledgment from the TACACS+ server that the authentication request has been received and is being processed. Also, because the two can communicate with a connection-oriented protocol, more sophisticated security mechanisms can be employed. For example, while RADIUS encrypts only the password in the packet that is passed from the RAS to the RADIUS server, TACACS+ encrypts the entire body of the packet including the information regarding the username and the service that the user is requesting. This makes TACACS+ a much more secure service than RADIUS. Of course, TACACS+ also keeps an accounting of all requests from a RAS, and that accounting can also be secured.

Network access control

Let's say that I have a device in a network that you can access and thereby gain access further into the network. That device may be a RAS or could be a wireless access point. It may not have the intelligence or the information to authenticate you, but it has a connection to a server that does. In this case, the device relays your credentials to the authentication server that does have the intelligence and the database to make the right decision. This is an example of *network access control*. The most common type of network access control is 802.1x, covered in the next section.

802.1x, posture assessment

802.1x is a standard developed by the Institute of Electrical and Electronics Engineers (IEEE). It defines a method for access control whereby the client computer (referred to as a *supplicant*) requests access to a network through a device such as a network appliance or a WAP (referred to as an *authenticator*), and the authenticator passes the request to the authentication server to be authenticated. The authentication server either accepts or rejects the request, based on its database, and then gives instructions to the authenticator to accept the request or reject it. It can also consider the applications that the supplicant is using as well as any configuration settings on the client. This is referred to as *posture assessment*. 802.1x is commonly used for both wired and wireless security in today's networks. The tricky part here is that the authenticator does not really authenticate the request at all—the authentication server does. The authenticator just acts as a gatekeeper.

CHAP

Challenge Handshake Authentication Protocol (CHAP) is a remote access authentication protocol that uses a password that is a shared secret between the server and client; however, the password is never sent in clear text. Instead, a three-way handshake is used in which the server sends the client a challenge to prove that it knows the password by inserting it into a challenge string sent by the server using a hashing algorithm. The client uses the hashing algorithm on the password to create a hash of the password, called a *message digest*, which it sends back to the server. When the server receives the message digest from the client, it compares it with the message digest of the true password using the same hashing algorithm. If the two message digests are the same, then the client knows the password, and the communication can continue. If they are not the same, then the communication will be terminated. In this way, CHAP establishes authentication without having to send a password in clear text. CHAP is the strongest authentication method that can be used when deploying a mixture of Microsoft clients and other types of clients, such as Novell, Unix, or Apple.

MS-CHAP

Microsoft Challenge Handshake Protocol (MS-CHAP) is Microsoft's variation on the CHAP protocol, which provides even greater security for authenticating Microsoft clients. Because MS-CHAP is specifically written for Microsoft, all clients must be running a Microsoft operating system. Although it's possible for any Microsoft client to use MS-CHAP, it is more likely that it will be used by Windows 95, Windows 98, and Windows NT Workstation clients. This is because the newer clients can use an even more secure protocol referred to as MS-CHAP v2.

Microsoft Challenge Handshake Protocol version 2 (MS-CHAP v2) is a much stronger form of remote access authentication that can be used only by Windows 2000 Professional and newer clients or by Windows 98 clients using a VPN. Many new features in MS-CHAP v2 strengthen the security of the authentication mechanisms. The most important of these is that MS-CHAP v2 offers a two-way authentication method. This means a client can verify that a server is legitimate and not a rogue RAS server before it reveals its credentials to the server for authentication. This prevents an attacker from inserting a server into a network environment for the purpose of collecting user credentials for later use. MS-CHAP v2 is a good solution for networks with Microsoft Windows 2000 Server and newer servers and Windows 2000 Professional and newer clients.

EAP

As the name suggests, *Extensible Authentication Protocol (EAP)* is an open set of standards that allows the addition of new methods of authentication. EAP can also use certificates from other trusted parties as a form of authentication. It is currently used primarily for smart cards, but it is evolving and will be used for many forms of biometric authentication using a person's fingerprint, retina scan, and so on.

Two-factor authentication

As I mentioned, I can prove that I am who I say I am by something I know, something I have, or something I own. Each of these is a method or factor of authentication. If I use two of these factors at the same time, this is referred to as *two-factor authentication.* A common example of this type of authentication is a smart card that also requires a PIN. This combines something I know (the PIN) with something that I have (the card).

Multifactor authentication

To take this a step further, I might be required to also have my hand scanned, or my iris, or I might have to give a voice imprint. These are all examples of something that I *am*. When I have to combine all three of these factors in order to authenticate to a system, it is said to be using *multifactor authentication*. This is generally accomplished by using biometrics (body measurements) in combination with the other two factors.

Single sign-on

If you log on to a Windows Active Directory network (for example) as a domain administrator, you are given the permissions and rights to manage all of the computers that are in your domain. You don't have to continually re-authenticate every time you want to connect to a computer in that domain and manage it. This is an example of *single sign-on* in action.

Although, at first glance, it may seem as if this is less secure than forcing you to re-authenticate repeatedly, it can actually turn out to be a more secure method. The principle is that the best way to keep a password secure is by not using it! In other words, the less an administrator needs to enter credentials to authenticate, the less chance an attacker has of discovering what those credentials are and exploiting that discovery. For this reason, single sign-on is used in Active Directory as well as many other systems such as web applications, and the like.

Exam Essentials

Be able to explain factors of user authentication.   User authentication involves a user proving their identity through network communication. This is generally accomplished by one or more of three factors—something the user knows, something the user has, or something the user is. Some protocols combine two or more of these factors.

Understand PKI.   PKI consists of the management of certificates that contain key pairs. One key, the public key, is used to encrypt data that will be sent to the user through the network. It cannot decrypt the message itself. The corresponding key, the private key, is used to decrypt data that has been encrypted with the public key. Many applications use PKI in creative ways to exchange information securely.

Understand Kerberos.   Kerberos is the default authentication protocol on the latest Microsoft and Novell server systems. It uses a series of tickets that expire after their use or after a specific period of time. It's designed especially to prevent replay attacks in which a user's credentials are recorded and played back to gain access to resources.

Understand AAA.   AAA is a general term for authentication, authorization, and accounting. Authentication is "Who are you?" Authorization is "What are you allowed to do?" Accounting is "What did you do?" Most security protocols involve one or more of these concepts.

Understand RADIUS and TACACS+.   RADIUS and TACACS are both services that provide a centralized system for AAA. A RAS acts as a go-between and actually gets its authority from an authentication server. Since every authentication request goes through the authentication server, the accounting can also be centralized.

RADIUS, the default AAA service used with Microsoft systems, uses UDP to broadcast requests between a RAS and the authentication server. TACACS works in much the same way but uses TCP to provide connection-oriented communications between the client and the RAS as well as the RAS and the authentication server. This allows for much more secure communication between the RAS and the authentication server.

Understand 802.1x.   802.1x is a type of network access control that can be used on wireless and wired networks to improve authentication procedures and security. The client computer, or supplicant, will give its credentials to the access point, the authenticator, but does not actually perform the authentication. Instead, the access point will give the credentials to a server with a database (usually a domain controller), and that server will authenticate the request and give the "authenticator" permission to let the traffic pass through it and into the network.

Understand CHAP, MS-CHAP, and EAP.   CHAP is a protocol that protects the secrecy of a password by not sending the password at all. Instead, a hashing algorithm is used, and the result of the hash (called a *message digest*) is sent to prove that the password is known. MS-CHAP is Microsoft's variation of CHAP that provides greater security for Microsoft clients. MS-CHAPv2 is a much stronger form of authentication that provides two-way authentication of the latest Microsoft clients and servers. Finally, you should know that EAP is an open set of standards that allows for the addition of new methods of authentication such as smart cards and various forms of biometric authentication methods.

5.4 Explain common threats, vulnerabilities, and mitigation techniques

It would be nice if we could just build our networks and manage them with the understanding that everyone had our best interest in mind. If that were the case, then we would just make sure that the resources were as available to the users as they possibly could be made available with little effort on their part or ours. As I say, that would be nice! The problem is that there are people out there who aren't so nice and who will steal your data, embarrass your company, confuse communication, and cause chaos...just because they can. You should protect yourself and your network from these people. In this section, I will discuss the most common threats against your network and the computers that it contains. I will focus on the vulnerability that makes the threat a reality and especially on what you can do to mitigate the threat.

Wireless

It seems as if I keep coming back to wireless communications over and over, doesn't it? I promise that this will be the last time in this book that I will discuss wireless! It is important, though, that we discuss some threats that are specific to wireless networks so that you will be able to recognize them and mitigate the threats. In the next section, I will discuss the most common threats that affect wireless networks.

War driving

War driving is the act of searching for wireless networks in a moving vehicle using a portable computer or PDA. It came about with the earliest of wireless networks because it was well known that many organizations were setting up wireless networks that they did not know how to keep secure. You might think that they are all secure now, but you would be wrong! There are still many organizations that use unsecure methods (WEP and WPA...or even less) to "secure" their networks and unwittingly open themselves up to attack. What began as curious geeks with "high-gain antennas" made from Pringles potato chip, coffee, or paint cans is now a full-blown science consisting of specialized software such as Kismet or NetStumbler that combine a Wi-Fi receiver with a GPS unit to pinpoint the location of a wireless network...your wireless network!

To keep your wireless network secure, you just need to make sure you really implement the measures that we spoke of earlier. You should use WPA2, know where your network ends, and know who is on it. Just as the new war drivers can use software to their advantage, you can use software such as Capsa from Colasoft to tell you who is on your wireless network and what they are doing. You should use the technology to stay ahead of the war drivers and let them go after "softer" targets.

War chalking

Starting in about June 2002, a group of people began indicating to others that they had found a wireless network so that others could use it. They developed a series of symbols that indicated that the network was nearby and whether it was secure, unsecure, protected by WEP (also unsecure), and so on. They marked these symbols onto a nearby wall or street sign to indicate the location of the network. This method has pretty much gone away, now that most people can find Wi-Fi when they need it and many cell phones are constantly searching for it. It is another reminder, though, of the lengths to which some people will go to get what they want! Figure 5.3 shows some of the symbols used by war chalkers.

WEP cracking

As I mentioned, a wireless network that is "protected" by WEP is not considered secure in today's terms. All the attacker has to do is determine the WEP key, and this can now be done in a matter of less than a few minutes! Once the attacker has determined the key, he can get inside your system and monitor traffic or even take on the role of administrator and change your settings while hiding the fact that he is even there.

FIGURE 5.3   War chalking symbols

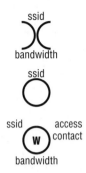

How can you prevent WEP cracking on your wireless network? You guessed it—don't use WEP! In fact, don't even use WPA, which we will discuss next. Use WPA2 because it is much more secure than WEP or WPA.

WPA cracking

As you may remember, WPA uses a security mechanism called Temporal Key Integrity Protocol (TKIP). That sounds really fancy and secure, doesn't it? Well, we had high hopes for it, but in November 2008 it was revealed to have a flaw that was a carryover from WEP. In 2009 and 2010 it just got worse. Now it has been discovered that there are ways that a determined and experienced attacker can decrypt all incoming traffic to a computer using WPA with TKIP. In other words, it's not secure anymore, even though many operating systems and applications use it as an option and maybe even a default. I think it goes without saying that you keep from being WPA cracked by not using it. Instead, you guessed it, use WPA2 with AES; as far as we know, it's secure for now!

Evil twin

An *evil twin* is a bogus Wi-Fi connection that fools people into believing that it is a legitimate connection for the purpose of phishing attacks and exploitation of data transactions. These types of attacks are becoming more common, so you should be aware of them and guard against them. They can affect you personally and professionally.

Have you ever been at the airport or a coffee shop on your laptop and noticed an "access point" that boasted "Free Internet Here" but the icon looked like a computer and not an antenna like a true infrastructure WAP indicator? I hope you didn't fall for it and try to use that connection. If you had, then you would have been asked to authenticate and create a password. How likely would it be that you would give the same password that might work for some of your other accounts and connections? Also, if you connected to your corporate accounts or, worse yet, bank accounts without using secure encryption techniques, the attacker would have access to all of that information because it would be going through his system.

You can protect against evil twin attacks by educating yourself and your friends and co-workers about such attacks. You can also use virtual private networks (VPNs) with SSL or

TLS to ensure that all email, passwords, and other sensitive information is encrypted during transmission. In general, you should never send highly sensitive information over any wireless networks of which you are not 100 percent certain of the origin and the security.

Rogue access point

A *rogue access point* is a wireless access point that has been installed without the explicit permission of the network administration team. It may have been connected for innocent means by a user who thinks he can get a better signal that way, or it may have been connected by an attacker in the hopes that the administrative team doesn't find it. In either case, it creates the potential for a man-in-the-middle attack whereby the security of the network has been breached because there is now a way in that does not go through your normal security measures. You may have taken painstaking effort to create a RADIUS server, of which we spoke earlier, but if a user (or an attacker) can come into the network through this point as well, then your network is not secure.

To prevent the installation of rogue access points, you should first educate the users about the dangers and make it known that these types of unsecure installations are not acceptable. In addition, you can monitor your network for newly installed access points using wireless intrusion prevention systems that can detect changes in the radio spectrum that indicate a new access point is installed and operational. Many of these systems can take automatic countermeasures as well by identifying the rogue and redirecting traffic away from it.

Attacks

A security threat to a network can be an attacker who attempts to gain information that they can use to exploit a network vulnerability. This type of attack is referred to as a *passive attack*. In another type of attack, the attacker is actually attempting to disrupt network communication and affect the productivity of the users of the network. This is referred to as an *active attack*. In the following sections, I will discuss the most common types of security threats.

DoS

A *denial of service (DoS)* attack overwhelms a network host with a stream of bogus data that keeps it from being able to process the data that it was designed to process. DoS attacks can be launched against computers as well as against network devices. Often a DoS attack is a security threat that indicates that a larger attack is in progress. The DoS attack is sometimes part of an attack that hijacks communication from a user who has already authenticated to a resource. While the user's computer is blocked by the DoS attack, the attacker accesses the resource and gets the information they want and then returns the control to the user who may not even know what has occurred.

DDoS

A *distributed denial of service (DDoS)* attack occurs when multiple systems are used to flood the bandwidth or resources of one server or a group of servers. The purpose of this type of attack is to saturate the resources so that they are no longer available for legitimate use. It can also be used as a decoy to hide an even more malicious attack that attempts to steal data or other sensitive information.

Conventional firewalls, switch and router ACLs, and even some IPS systems are not completely effective against DDoS attacks. This is because they often have legitimate content but bad intent. In other words, the system doesn't necessarily see that traffic as something that shouldn't be there, but the volume of the traffic is the problem. Specialized software called DoS Defense Systems (DDS) is able to effectively block traffic that has legitimate content but bad intent.

Man in the middle

A *man-in-the-middle attack* occurs when a person places equipment or logical connections between two communicating parties. The two communicating parties still assume they are communicating directly to each other, but their information is actually being sent to the man in the middle who then forwards it to the intended recipient. The man-in-the-middle attack may just listen in on the communication and learn new information, or it may begin to change the communication between the parties so as to confuse or sabotage the communication. In either case, man-in-the-middle attacks are harmful to an organization. Most organizations adopt measures including strong authentication and the latest protocols such as L2TP/IPsec with tunnel endpoint authentication.

Social engineering

Social engineering attacks do not rely on protocols or technology to succeed, but instead they rely on human nature. People generally want to trust each other, and that's where social engineering attacks start. They could consist of something as simple as getting to know someone well enough to guess their password or tricking someone into giving their credentials on the phone. They could also consist of false websites that ask for information from unsuspecting web surfers. This type of attack is referred to as *phishing*. Social engineering attacks can be prevented best by simply training all users not to give out their credentials and to be very careful about anyone who asks for this information on a web page.

Viruses

A computer *virus* is a program that can infect a computer and then copy itself without the consent of the user. Viruses began infecting computers in the early 1980s and have continued to evolve with technology ever since. Some viruses are able to change themselves after they infect a computer to attempt to "hide" from antivirus software. As viruses have changed over the years, companies such as Symantec and McAfee have specialized in software that can detect and eradicate viruses from computer systems or even keep them from infecting the computer in the first place. These programs are kept up-to-date by downloading the latest list of virus signatures that can detect the very latest viruses. There are more than 75,000 known viruses today, but most if not all of them are defeated by just keeping your antivirus software up-to-date on all servers and clients.

Worms

A *worm* is different from a virus in that it is a program and not just an "infestation." Worms use the computer network to send copies of themselves to other computers without the user's consent. Unlike viruses, worms do not need to attach themselves to an existing program but can instead work on their own. They are generally designed to cause network problems including bandwidth and resource utilization issues. Famous worms like the Mydoom and Sobig worms have affected thousands of computers and servers in the past. Worms typically spread by exploiting vulnerabilities in operating systems. You can prevent their spread by keeping clients and servers up-to-date with the latest security patches.

Buffer overflow

A buffer overflow attack is an anomaly created by a rogue program that while writing data to a buffer intentionally overwrites the buffer memory and then overwrites the adjacent memory. This may result in erratic behavior and memory errors and even a crash or a breach of system security. It is often used to confuse or "soften" a computer system as a prelude to another more malicious attack. You can use products such as Stackguard and ProPolice to prevent buffer overflow attacks from succeeding.

Packet sniffing

An attacker can use a protocol analyzer to launch an attack by *packet sniffing.* This is a process in which the attacker collects a data sample with hardware or a software device that allows the inspection of the data at the packet level. At this level, the attacker might see IP addresses, MAC addresses, unencrypted passwords, and other sensitive data. There might not be one key piece of information that gives the attacker an advantage, but it might just be a combination of the information gained that reveals the vulnerability that the attacker seeks. After the vulnerability is discovered, then the attacker can begin the active attack. The best way to prevent this type of attack is to forbid anyone except a trusted network administrator from placing a packet analyzer on your network. Most packet analyzers can detect the presence of other packet analyzers, unless the attacker has used software to make his attack invisible.

FTP bounce

The FTP bounce attack is a legacy attack that likely will not work on the latest FTP software. It used the `port` command to request access indirectly through the victim machine. Once in the ports, the attacker could gain information or disrupt network communication.

Smurf

A *smurf* attack exploits a common network tool, specifically `ping`. As you know, when you ping a host, you will get a reply from that host. Well, let's say you are in a network with hundreds of hosts. If you were to ping the broadcast address of your network, then all the hosts would reply to you. That means you would be flooded with replies from all over the network; however, you asked for it! Now let's say you didn't ask for it but instead someone else pretended to be you and sent a ping using your source address to the broadcast address of the network. You would still get flooded with replies even though you didn't ping anyone. You would then be the victim of a smurf attack. To prevent this type of attack, simply install the latest security patches. One of the changes that the patches will make is to disallow any network host to ping their own broadcast address. This will put a stop to the smurf attack.

Mitigation techniques

Now that I have discussed the main security threats against your network, let's look deeper into the ways that you can protect against these threats. The method you will use to mitigate a threat is largely dependent upon the type of threat. Methods from which you can choose include policies and procedures, user training, and patches and updates. In the following sections, I'll discuss each of these mitigation techniques.

Training and awareness

Although it may not seem to be the most convenient form of security at the time that it's done, user training is one of the most effective and least expensive mitigation techniques. The best way to keep users from making the mistakes that can lead to the success of a social engineering attack is to educate them about what to expect and how to handle it. In regard to IT personnel, the more they know about the policies, procedures, and protocols, the better they can assist you in the security of the network. In either case, training users provides a real benefit for a relatively low cost.

Patch management

When an operating system or an application is released, it is typically not perfect from a security perspective. After its release, security patches and updates are also released on an ongoing basis that can be added to the software to make it more secure or give it more functionality. For example, Microsoft releases security patches on the second Tuesday of each month, "patch Tuesday," for most of its operating systems. The Windows Update system that is installed in all the latest clients and servers can be configured to download and install these patches automatically from the Microsoft Update site. In addition, hotfixes may be released on other dates when there is a security reason to do so. Network administrators can also use Windows Server Update Services (WSUS) to download these patches to servers and test them before applying them to the bulk of clients on their network.

Policies and procedures

Security policies and procedures should be clearly outlined in writing in your organization. They should be written by those who know the network best and signed off on by upper management to give them authority. They should clearly define acceptable behavior on the organization's computers and networks and the consequences for violating acceptable behavior standards. Anyone who uses computers should be required to read these policies and procedures and sign a form agreeing that they have read and understood them. Finally, when someone does violate the acceptable behavior standards, the rules should be enforced to provide a deterrent to those who might "test" the policies next.

Incident response

If you are "first on the scene" when an intruder has enacted a successful attack on your network, your first instinct may be to get the users back to work as soon as possible regardless of what it takes. In the short run, this makes a lot of sense, but in the long run it may be the wrong move. If you have to reinstall software that has been damaged by the attack, the reinstallation itself may cover the tracks of the attacker and prevent you from finding and prosecuting him. This means that he will continue to attack and maybe with more vigor next time. On the other hand, if you preserve as much evidence as possible for a computer forensics expert to examine, then you might just get the upper hand on the attacker. The users might have to wait a little longer this time, but they will also be much better off in the long run if you can catch or at least scare away that attacker. Of course, you shouldn't be waiting until that attack happens to decide what to do. Instead, you should have a written incident response plan that details who should be contacted, which ports should be left open and which should be closed, and any other security measures that should be taken in the event of an attack.

Exam Essentials

Understand the main security threats affecting networks.   Be familiar with the main security threats affecting networks such as DoS attacks, viruses and worms, man-in-the-middle, smurf, and social engineering attacks. You should know how each type of attack operates and how it creates a security hole.

Understand the main mitigation techniques.   You should understand what should be included in security policies and procedures and who should be involved in their creation. In addition, you should understand why training users is an effective and efficient method of guarding against social engineering threats and other network weaknesses. Finally, you should understand that security patches should be used to update your operating systems and applications.

5.5 Given a scenario, install and configure a basic firewall

A firewall is a hardware or software system that is used to separate one computer or network from another one. The most common type of firewall is used to protect a computer or an entire network from unauthorized access from the Internet. Firewalls can also be used to control the flow of data to and from multiple networks within the same organization.

Additionally, firewalls can be programmed to filter data packets based on the information that is contained in the packets. In the following section, I will discuss the different types of firewalls that you might use on your network and their configuration.

Types

Not all firewalls are the same. In fact, firewalls have changed tremendously over the past 10 years as technologies have evolved. Firewalls that first could filter packets only by their addresses and their protocols can now filter them by the data they contain. As technologies used to examine packets and make filtering decisions improve, the sophistication of the firewalls and their ability to provide granular decision making also improves. In general, there are two broad categories of firewalls, software and hardware. In the following section, I'll discuss each of these types of firewalls and their configuration.

Software and hardware firewalls

Software firewalls either are generally part of an operating system or are a third-party application that installs onto the operating and can be configured in addition to and sometimes instead of the operating system firewall. They are configurable for a single host and are therefore flexible for configuration for that host alone.

Hardware firewalls are specialized appliances that are built to filter packets between networks. The most common type of hardware firewall is used to protect a computer or an entire network from unauthorized access from the Internet. Firewalls can also be used to control the flow of data to and from multiple networks within the same organization. Firewalls can be programmed to filter data packets based on the information that is contained in the packets. Some examples of third-party hardware firewalls include Barracuda and BlueCoat.

Port Security

One of the best ways to keep ports secure is to keep them disabled when they are not in use. Out of sight is out of mind to you, but you can bet that it's in the mind of the attacker. As I mentioned before in this chapter, ports are address extensions contained within a packet that indicate the purpose of a packet and thereby allow a computer to do many different things at once over the wire. If you are using an application that requires a specific port, then the port will have to be open in order to use that application. There are some ports that you should definitely close or disable if you are not planning on using the application that is associated with them. If you would like to check your own system for vulnerabilities in regard to port security, you can use a free program called Superscan to determine which ports are open and causing a vulnerability to attack but are not being used by your applications. Once you determine your vulnerabilities, then you could adjust the individual settings of host operating systems, but it is much easier to configure your firewall and thereby protect many hosts at once. Next I will discuss different types of firewalls and what they offer.

Stateful inspection vs. packet filtering

The difference between a stateful firewall and a packet filtering (stateless) firewall is one of the intelligence with which the firewall examines the packets. A packet filtering firewall is configured only to recognize static attributes in each packet, such as the source IP address, destination IP address, and protocol. It does not take into account a stream of data that would be normal for a protocol and therefore what packet it should be seeing next in the normal flow for that protocol. In contrast, a stateful firewall is able to hold in memory the significant attributes of each connection. The attributes, which are known as the *connection state*, might include IP addresses, ports involved in the connection, and sequence numbers that are being used for the connection. The most CPU time is spent at the beginning of the connection, because after that, the stateful firewall can identify packets that are just part of an already established and "prescreened" session. This makes the filtering more efficient and more accurate for most communication sessions. Stateful firewalls were the first step in the technical evolution toward IDSs and IPSs, which we will cover in the next section.

Firewall rules

Firewall rules allow you to determine what types of packets will be allowed through the firewall. Packets can be identified by protocol, IP address, MAC address, or even the data that they contain. Once the packets are identified, they will be subject to the rules that are configured for the firewall. In the next section, I will discuss the options that you can use in the rules of most firewalls.

Block/allow

In most cases, the decision made by the rule is a simple one, "Do I allow this packet to traverse the firewall, or do I block its passage?" When most people think of firewalls, they are thinking of keeping things *out*, but you can also use firewall rules to keep things *in* your network. In other words, based on the protocol, IP address source, IP address destination, MAC address, or even content of the message, you can configure a rule to not allow traffic out of your network. This can be especially useful to keep users from sending sensitive data out of your company "walls."

Implicit deny

Probably the best types of firewall settings are those that will block all traffic unless that traffic is specifically allowed, referred to as *implicit deny*. The reason that implicit deny is best is that if you miss something, the users won't get to the services that they need. Wait... are you not seeing the benefit here? Well, then consider the alternative of a system that allows users (and attackers) access to everything unless you specifically remember and configure a rule that says they can't get to it. Which one is more secure? As you can see, the more secure type of configuration is the one that does not allow a user (or attacker) access to a resource unless you specifically configure it. The trade-off is that it may be more work to configure all options for the user in the short term, but implicit deny will be much more secure in the long run.

ACL

As I said before, the decision that the firewall must make is whether to let the packet through or not. Firewall rules often contain *access control lists (ACLs)* that can be used to determine the fate of a packet based on its protocol, source and/or destination IP address, MAC address, or even combinations of these. ACLs are used to identify traffic, and then the rule itself is used to control the traffic.

NAT/PAT

As I mentioned earlier, NAT is a service that translates one set of IP addresses to another set of IP addresses. Does that sound dangerous to you at all? Well, NAT is a service in the right hands, but it's more like a "weapon" if it's in the wrong hands. If an attack can corrupt your NAT tables and thereby change your real addresses to the attacker's intended addresses, then it can certainly disrupt your network. You can secure your NAT routers and appliances by requiring strong passwords for local and remote access and controlling who gets those passwords.

When you have two or more computers on the inside of a network that share one address as represented on the outside of the network (usually the outside interface address of the router), the only way to keep their network communication channels separate and organized is by port designation on each packet. PAT changes the source address of a packet as it passes through the router or other device using PAT, appending it with a specific port number. Likewise, an attack on a device using PAT could disrupt your network flow by confusing the addressing schemes and causing the network to fail. You can protect your PAT devices by using strong passwords for local access and especially remote access.

DMZ

In general, three zones are associated with firewalls: internal, external, and demilitarized (DMZ). The internal zone is the zone inside of all firewalls, and it is considered to be the protected area where most of your critical servers, such as domain controllers and sensitive information, are located. The external zone is the area outside the firewall that represents the network against which you are protecting yourself. This is generally, but not always, the Internet. The DMZ comes into play only when you have more than one firewall. It is a zone that is between two firewalls. It is created using a device that has at least three network connections, sometimes referred to as a *three-pronged* firewall.

You should place your servers that are used by hosts on both the internal network and the external network in the DMZ. Servers that might be placed in the DMZ include web, VPN, and FTP servers. Higher-security servers, such as domain controllers and DHCP servers, should be placed in the internal zone behind both firewalls. A DNS server that connects to the Internet might be placed in the external zone. Placing the proper resources in the proper zones is essential to the security of your network.

Exam Essentials

Know the difference between stateful inspection vs. packet filtering.   The main difference between stateful inspection and packet filtering is the intelligence with which the firewall examines the packets. Packet filtering firewalls examine only the static attributes of packets such as source protocol and source/destination addresses. A stateful inspection firewall is able to hold in memory the significant attributes of each connection; therefore, it can identify packets that are part of an already established and prescreened session. This makes filtering more efficient and more accurate.

Understand firewall rules.   Firewall rules determine what packets will be allowed through a firewall. Packets can be identified by protocol, IP address, MAC address, or even the data they contain. Rules will simply either block passage of a packet or allow passage based on the rule. An implicit deny setting is the best type of firewall setting because if you miss something, the users are blocked instead of allowed. ACLs are used to identify traffic, and then the rule itself is used to control the traffic.

Understand NAT and PAT in relation to security.   NAT and PAT use a table that changes the apparent source address of a packet to a different address. An attack on that table could wreak havoc on your network by disrupting communications and even redirecting traffic. You can protect your NAT and PAT devices by using strong passwords for local access and especially remote access.

Know the purpose of a DMZ.   A DMZ is a zone between two firewalls. You should place your servers that are used by hosts on both the internal network and the external network in the DMZ. These might include web, VPN, and FTP servers.

5.6 Categorize different types of network security appliances and methods

You can use many appliances and methods to secure your network and to test its security. They are available to anyone who chooses to use them. The ironic thing is that if you choose not to use some of these tools, then you may miss the very vulnerability that an attacker might find using the tools that you should have used. You can also employ proactive security appliances and methods to trap and catch an attacker.

In this section, I will discuss the various methods of intrusion detection and prevention that you can employ on your network. In addition, I'll discuss some vulnerability scanners that you can use or that can be used against you. Finally, I'll discuss more advanced and proactive methods used to decoy, trap, and catch would-be attackers.

IDS and IPS

An intrusion detection system (IDS) is much more than a firewall. In effect, an IDS is an intelligent monitor of network traffic that "understands" what normal traffic is supposed to look like and what it is supposed to do and can therefore identify abnormal traffic as a threat. "How does it know?" you may ask. Well, either it's configured with the latest attack signatures from its vendor (much like antivirus software) or it simply "watches" your network for a while to learn what normal traffic looks like. Of course, the best system is a combination of the two. In addition, an IDS can be configured to alert the network administrator when it detects a threat. In fact, the only action that a true IDS takes in response to a threat is to alert the administrator with an email message or network message if configured properly. Often an IDS just logs the threat so the network administrator can address it later.

An intrusion prevention system (IPS) is very similar to an IDS but can take more action in response to a threat than an IDS. An IPS can address an identified threat by resetting a connection or even closing a port. Of course, the IPS can also be configured to alert the administrator of the threat and the action that was taken. In fact, in practice, the main difference between an IPS and an IDS is one of software configuration. Four methods are used by IDS and IPS. In this section, I will discuss each of these four methods.

Behavior based

A behavior-based IDS/IPS is generally software that is installed on the host to monitor it as an agent that can detect and potentially respond to anything or anyone attempting to circumvent the security policy. It can dynamically inspect network packets and determine which programs use which resources during a normal working day. After it has learned what is "normal," then it can also detect an event that is not normal and alert the administrator or even take action to close ports and connections. Because it does maintain a database of attacks, it must gradually learn what is normal and what is not.

Signature based

A signature-based IDS/IPS starts off with a database of known attacks and is capable of recognizing those attacks. This allows some protection in a quicker manner than that of behavior-based systems. The catch is that if the attack that is occurring is not in the database of signatures, then it won't be recognized by a purely signature-based IDS/IPS. As you can imagine, the most effective appliances use a combination of behavior-based and signature-based methods.

Network based

A *network-based* appliance is generally located on the edge of a network where that network comes in contact with another network such as the Internet. Some network appliances are used between two corporate networks to control the flow of information between the two divisions, such as between departments in the same company. In either case, the advantage of a network-based appliance is that it provides general protection for all the hosts behind it. However, the disadvantage is that the settings on the firewall will affect all the hosts behind it and therefore tend to be general settings and not specific settings for specific network hosts.

Host based

Software-based firewalls that are used to control traffic to a single host are referred to as *host-based* system. The Windows Firewall on Microsoft Windows operating systems is a prime example of a firewall that comes with the operating system software. In fact, the latest version of Windows client, Windows 7, will warn the user if it does not detect the use of either the native Windows Firewall or some third-party application to take its place. Applications that could provide this service include Norton and McAfee antivirus and firewall products. The configuration of the Windows Firewall is typically a "no-brainer" for most client computers. The default settings will provide the required security, so it just needs to be kept on. The configuration of Norton and McAfee products can be more complex and defined, but often the default settings will suffice as well.

Vulnerability scanners

As I mentioned, the reason that a threat might harm your network is that your network has a vulnerability that it can exploit. You cannot eliminate the threats; some people are just mean and nasty! You can, however, reduce your vulnerability to the threats. To do this, you may want to use a vulnerability scanner to determine where you are weak and where you are strong. You may as well, because you can bet that the attacker will! In the following section, I'll review two of the most common vulnerability scanners.

NESSUS

Nessus is a proprietary vulnerability scanning program that can detect misconfigurations or open ports that might allow an attacker to gain control of your system or its sensitive data. For example, it checks for default passwords, weak passwords, missing patches, and the like. At the time of this writing, this tool was free, and it is estimated to be used by more than 75,000 organizations worldwide.

NMAP

Nmap (Network Mapper) is a security scanner that can discover hosts on a computer network and thereby create a map of the active network. It sends special packets to the target host and then analyzes the responses it receives. It can determine open ports, the presence of firewalls, and other capabilities of the devices that it discovers. Nmap runs on Windows, Linux, Solaris, and other operating systems as well.

Methods

Sometimes to catch attackers you have to think like them. What would attract attackers and cause them to want to attack? Once you are "in the attacker's mind," then you can create environments that look like a good target for them but are really just a decoy to, at the very least, distract them from finding the real sensitive data and, at the most, a trap that will cause them to slip up and get caught. Two of these "decoys" are honeypots and honeynets.

Honeypots

Honeypots are security devices that are used as a decoy to look like a valuable server target to an attacker. They also appear to be vulnerable to attack and undefended, when in fact they are monitored and are isolated from any truly sensitive computer data. The idea is to get the attacker to take the bait, and then while he is wasting his time in the honeypot, your real data is safe, and you can gather information about the attacker and give it to the correct authorities.

Honeynets

Two or more honeypots on the same network form a honeynet. This is used when an organization is very large and a single honeypot server won't do the job. The honeynet simulates a production network but is actually heavily monitored and isolated from the true production network. It can be used to draw the attacker deeper in and give him that much more opportunity to make a mistake that will get him caught.

Exam Essentials

Know the difference between an IDS and an IPS.   An IDS can watch your network for normal traffic and other traffic that looks suspicious and alert the administrator when it sees suspicious traffic. An IPS can also watch the network for suspicious traffic, but it can do more than just alert the administrator. An IPS can automatically reset a connection or close a port on suspicious traffic.

Know the difference between behavior-based and signature-based IDS/IPS.   Behavior based systems can also be appliances and can protect an entire network, not just a host. After it has learned what is normal, then it can be used to dynamically detect suspicious traffic, but this takes time. A signature-based IDS/IPS starts off with a database of known attacks that it is already capable of recognizing. This means that it can get a "head start" on the behavior-based system. The most effective systems use a combination of methods.

Know the difference between network based and host based.   A network-based system is usually an appliance that is located on the edge of the network. It provides general protection for all of the hosts behind it but does not usually provide for customization of host protection. Host-based firewalls are used to provide customized protection for a single host. The Windows Firewall on Windows 7 is an example of a host-based system. Other examples include Norton and McAfee products that are often bundled with antivirus software.

Be familiar with vulnerability scanners.　Vulnerability scanners include software such as Nessus and Nmap. You can use these programs to test for weaknesses in your network security; unfortunately, so can an attacker.

Know the difference between honeypots and honeynets.　Honeypots are security devices that are made to look to a hacker like a sensitive and valuable target. They are used as a decoy to draw the hacker in to catch him or just to keep him distracted from the real sensitive targets. Two or more honeypots on the same network form a honeynet.

Review Questions

1. Which type of firewall examines only the static attributes of a packet such as the IP address and protocol?

   A. Stateless

   B. IDS

   C. IPS

   D. Stateful

2. Which of the following is an advantage of signature-based IDS? (Choose two.)

   A. The administrator's signature is required.

   B. It lets you benefit from the previous security issues of others.

   C. Signatures are identified by the vendor.

   D. It does not require programming or configuration.

3. Which of the following servers would most likely be placed in the DMZ? (Choose two.)

   A. Web

   B. FTP

   C. Domain controller

   D. DHCP

4. Which of the following are common tunneling protocols? (Choose two.)

   A. PPP

   B. VPN

   C. PPTP

   D. L2TP

5. Which of the following remote control protocols is installed by default on the latest Microsoft clients and servers?

   A. UDP

   B. TCP/IP

   C. ARP

   D. RDP

6. In PKI, which key is typically used to decrypt a message?

    A. Only the public key.

    B. Only the private key.

    C. Both the public key and the private key.

    D. Neither key is used for decryption.

7. Which of the following is a remote access service that uses TCP?

    A. RADIUS

    B. WEP

    C. TACACS+

    D. WPA

8. In 802.1x, what is role of the client machine?

    A. Authenticator.

    B. Authentication server.

    C. Supplicant.

    D. The client does not have a defined role.

9. Which of the following protocols is an open set of standards that allows the addition of new methods of authentication such as smart cards and biometric authentication?

    A. EAP

    B. CHAP

    C. MS-CHAP

    D. MS-CHAPv2

10. Which of the following is a type of social engineering attack?

    A. Man-in-the-middle attack

    B. Smurf

    C. DoS

    D. Phishing

Appendix A

Answers to Review Questions

Chapter 1: Domain 1 Network Technologies

1. C. A Media Access Control (MAC) address is a unique physical address that is assigned to each network interface card. MAC addresses are "burned in" to the card at the manufacturer.

2. C. An IPv4 address is a 32-bit address. It is composed of four sections of 8 bits each, called octets. Each octet is converted to decimal for configuration purposes, but the computer uses the entire 32-bit address for communication.

3. B. If you have a Class B address with a default subnet mask, then the current subnet mask is 255.255.0.0. This means you have 16 bits for networks and 16 bits for hosts. If you want to create eight subnets, then you need to solve for $2^s > 8$. Solving for s, you can determine that you need to use the first 3 bits from the network address to create the subnets. The values of the first 3 bits total 224 (128 + 64 + 32), so the new subnet mask is 255.255.224.0.

4. A, B. The valid private address ranges include the following:
   - 192.168.0.0–192.168.255.255
   - 172.16.0.0–172.31.255.255
   - 10.0.0.0–10.255.255.255

   Only answers A and B fall into these ranges.

5. C. FTP is an Application layer protocol that uses TCP ports 20 and 21. It is the standard protocol used for file transfer over the Internet.

6. D. The Network layer of the OSI model is responsible for logical addressing. In most networks today, this is in the form of an IP address.

7. C. The Application layer of the TCP/IP protocol suite loosely aligns to the Application, Presentation, and Session layers of the OSI model.

8. A. Session Initiation Protocol (SIP) is a Session layer protocol that is primarily responsible for setting up and tearing down voice and video calls over the Internet. It also enables IP telephony networks to utilize advanced call features such as SS7.

9. C. An IPv6 address is a 128-bit binary address that is expressed as a hexadecimal address. Leading 0s can be omitted and successive fields of 0s can be represented as ::.

10. A. A Class B network will by definition have a subnet mask of 255.255.0.0. This means you have 16 host bits with which to work to create 100 subnets. To determine the number of subnets you need, you use the formula $2^s \geq 100$. Solving for s, you can determine that you need 7 host bits, since $2^6 = 64$ but $2^7 = 128$. This means that the 128, 64, 32, 16, 8, 4, and 2 values in the third octet will now count in the subnet mask. Adding these values, you get 254, so the new subnet mask is 254.

Chapter 2: Domain 2 Network Installation and Configuration

1. A, D. NAT is a service that translates one set of IP addresses to another set of IP addresses. Computers often connect to the Internet through NAT, but it is not a requirement. NAT services can be provided by computers, routers, or other specialized devices.

2. D. A VLAN is a layer 2 network (virtual subnet) that is created using a switch. VLANs increase the flexibility and security of a network by separating the logical from the physical. A MAC address is a layer 2 address of a computer or device. WPA and WEP are wireless security protocols.

3. C, D. Wireless networks are not necessarily easier to maintain, because you must then maintain the wired portion as well as the wireless portion of your network. WAP and/ or antenna placement is very important in a wireless network. Improper placement can cause signal loss, can cause interference, or can cause the network to broadcast to areas to which you did not intend. Bluetooth devices can cause interference on wireless networks, especially if the wireless signal is weak or the Bluetooth device is very close to the WAP or wireless card. The most common channels for a wireless networks are 1, 6, and 11.

4. A, D. Wireless standards have evolved and continue to evolve. Most devices purchased today can be used for 802.11b/g/n, but some devices can also be used for 802.11a. If a device can be used for 802.11a, it is because it has specialized orthogonal frequency division multiplexing (OFDM) hardware in it. 802.11a is not considered compatible with 802.11b/g but is compatible with 802.11n.

5. C. A Dynamic Host Configuration Protocol (DHCP) server can assign much more than just an IP address to a client computer. It can also inform the computer of the addresses of the DNS server, default gateway, and much more. DHCP servers are not also DNS servers, although both services could run on the same box. You can reserve an address for a computer or device that is not always connected but that you want to have a predictable address when it is connected. This will generally be based on the MAC address of the computer or device. In general, other servers, printers, and routers should be statically configured and should not obtain their addresses from the DHCP server.

6. C. Maximum Transmission Unit (MTU) is a configuration that controls the largest size packet that an interface can forward. If MTU is improperly configured between two connected devices, it can cause the packets to be consistently dropped instead of being forwarded since the TCP handshake could succeed and the connection could still hang when data is sent. This condition is referred to as MTU black hole, and the router that is misconfigured is sometimes referred to as a black hole router.

7. B. Small office/home office (SOHO) networks contain the same types of components as larger enterprise networks but on a much smaller scale. They may contain servers, but this is not a requirement. They may use wireless communication, wired communication, or a combination of the two.

8. C. If you use twisted-pair Ethernet cables in your network, you should remember the "100 meters without repeaters" rule; 100 meters is approximately 328 feet. This is the maximum distance that you should run a cable from the switch to the computer.

9. A, D. DHCP scopes contain a range of IP addresses that can be assigned by the DHCP server. You should take care that these ranges do not overlap, because this could cause IP address conflicts in your network. DHCP scopes are not typically configured based on the MAC addresses of computers.

10. B. QoS is a network technique that divides traffic into categories based on the protocol of the traffic and then allows for the prioritization of each category. WEP and WPA are security protocols for wireless communications. PAT is a specialized form of NAT that uses a port designator as well as an IP address.

Chapter 3: Network Media and Topologies

1. C. Singlemode fiber is the only choice here that will give you the distance that you need and provide a high-speed connection. Coaxial cable and twisted would not provide a high-speed connection at that distance. Multimode fiber would be appropriate for fiber connections within buildings.

2. B. This is kind of a tricky question in that a PC actually functions much like a router on a network. In fact, it's possible to create a router from a PC. The thing to remember here is that similar devices connect to each other with a crossover cable. A straight-through cable is used to connect dissimilar devices. A rollover cable is used to connect to a device for management purposes. A T1-crossover cable connects a CSU/DSU to a router.

3. A. The local connector (LC) is a fiber connector that is built into the body of an RJ-style jack. It is perfect for connections in the network closet or telecom room. The DB-9 connector was the standard used for serial connections such as modems.

The SC connector uses a push-pull mechanism similar to common audio and video plugs. The straight tip (ST) connector uses a half-twist bayonet type of lock.

4. B, C. The wireless standard 802.11a is not compatible with 802.11b. The wireless standards 802.11g and n are compatible with 802.11b. In addition, the wireless standard 802.11 n is compatible with 802.11a. 802.11y is not a current wireless standard.

5. B. A T1 provides for 24 64Kbps channels for a total of 1.544Mbps bandwidth. A T3 provides for 672 channels or an equivalent of 28 T1s. An OC3 provides for 150Mbps. An E1 provides 32 channels for a total of 2.048Mbps bandwidth.

6. C. The ATM technology uses fixed-length cells of 53 bytes. Frame Relay is packet-switching technology used by companies to save money vs. having dedicated lines. DSL is a technology that uses telephone lines for Internet communication. Ethernet uses variable length frames, not fixed-length cells.

7. A. MPLS is a mechanism used to create a logical network topology with no dependence on the underlying protocol. Instead, it uses labels to make frame forwarding decisions, giving the network designer a wide range of flexibility. Point to point, ring, and mesh topologies do not use labels.

8. C. If you chose to create a full mesh, it would take [n(n − 1)]/2 connections. This works out to [5(5 − 1)]/2 = 10. To clarify, this would be 20 connectors and 10 connections, and each computer would need to contain 4 network interface cards.

9. A. If you have TX and RX reversed on a connection because of an improper installation of a wall jack or patch panel or because of the wrong type of cable being used, then the result will be a total lack of connectivity, not a partial or intermittent one.

10. B. The point at which the control and ownership changes from your company to the service provider network is referred to as the demarc or demarcation point. The IDF is a rack that holds communications lines and is located in the equipment or telecommunications room. The MDF is a reference point generally used for telephone lines. A CSU/DSU is a device used to connect a router to a digital circuit, such as a T1 or T3 line.

Chapter 4: Network Management

1. C, D. Routers and switches are considered network devices since they are core components of a network with varied uses. Network appliances are devices such as load balancers, and content filters are specialized devices that perform a specifically defined function.

2. A. A butt set is a legacy tool still used by telephone technicians to test and communicate on standard telephone lines. A crimper is used to create network cables. A toner

probe is used to follow a wire from end to end, even through thin walls. A protocol analyzer can be used to look inside a packet and get detailed information.

3. A. A TDR would be your best tool to determine the location of a break in a copper network cable. An optical time domain reflectometer (OTDR) would be best only if the break were in a fiber-optic cable. Neither a protocol analyzer nor an environmental monitor would assist you in determining the location of a break.

4. C. Throughput is best described as the amount of data that a network can pass in a given period of time. The size of the pipe would more accurately be stated as bandwidth. The average size of a file has nothing directly to do with the description of throughput. The amount of time it takes to pass data from sender to receiver would better be described as latency.

5. A. The ping tool is used primarily to verify connectivity between two devices. The ipconfig tool is used to gather information about the current IP connection. Nslookup is used to query for information about the DNS server. DHCP is a protocol used to automatically assign IP addresses and other information such as default gateway, DNS addresses, and so on.

6. A. Netstat is a command-line tool that you can use to get information about open and active ports. Nbstat is a command-line tool that you can use to get information regarding NetBIOS over TCP/IP. Ping is a tool that allows you to verify connectivity between two devices. Dig is a simple tool that gives you information about DNS configuration for a host.

7. A, C. All SNMP versions allow you to gather information about your network devices, but they are not all secure. SNMPv2 is more secure than the original, but SNMPv3 is the most secure of all.

8. C. QoS is a service that allows you to manage different types of traffic and establish priorities between them. Traffic shaping is controlling network traffic by slowing down some traffic on specific connections. High availability is a system design that sets a limit on unplanned downtime. Caching engines make it faster to do something after the first time.

9. B. CARP provides for failover redundancy whereby two devices can share the same IP address; referred to as a group of redundancy. Fault tolerance does provide for failover redundancy but does not use a group of redundancy. Caching engines speed operations by holding repetitively used data in a location where it can be accessed faster than it was the first time. Baselines are used to compare a normal state of a network to what is occurring to isolate the differences and thereby determine the problems.

10. A, D. VoIP and video traffic are certainly considered high-bandwidth traffic. Your users will be affected if you do not set aside enough bandwidth to support these services. Printer sharing is generally considered low-bandwidth traffic. Even if many documents are to be printed, the total bandwidth consumed is nowhere near that of VoIP or video traffic. In addition, the printer operations can work with delays and inconsistencies that VoIP traffic cannot. Network management should never be high bandwidth. Your job as a network administrator is to preserve as much available bandwidth for the user after you subtract your network management overhead.

Chapter 5: Domain 5 Network Security

1. **A.** A stateless firewall examines only those static attributes of a packet such as the IP address and protocol. A stateful firewall identifies a packet stream and determines whether it is the normal stream that it should be seeing for that protocol. IDS and IPS are intrusion prevention/intrusion detection systems, which are not the same as a firewall.

2. **B, C.** Signature-based IDS is a method by which administrators can determine what they are filtering on a firewall. Security threats are identified with a signature, and the prevention technique can be deployed using the signature ID. You can also combine IDs into common groups to increase security and make sure nothing is forgotten. Since these can be programmed and don't have to be learned, it lets you benefit from the previous security issues of others.

3. **A, B.** Servers that are likely to be used from the inside and the outside of the same organization should be placed in the DMZ. These include web, FTP, and VPN servers. Servers that are of higher security should be placed in the internal zone behind both firewalls. These include domain controllers, DHCP servers, and internal DNS servers. Servers that are used only on the outside, such as an external DNS server, may be placed in the external zone.

4. **C, D.** The most common tunneling protocols are PPTP and L2TP. VPN is not a protocol but instead a type of network connection. PPP is used for serial point-to-point connections and for dial-up, but it is not a tunneling protocol.

5. **D.** RDP is installed by default on all the latest Microsoft clients and servers. UDP is not a remote control protocol. TCP/IP is an entire protocol suite and not a remote control protocol. ARP resolves IP addresses to MAC addresses and is not a remote control protocol.

6. **B.** PKI typically uses key pairs such that when a message is encrypted using the public key, the only key that can decrypt the message is the private key of same key pair. The public key is never used to decrypt a message but may sometimes be used to verify a signature.

7. **C.** TACACS+ is a remote access service developed by Cisco that centralizes authentication, authorization, and accounting (AAA). It is connection-oriented and uses TCP

for communication. RADIUS is another remote access AAA service, but it uses UDP instead of TCP. WEP and WPA are wireless protocol security standards and are not remote access services.

8. C. 802.1x is often used for wired and wireless network access control. In 802.1x, the client is the supplicant that supplies the credentials to the authenticator and requests access. The authenticator does not authenticate the request but instead passes it to the authentication server. The authentication server authenticates the requests and gives the authenticator the permission to open the port and the client to communicate through it.

9. A. EAP is an open set of standards that allows for the addition of new methods of authentication. These may include smart cards, biometric authentication, and other forms of authentication. CHAP, MS-CHAP, and MS-CHAPv2 are challenge handshake protocols that have evolved over time. MS-CHAP and MS-CHAPv2 are proprietary to Microsoft, and the latter protocol can be used only on the latest clients and servers.

10. D. A phishing attack is a type of social engineering attack because it relies on the behavior of the user who trusts a bogus website. A man-in-the-middle attack is a rather sophisticated attack by which the attacker places himself in the data stream between two hosts without the knowledge or consent of the users. A smurf attack uses the ICMP protocol and a bogus source address. The user is the victim and is not directly involved in the attack's success or failure. A DoS attack floods the network with useless data that takes up resources and keep systems from functioning properly.

Appendix B

About the Additional Study Tools

IN THIS APPENDIX:

✓ Additional Study Tools

✓ System requirements

✓ Using the Study Tools

✓ Troubleshooting

Additional Study Tools

The following sections are arranged by category and summarize the software and other goodies you'll find from the companion website. If you need help with installing the items, refer to the installation instructions in the "Using the Study Tools" section of this appendix.

 The additional study tools can be found at www.sybex.com/go/netplusrg2e. Here, you will get instructions on how to download the files to your hard drive.

Sybex Test Engine

The files contain the Sybex test engine, which includes two bonus practice exams.

Electronic Flashcards

These handy electronic flashcards are just what they sound like. One side contains a question, and the other side shows the answer.

PDF of Glossary of Terms

We have included an electronic version of the Glossary in .pdf format. You can view the electronic version of the Glossary with Adobe Reader.

Adobe Reader

We've also included a copy of Adobe Reader so you can view PDF files that accompany the book's content. For more information on Adobe Reader or to check for a newer version, visit Adobe's website at www.adobe.com/products/reader/.

System Requirements

Make sure your computer meets the minimum system requirements shown in the following list. If your computer doesn't match up to most of these requirements, you may have problems using the software and files. For the latest and greatest information, please refer to the ReadMe file located in the downloads.

- A PC running Microsoft Windows 98, Windows 2000, Windows NT4 (with SP4 or later), Windows Me, Windows XP, Windows Vista, or Windows 7
- An Internet connection

Using the Study Tools

To install the items, follow these steps:

1. Download the `.zip` file to your hard drive, and unzip to an appropriate location. Instructions on where to download this file can be found here: `www.sybex.com/go/netplusrg 2e`.
2. Click the `Start.exe` file to open up the study tools file.
3. Read the license agreement, and then click the Accept button if you want to use the study tools.

The main interface appears. The interface allows you to access the content with just one or two clicks.

Troubleshooting

Wiley has attempted to provide programs that work on most computers with the minimum system requirements. Alas, your computer may differ, and some programs may not work properly for some reason.

The two likeliest problems are that you don't have enough memory (RAM) for the programs you want to use or you have other programs running that are affecting installation or running of a program. If you get an error message such as "Not enough memory" or "Setup cannot continue," try one or more of the following suggestions and then try using the software again:

Turn off any antivirus software running on your computer. Installation programs sometimes mimic virus activity and may make your computer incorrectly believe that it's being infected by a virus.

Close all running programs. The more programs you have running, the less memory is available to other programs. Installation programs typically update files and programs; so if you keep other programs running, installation may not work properly.

Have your local computer store add more RAM to your computer. This is, admittedly, a drastic and somewhat expensive step. However, adding more memory can really help the speed of your computer and allow more programs to run at the same time.

Customer Care

If you have trouble with the book's companion study tools, please call the Wiley Product Technical Support phone number at (800) 762-2974. 74, or email them at http://sybex.custhelp.com/.

Index

Note to the Reader: Throughout this index **boldfaced** page numbers indicate primary discussions of a topic. *Italicized* page numbers indicate illustrations.

Q

S

T

X

Z

Free Online Study Tools

Register on Sybex.com to gain access to a complete set of study tools to help you prepare for your CompTIA Network+ Certification Exam

Comprehensive Study Tool Package Includes:

- **Two Full-Length Practice Exams** to test your knowledge of the material

- **Electronic Flashcards** to reinforce your learning and give you that last-minute test prep before the exam

- **Searchable Glossary** gives you instant access to the key terms you'll need to know for the exam

Go to www.sybex.com/go/netplusrg2e to register and gain access to this comprehensive study tool package.